welsh writing  ᴊוׁ

a yearbook of critical essays

Acknowledgements

Welsh Writing in English: A Yearbook of Critical Essays is published with the financial support of the Welsh Books Council; the editors also gratefully acknowledge the support of the Association for Welsh Writing in English, Research Centre Wales (University of Wales, Bangor) and the Department of English, University of Wales, Bangor. We are as ever indebted to those scholars who have found time in busy schedules to act as readers of papers submitted for publication; their advice and guidance is quite indispensable. The editor is especially grateful to Linda Jones, Research Administrator in the Department of English, University of Wales, Bangor, for her scrupulous checking of proofs; her expertise is a welcome support and constant reassurance. We are also grateful for the advice and support of Francesca Rhydderch at *New Welsh Review* and to Owain Hammonds for the rapidity and professionalism with which he has produced proofs.

Information for Contributors

Correspondence and contributions for publication should be addressed to the editor: Dr Tony Brown, Department of English, University of Wales, Bangor, Gwynedd, LL57 2DG (e-mail: els015@bangor.ac.uk). The *Yearbook* publishes essays on literary topics, not on purely Welsh historical matters. While its primary concern is the study of Welsh writing in English, papers on Welsh-language authors, written in English, will be considered; the *Yearbook* will also consider papers which relate the two literatures of Wales. Papers should not normally exceed 8,000 words in length. The *Yearbook* also welcomes shorter papers of a factual nature for consideration for the "Notes" section and responses to published papers for its "Forum" section.

Manuscripts (two copies) should be typed on one side of the page, double spaced, and produced according to the *M.L.A. Style Manual*. Include a computer disk with the hard copies, and note the word-processing programme used.

All contribution will be refereed. While a decision will be made as expeditiously as possible, allow three months for a decision. Contributors of published papers receive four complimentary copies of the issue in which their paper appears.

The *Yearbook* web page, which includes information on past issues, is at: www.bangor.ac.uk/english/periodic/welshwrit.

© Contributors and the *Yearbook*

ISBN 0-70831-829-0

welsh writing in english

a yearbook of critical essays   VOL 9 | 2004

Editor:
Dr Tony Brown, University of Wales, Bangor
Associate Editors:
Professor Jane Aaron, University of Glamorgan
Professor M. Wynn Thomas, University of Wales, Swansea

CONTENTS

Welsh Periodicals in English 1880-1965: Literary Form and Cultural Substance

Malcolm Ballin
University of Wales, Cardiff

L iterary journalism in Wales is an under-researched topic, especially given the significance periodicals have had in promoting new writers and producing literary and cultural dialogue. The periodical is rarely looked as a literary artefact in its own right, repaying study in terms of its form as well as its content. It will be argued here that Anglo-Welsh periodicals in the first part of the twentieth century adopted, more or less consciously, particular genre formats that had been well-established in literary history. In particular it will be shown that these periodicals tend to start their production in one genre, often the little magazine, but, for a variety of reasons, migrate into another: the serious liberal miscellany. To demonstrate this it will be necessary to trace in some detail the nature of the Welsh periodicals written in English during the fifty years before the first Anglo-Welsh little magazine of the twentieth century, Keidrych Rhys's *Wales*, appeared in July 1937. This historical excursus will give some insight into the unique genre history of Welsh magazines. The first models for later Welsh magazines appear in the nineteenth century, initially almost solely written in Welsh but later produced as English-language periodicals, mostly cast in the miscellany genre.

Welsh periodicals in English also need to be read in the context of Welsh society and culture. Historically, Welsh nationalism has differed from that of other countries, and particularly that of Ireland, in that, although intensively political in character, "separatism in Wales was relatively muted" and demands for Home Rule were seldom voiced.[1] There was indeed, throughout most of the nineteenth century, widespread acceptance of the concept of a dual British/Welsh idea: "the land of their fathers still lacked for most Welshmen the essential attributes to turn a static sense of national consciousness into a more dynamic sentiment of nationalism".[2] Although from 1880 onwards this changed in degree, it remained the case into the twentieth century and especially in the context of the Second World War, that "most Welsh people still differed profoundly in their priorities from their Celtic counterparts across the Irish Sea. They rejected an inwards-looking exclusiveness and sought rather to make Wales a recognised, dignified partner within a wider world".[3] This sense of dignity, a desire to be taken seriously and to be recognized beyond national boundaries, is a determining factor in the character of many of the Welsh periodicals to be considered here.

It is against this background that the sense of an Anglo-Welsh identity begins to crystallize. Glyn Jones argues in his critical work, *The Dragon has Two Tongues*, that there are few resemblances in Welsh culture to the concept of the Anglo-Irish Ascendancy tradition which lies behind the work of Yeats or Synge. He argues rather that polarization takes place in Wales more around the language issue and between the cultures of rural and urban working-class communities.[4] Paul O'Leary points out that early Welsh journalism was predominantly written in Welsh and reflected the predominance of print-culture and literacy in Wales, strongly associated with that Protestant Nonconformity which, from the eighteenth century onwards, was an essential element in national identity. This contrasts with the division in Irish culture where the oral culture was predominantly Gaelic and the print culture was expressed in English almost exclusively. O'Leary draws attention to the stark contrast between the development of separatist political nationalism in Ireland up to 1916, the year of the Easter Rising, and in Wales, where, later in the same year, David Lloyd George became Prime Minister of the British Empire at war.[5]

Before looking at the range of periodicals in some detail it will be helpful here to refer briefly to the nature of periodical genres. Categorization of literary works is not of any especial value for its own sake; many periodicals are ambiguous in their choice of genres or change genres as their history causes them to develop different positions. However, a well-established body of genre theory (associated with such practitioners as Mikhail Bakhtin) suggests how the adoption of a particular genre sends signals to readers and potential contributors about the style of writing expected by editors, and the cultural or political stance of the magazine.[6] Such messages are often derived from a historical consciousness of the nature of other perodicals in the same genre. Raymond Williams describes persuasively how genres provide "indicative bearings within the sheer vastness of production":

> There are clear social and historical relations between particular literary forms and the societies and periods in which they were originated or practised. . . . [T]here are undoubted continuities of literary forms through and beyond the societies and periods to which they have such relations. In genre theory everything depends on the character and process of such continuities.[7]

Thus, for example, magazines cast in the review genre invoke the memory of such historic exemplars as the *Quarterly Review*, the *Edinburgh* or the *Westminster*. They want to be read as sources of weighty commentary, directed at exclusive groups, their anonymous contributors often appearing to address themselves over the heads of their contemporaries to the judgement of posterity. Some of this lofty poise comes from their self-awareness as part of a potent generic tradition.

The miscellany periodicals, however, stem from a different lineage, established by such predecessors as *The Gentleman's Magazine*, the *London Magazine* or the *Cornhill*. They are examples of what Bakhtin characterized as "mixed genres" that are "deliberately multi-styled and hetero-voiced" having a "pointed interest in the topics of the day".[8] Miscellanies tend therefore to provide serious, though sometimes satiric, analyses of the contemporary world. "Little Magazines", on the other hand, have a generic history extending back to eighteenth-century pamphleteering but reaching the twentieth century via such controversial publications as *The Yellow Book* or Wyndham Lewis's *Blast*. The Modernist movement, with its emphasis on the manifesto, greatly encouraged the development of the little magazine, seen by Malcolm Bradbury as "the obverse to the solemn, serious, debating magazine".[9] T. S. Eliot, reported in *The Welsh Review* in 1944, paid generous tribute to the little magazines' role and importance, especially in providing early publication opportunities for new poets:

> These small magazines often circulate only among contributors and would-be contributors; their condition is usually precarious, their appearance at irregular intervals, and their existence brief, yet their collective importance is out of all proportion to the obscurity in which they struggle.[10]

Roland Mathias in his short monograph about Anglo-Welsh Magazines seems to see all of them as belonging to this category, in as much as they "are tied to life by the merest thread".[11] However, as the present paper will show, most of the magazines produced in Wales in the middle of the twentieth century come to display characteristics that differentiate them from the little magazine. Looking at periodicals in this way, through the perspective of genre, encourages the reader to give attention to the holistic character of a journal, to the way it develops a special identity through the total effects of the combination of presentation, content, tone and style.[12]

The earliest periodical writing in the English language on Welsh subjects appears to have been a group of publications between 1795 and 1830, published in London, mainly attempting to preserve Welsh myth and legend and appealing to antiquarian interests.[13] However, the direct and influential predecessors of twentieth-century periodicals start with a number of Welsh miscellanies, including *The Red Dragon* in the 1880s, edited by Charles Wilkins, and *The Welsh Review* (1891-93), edited by Ernest Bowen Rowlands. These are followed by two separate magazines, both called *Wales,* one edited by Owen M. Edwards, between 1894 and 1897, and the other by J. Hugh Edwards, between 1911 and 1914. All these magazines speak for the dominant Liberal ascendancy of the time and each of them, in its time, was described as being, in some sense, a "National Magazine of Wales".[14] These rather solemn instances of the miscellany periodical, with their self-declared mission to speak for Wales as a whole, set a particular pattern of expectation.

The Red Dragon: The National Magazine of Wales (1882-1887)

The Red Dragon's title page displays twin shields, a crown over the top of them and the motto "Dieu et Mon Droit", clearly signifying a loyalist message. The mix of creative writing, reporting, cultural comment and reviewing is typical of the miscellany genre. Charles Wilkins, born in Gloucestershire, became a postmaster and librarian in Merthyr Tydfil and produced numerous works of local industrial and literary history. He is credited in the *New Companion to the Literature of Wales,* with "a brave attempt to create a relatively cultured reading public in English where none sufficient yet existed".[15] The first issue of *The Red Dragon* offers a series entitled "Welsh Poetry in English Dress: the Shake of the Hand", providing an early instance of the wish to negotiate around the language tensions. It also includes a discussion of the differing arguments about the best location for the new University of Wales.[16] *The Red Dragon* includes, from No. 3 onwards, regular reports of activities of Welshmen in the Oxford Colleges as well as from Lampeter and Aberystwyth. One of these reports criticizes the inclusion of Welsh-language journals in preference to their own magazine in the set of periodicals on offer in the reading room at the Oxford Union.[17]

Consideration of the contents of a typical issue of the magazine illustrates the characteristic editorial practice of the miscellany periodical, essentially using creative materials to reinforce the messages implied by its reportage and critical articles. The January 1883 issue opens with one of a series of articles about "Notable Men of Wales", on this occasion in the form of an obituary of the recently-deceased Judge John Maurice Herbert. He was born in Montgomery, educated at Hereford Cathedral School and St. John's College, Cambridge. This account records his athletic prowess as the cox of his college boat, pays tribute to his professional acumen and incorruptibility and admires his active social life.[18] The article is preceded by an impressive portrait in sepia. *The Red Dragon's* aspiration to a place in Welsh society is thus set early. The magazine's adherence to well-established middle-class values is reinforced by the extract from Charles Gibbon's novel of manners that follows, commencing with a chapter titled "Tragedy in the Drawing Room".[19] The second part of a series about the Cromwell family and their Welsh connections seeks to recuperate the "prejudice generated by the very name of Cromwell" and "to convince some minds that Oliver Cromwell was a member of one of the most *notable families to be found in English history*" [my italics].[20] The concept of the "notable" (repeated in this different context) suggests that participation in powerful roles in *England* is the accepted objective of ambition for Welshmen.

A poem, "A Romance of Pennard-Gower" echoes Tennyson or Longfellow:

> Hers were not tears of sorrow—joy gleamed upon the morrow
> Far away from haughty knights and haughtier sire,
> For a little skiff did lay 'neath the shadow in the bay
> And in it was Llewellyn of the Lyre.[21]

The other verse in this issue again romanticizes the mediaeval in the shape of "Welsh Poetry in English Dress" which presents translations from fourteenth-century bards.[22] Overt references to Tennyson and to Longfellow appear in the series "In Pembrokeshire with a Sketch Book" where two brothers explore Carew Castle and meet with a mysterious stranger who tells tales of apparitions he has encountered there.[23] A scholarly article about the Welsh origins of Latin place-names follows, in the shape of a critique of an edition of London matriculation papers set in 1882.[24] "Gossip from the Welsh Colleges" and "Our 'Red Dragons' at Westminster" are regular series, as is the literary gossip article, "Marginal Notes on Library Books".[25] "Welsh Character Sketches" presents an account of Women's Clubs in Wales, apparently common in the writer's youth, now out of fashion but said to be an amusing phenomenon to be thought of "with kindly hearts".[26] The issue closes with two more regular features: "Literary and Art Notes of the Month &c." and "Draconigenae", a set of humorous snippets that might furnish a gentleman with material for an after-dinner speech.[27]

This typical issue of *The Red Dragon* is liberal and tolerant. It sees Wales as an exotic source of antiquarian materials and historical events. It enshrines many of the traditional values of more cultivated late-Victorian society. It is rarely philistine and it seems quite confident at this stage of the presence of a reliable audience of like-minded individuals. Charles Wilkins is at pains, indeed, to create a club-like atmosphere, enhanced by the presence of a number of regular series to be continued through future issues. The tone is high-minded, somewhat puritanical, and the dominant ideology is consistently reproduced in a sequence of articles, some factual and academic, others fictional or critical. The Wales invoked here is that of established families, providing to the nation the parsons, lawyers and respectable Nonconformist ministers that feature regularly in the magazine's accounts of "notable" individuals. *The Red Dragon* is an entirely typical miscellany periodical, in the same mould as popular late nineteenth-century English contemporaries such as *Blackwood's*, *The Fortnightly Review*, or the *Cornhill Magazine*. It has much in common, too, with its immediate successors in Wales.

The Welsh Review (1891-92)

This short-lived example of a Welsh miscellany opens in November 1891 with the assertion that it is intended to be a monthly magazine "worthy in every sense of the word national". The editor aims to create "a literary organ" in which the views of the Welsh could be interchanged with those of other nations. In a further expansion of the search for readership, it appeals for support from the Welsh diaspora in the United Kingdom and overseas. The editor, Ernest Bowen Rowlands, undertakes to give adequate space to contemporary literature and to publish suitable original writing. The rhetorical tone of this editorial is elevated:

> Its purpose is to make known the country of Wales, to afford an outlet to Welsh genius, and to act as a medium of communication between Wales and other countries as a means of bringing in to closer association the minds of Welshmen living in all parts of the world. The success of the REVIEW will be the elevation of Wales, and it behoves you her sons to put each his shoulder to the wheel and increase the velocity of the ascent.[28]

This sense of placing a patriotic and moral obligation on the readership to support a means of national cultural expression is to recur in other Anglo-Welsh periodicals. The editor publishes nine pages of facsimiles of the signatures of letters of support for the magazine from "all sorts and conditions of people".[29] The generic self-consciousness of this production is underlined by the presence in the opening issues of a two-part article about Welsh periodical literature by D. Tudor Evans. This begins by pointing out the origins of Welsh periodical writing in the secular almanacks of the eighteenth century. The article's emphasis on the "earnest desire of educated Welshmen to impart useful information to their fellow countrymen" sets a didactic tone that is to be heard many times in the future history of Anglo-Welsh journals.[30] In the second part of the article the role of bards, "uninfluenced by sect or party" working on the "purely national and patriotic lines" associated with the Cymmrodorion Societies is recorded. It also underlines the predominance throughout the nineteenth century of Welsh-language religious periodicals with their bases in particular Nonconformist denominations. The only English-language periodical mentioned is the *Cambro-Briton,* said to have lasted three years only, from 1819-22. There is no mention of *The Red Dragon*.[31]

The May 1892 issue shows how *The Welsh Review* operated the typical editorial practice of the miscellany, mingling major topics of the day with more diverting entertainment for its readership. It also demonstrates the familiar technique of presenting both articles and fiction in series, while at the same time encouraging internal debate and controversy, thereby seeking to create a mild form of dependency in its audience. The issue opens, for instance, with the first part of a scholarly article on temperance, citing historical precedents from Greece and Rome as well as from earlier British history to prove that legislation can contribute to controlling this "intolerable nuisance". Nora Phillips responds to an attack on her earlier essay in the February issue, which had argued the case for women's rights and suffrage. Her critic, Eliza Orme, had complained that Phillips had effectively sought to expel from the Liberal Party all those who disagreed with her; Phillips claims, in rejoinder, that she has the constitution of the party on her side and says acidly that "Miss Orme in her 'Commonplace Correction' is more successful in being commonplace than in being correct". James A. Duncan discusses the case for Members of Parliament to be paid salaries, dismissing the Conservative argument that this will lower standards and arguing that payment will allow direct representation of the working classes. One of a series of satirical skits giving semi-fictional accounts of political gossip but using the real names of political figures, such as Joseph Chamberlain, Lord Roseberry, Gladstone or Randolph Churchill appears under the presumed pseudonym of the "Duchess of Treorky".[32] In its mix of reportage, deliberate exaggeration and ironic commentary the contribution appeals to much the same taste for sensation and humour as today's *Private Eye*.

These articles, then, generally comprise weighty treatments of serious matters, much enlivened by the argumentative and satirical style of some of the contributors. However, the creative and critical writing in *The Welsh Review* is, on the whole, less impressive than that in *The Red Dragon*. "The Blue Bandit of the Bread Mountains" is actually intended as parody, a romantic fiction much given to the use of asterisks to represent the bandit's language, and presented in the name of "Rider-Haggard-Dumas-Stevenson-Flaubert-Longbow". But "The Chaplain's Secret", which appears a little further on, is an example of just such a fiction, full of improbable coincidence. So is the serialized novel, *Owain Seithenyn*, with its story of Owain and Nesta (with her "raven locks") and the lovers' thrilling encounters with the aged harpist Gwilym and with fiery, jealous Jestyn. The theatre criticism welcomes the use of music halls for theatrical performances despite the objections of Sir Henry Irving, and goes on to review current London productions, including *A*

Doll's House and *Lady Windermere's Fan*. This suggests something of the metropolitan aspirations of the middle-class audience being sought for the magazine. The only book review in this issue is of a sympathetic biography of the German Kaiser, whose character is, however, much excoriated by the reviewer as a brutal and unfilial son, compared unfavourably to Count Bismarck.[33] There is no poetry. The relatively lightweight character of the magazine's handling of cultural material means that, ultimately, *The Welsh Review*'s initial ambition to elevate debate and to be a significant "literary organ" in Wales is not achieved. The somewhat jarring combination of serious articles and frippery fiction may be related to its apparent need to serve a limited and divided audience at home and in the diaspora.

Wales: A National Magazine for the English-Speaking Parts of Wales (1894-97); *Wales: The National Magazine for the Welsh People* (1911-14)

Owen M. Edwards's *Wales* is another example of the miscellany genre, once more adopting a lofty social tone. However, the editor's concern about widening the range of his readership appears in the introduction to the second volume (signed as from Lincoln College, Oxford):

> [T]he farmers, the artisans and the labourers of the English-speaking parts of Wales have not welcomed it with the enthusiasm that their Welsh [-speaking] brethren showed when *Cymru* and *Llenor* were offered to them. *Wales* is gradually, but very slowly, making its way into the peasant homes of the Severn valley, and to the cottages of the great industrial centres of South Wales. I desire above all things, to see the peasants of eastern and southern Wales becoming readers. No man is too poor to enter into the glorious world of thought which is around him and within him. For this purpose, the third volume will be of a more popular character; while at the same time its interest to scholars will be kept up. An attempt will be made at illustrating the humour and the pathos of typically Welsh life.[34]

This passage, with its mixture of missionary seriousness, its recognition of the primacy of print culture in the Welsh language, expressing both some condescension towards "the peasants" and also concern about their reception of English-language writing, nods to many of the problem areas that will recur in this analysis. The habitual resort among many future writers to presentation of the Welsh as being, in Harri Webb's words, "a marginal, picturesque people" is hinted at in that final, slightly despairing sentence.[35]

Rural issues also feature prominently in John Hugh Edwards's later miscellany, *Wales*, which has, however, a stronger nationalist tone. An opening article about the problems of Welsh agriculture both highlights the predicament of the labourer and the poverty, squalor and demoralization of the small farmer and also attacks the laziness and detachment of the gentry.[36] The article goes on to advocate "democratisation of the land". In this miscellany the fiction also addresses countryside concerns, through its serialization of "Owen Owen: a tragedy of misunderstanding", which tells of difficult relationships between the Welsh-speaking hero and the "Saxon" master of *Plas-y-Graig*.[37] An article about Welsh Nationalism by a journalist from the *Manchester Guardian* is basically a threnody for Welsh Liberalism, marking the achievements, during what Kenneth O. Morgan calls its "Antonine period", of a degree of national independence. This was the period of the founding of the University of Wales and the National Library, and the establishment of the Central Welsh Board for Education.[38]

John Hugh Edwards, was an active Liberal politician, a Member of Parliament, a former Minister with the Independents and a regular contributor to such British publications as *The British Weekly* and *The Empire News*.[39] He had also written a recent biography of Lloyd George, which made much of Lloyd George's folk-hero image, as the country boy who had "trod the primrose path" to fame and fortune in England.[40] J. Hugh Edwards epitomizes the intensely respectable nature and gentlemanly ethos of these early Welsh periodicals. They are, in terms of genre analysis, clearly miscellanies in terms of their mix of creative writing, polemical and documentary articles. It is interesting that there do not appear to be any early instances of the review genre among nineteenth-century Welsh periodicals. Indeed, these rather solemn Victorian and Edwardian miscellanies could be regarded as filling that gap in the range of periodical genres available to Welsh middle-class readers in this period.

Other English-language journals, such as *Cymru Fydd* (1888-91) and *Young Wales* (1895-1903) appear more radical and nationally conscious. *Cymru Fydd* mixes English writing with Welsh-language articles and has a lively correspondence column, dealing with religious and educational issues. *Young Wales* is also edited by J. Hugh Edwards. While it appears in a much slimmer format than his *Wales* (rarely more than twenty-five pages), it still carries some heavy-weight articles comparing Welsh-language problems to those in Flanders and advocating the use of Welsh for juries in trials of monoglot Welshmen.[41] These earlier examples of periodical writing in the serious miscellany mode, aiming at speaking for and to a Welsh national community, set a tone and a pattern towards which many later Welsh magazines in English came to aspire. Later periodicals like *Welsh Outlook* and the later *Welsh Review* reflect a similar moderate politics and seriousness of tone.

The Welsh Outlook: A Monthly Journal of Social Progress
[later *New Welsh Outlook*] (1914-33)

The Welsh Outlook's strapline, "Where there is no vision the people perish", reflects the beliefs of its founder-editor, Thomas Jones, whose career included being Secretary to Lloyd George's Cabinet, the inspiration behind Coleg Harlech and one of the founders of C.E.M.A., the precursor of the Arts Council of Great Britain.[42] Working closely with the magazine's sponsor, the wealthy industrialist Lord Davies of Llandinam and a carefully-selected Board of Management, Jones produced a magazine described as "liberal, internationalist, moderately de-centralist but often rigidly conservative over ideological questions".[43] In many of these respects it echoes its predecessors. *The Welsh Outlook*, however, adopts a stance of high seriousness more apposite for a review. The periodical is stylish in presentation, with a reproduction of Millet's *Going to Work* facing the opening page of its first issue in January 1914. There are two columns to a page, closely printed, and most articles in it are anonymous. There is one poem but no other creative writing. These are all characteristics of the review genre. The serious and weighty tone of this periodical is well illustrated by an article in the first issue, "The Religious Outlook in Wales". This accepts that "hitherto our language has served as a mighty bulwark to keep out the good and the evil that the alien might send us". Given the rate of increase in contacts with the outside world and the triumph of scientific investigation, "if Theology still claims to be the queen of the sciences she knows that she must rule as a constitutional monarch". There are articles reviewing a wide range of topics, including the weaknesses of Welsh medicine, the problems of Welsh writers (given the lack of a viable native publishing industry), the apathy of the nation in relation to art and architecture and the deplorably infantile nature of contemporary Welsh drama. There are some six pages of reviews.[44] *The Welsh Outlook* is credited with helping to influence Welsh public opinion (which had a strong pacifist element) in favour of the prosecution of the 1914-18 war, especially by producing a philosophical basis for opposition to Prussian nationalism and the influence of Nietzche.[45] Some degree of overt censorship had to be employed by the Board of Management to secure this end.[46]

　　Thomas Jones handed over the day-to-day editorship in 1916 to Edgar Chappell, a life-long Socialist, but Jones still retained overall control and his practice of referring potentially controversial material to his sponsor continued.[47] Chappell aimed at a less academic approach, with more "*strong virile outspoken* stuff".[48] However, the periodical had some difficulty in coming to terms with contemporary turbulence in labour relations. For example, in January 1916 a restrained article argues that "it is in the interests of labour to support the stability of the safer ventures by arranging to prevent any dislocation as far as possible". However, Chappell's own article (written under the pseudonym "Observer" some six months later) praises the activism and independence of the South Wales Miners' Federation and deplores "the *Western Mail* sneer" about the Kaiser sending them sixty thousand iron crosses for distribution.[49] Chappell overstepped his sponsors, however, in his proposed article for the December 1916 issue, attacking capitalism and advocating workers' control. The article was referred by Thomas Jones to Lord Davies who annotated it as "rubbish" (his mildest comment) and caused Chappell to withdraw it.[50] In 1920, following a substantial reorganization, including moving the journal's base from Cardiff to Newtown, *The Welsh Outlook* deliberately shifted attention away from the South Wales scene.[51] Under successive editors, Robert Roberts (Silyn), Thomas Huws Davies and William Watkin Davies, serious articles continue to predominate but the magazine now skirts gingerly around controversial contemporary events. The first mention of the 1926 General Strike was in the month following the return to work. The collapse of the strike was described as "a victory for sanity" which should lead to organized labour embracing policies based on "a system of co-operation rather than of war".[52] Under William Watkin Davies, following a threatened libel case by Professor T. Gwynn Jones, circulation fell sharply to around seven hundred copies a month and Lord Davies withdrew his financial support in 1927.[53]

At this point the editorship passed to Elias Henry Jones. *New Welsh Outlook* retained its original format but there is a sense of the material having become thinner. Physically, the January 1930 number is only twenty-eight pages long as against the first issue's thirty-eight pages. Articles are now signed and there is more creative writing in the shape of short stories. There are three pages of reviews.[54] The magazine is now more of a miscellany than a review. Three years later, the final issue is much more downhearted in tone. An editorial records the devastation of the war and the subsequent depression, regrets that there has been "no national effort to counter the evil", and concludes, rather sadly, that "all we have to do, after all, is to hand on the torch . . . " This terminal issue recapitulates the reviews of religion, art, literature, music, drama in Wales that appeared in the first issue, regretting the loss of "happy days of more uniform opinions".

This article records a few bright spots, improvements in music provision being one of them. But in drama, the scene is marked by the further decline of the language and the "deterioration of social values". The increase in tuberculosis outweighs the improvements in health provision elsewhere. T. Huws Davies observes that the first issue wore "a Greyfriars robe" and almost ignored politics. "Today", however, he concludes, "the present position of

Welsh politics is utterly confused".[55] *The Welsh Outlook* engages with Welsh life throughout a damaging and problematic transitional period, involving massive social distress. There is some dissonance between its original form as a review serving an audience devoted to high culture and the nature of the material it is later required to deal with as social tensions within Wales were exacerbated in the aftermath of the First World War. This tension contributed to the significant shift in genre during its final period of production.

The Welsh Review: A Quarterly Journal about Wales, its People and their Activities (1939 [February to November]; 1944-48)

A second periodical called *The Welsh Review*, once more a monthly, this time edited by Professor Gwyn Jones, was launched in February 1939. Despite the word "review" in its title, *The Welsh Review* appears essentially as a serious-minded miscellany, trying to look outwards in the name of a group of young writers seen as "interpreting Wales to the outside world". These writers regard themselves as the Welsh equivalents of the poets and dramatists of the Irish revival. It declares itself as definitely "*not* a successor to *Welsh Outlook*" but "a new journal for a new day. . . . Briefly we speak to and for the people of mind".[56] It has a liberal-humanist agenda, finding it necessary to declare overtly its preference for democracy over totalitarianism. The pre-war issues of this miscellany seem to experience considerable difficulty in adjusting from the Edwardian consensus that is apparent in its predecessors to the circumstances of a changed world. During its first six issues, *The Welsh Review* betrays, for a periodical with a declared ambition to be outward looking, a surprising lack of awareness of the international situation immediately before the outbreak of World War II, only acknowledging it for the first time in October 1939.[57] Some of the fiction in *The Welsh Review* reflects the taste for "the quaint and grotesque" identified by Harri Webb as a recurring expectation of the audience for Anglo-Welsh writing.[58] "An Afternoon at Uncle Shad's", by Glyn Jones, typically represents some dark social themes through the consciousness of children. Two boys play on old pit workings on the same day that Uncle Shad, who has become demented as a result of a long period of unemployment, sets his bedclothes on fire and then tries, unsuccessfully, to cut his own throat. Uncle Shad

was a funny-looking man, pale, with a big oval face and round popping eyes, whitish grey and very shiny and wet-looking. On his head he had a brown covering of my father's armpit hair, and now that he had taken off his red flannel muffler I could see the swelling wen hung in his neck like a little udder, half of it grimy and half of it clear and white. When I went into the kitchen he was rubbing his back up and down against the edge of the open pantry door to scratch himself. Then he sat down and read the tablecloth with his head twisted on one side.[59]

The story speaks through the consciousness of the two boys about earthiness, the pits, homely food, unemployment, squalor and despair, together reflecting elements of Glyn Jones's Socialist vision of contemporary South-Wales society.

An editorial in July 1939 notes the recent closures of *Criterion* and the *London Mercury* ("[T]hese are not good days for literary journals. The publishers of books say that these last nine months have been the worst they have ever known") and the Gwyn Jones appeals for more subscribers.[60] In commenting about the Manchurian crisis, he deplores the activities of "the new-style imperialist who grants to aggressors the exact rights of smash-and-grab we found so profitable *in our own empire-building days*" [my italics].[61] This acceptance of an association of Wales with British imperial history reads strangely in a new periodical intended to express the idea of Wales to the world at large and it reflects, maybe inadvertently, some of the attitudes of *The Red Dragon* in the previous century. In the last editorial of this series, Gwyn Jones reasserts traditional liberal values, and claims that "*The Welsh Review* stands for just those values of creativeness, tolerance, goodwill and understanding that we are fighting this war to maintain".[62]

These worthy editorial sentiments are oddly at variance with a short story by Alun Lewis that follows immediately afterwards. "The Wanderers" is about a gypsy couple who visit a shop where "a shrivelled little Jew with scant mousy hair and watery peering eyes popped up ingratiatingly from behind the counter. His withered smile hardened as he looked at the gypsy" and "he fondled with his skinny fingers" the earrings they want him to pawn. The story also includes an encounter with a charming Welsh milkmaid and a meeting with a sexy Breton onion-seller. Read at this distance in time, it appears ironic that these stereotypes are being canvassed, apparently without question, in a liberal periodical advocating tolerance and understanding as major values to be defended in the first months of a war against fascism. *The Welsh Review*'s uncertain editorial practice at this stage in its life is further highlighted in the positioning of a well-argued article about the need for greater ambition in the British industrial novel, in the midst of several unconvincing creative contributions.[63] This article appears accompanied by two sentimental tales of childhood, "The Dog in the Sky", a picture of the imagined impact of bombing on a child, and "Pikelets and a Penny", about a child's reaction to his mother's grief over his father's death. These are preceded by a simplistic poem by Idris Davies:

Once in a mining valley
I heard the night winds say
"Beyond our sunless sorrows
There dawns a kinder day."[64]

The editors of miscellanies have the opportunity of using artful juxtapositions to reinforce the messages they are trying to communicate. However, here, *The Welsh Review* risks undermining its ideological position by the contrast between the powerful demands of its editorial rhetoric and critical writing, and the relative poverty of the creative materials accompanying them.

When the magazine reappears, as a quarterly, in March 1944, it repeats its intention to provide a platform for younger writers and "to keep the English speaking Welsh bound to their homeland".[65] The magazine now seems more alert to world events and it is soon to demand "stern justice" for a different kind of stereotype, this time "the spruce, handsome, metallic creatures of both sexes", those "thugs and perverts" who served as guards in concentration camps. Gwyn Jones goes on to record Lloyd George's many achievements, in the aftermath of his death in March 1945, especially the social legislation through which "he saved this country from revolution in the longest trade depression that we have had since 1929. . . . We claim him with satisfaction as a great Welshman".[66] Alun Lewis writes (this time very sensitively) about India, anticipating the post-war conflicts about Britain's withdrawal from Empire, and perceiving "a perpetual undercurrent of mockery and hostility towards us among the people". This factual account of his experience has none of the stereotyping of his earlier short story, nor does it reflect the personal ambivalence about colonial subjects observed by recent critics of his work.[67] The creative writing in the magazine is now much more impressive. There is a translation of a powerful short story by Kate Roberts and some excerpts from the journals of Caradoc Evans. Some sense of the passing of a generation appears in a speech at Aberystwyth by Thomas Jones: "[O]ne of the hundred definitions of education is that it is the enforcement on the young of the prejudices of the old".[68]

Peter Macdonald Smith, in his discussion of the making of the Anglo-Welsh tradition (written for the *New Welsh Review's* first issue in 1988) points up the miscellany nature of *The Welsh Review* when he says that "its second series (1944-48) appealed to the general but educated reader. Short stories appeared alongside essays on Welsh literature, poems appeared above erudite discussions of public health".[69] Indeed, as has been observed above, *The Welsh Review* sometimes had problems in separating itself from a nineteenth-century liberal set of social attitudes, more inclined to be vested in a class-based orientation which perceived advancement within English society and government as the natural pinnacle of Anglo-Welsh ambition. In this respect it perhaps reflected the attitudes of the generation from which it drew its core readership.

This survey of the serious liberal miscellany in Wales shows it to be the genre that dominated periodical production in the country for the period between 1880 and 1939. This is not to ignore the existence of a number of other more radical, politicized magazines and newspapers, such as *Plebs* (1909) or the *Rhondda Socialist*, ominously subtitled "the BOMB of the Rhondda Workers" and later re-titled the *South Wales Worker* (1911).[70] These were also to have their successors, later in the century. They were not however, unlike the miscellanies, to influence the sequence of twentieth-century little magazines to any perceptible degree. The first of these little magazines did not appear in Wales until 1937, with the publishing of yet another periodical called *Wales*, this time initially in a wholly different genre, edited by Keidrych Rhys.

Wales [later subtitled *The National Monthly Magazine*] (1937-39; 1943-1948; 1958-1960)

The first edition of *Wales* appears in a red and buff cover, priced at a modest one shilling, bearing no national symbol, but carrying, as its strap-line, a defiant quotation from the opening of its first offering, a short story by Dylan Thomas: "Prologue to an Adventure": "As I walked through the wilderness of this world, as I walked through the wilderness, as I walked through the city with the loud electric faces and the crowded petrols . . ."[71] This *Wales* is new, vibrant, urban, modern in tone. It has a list of contributors on the front cover but it eschews a conventional contents page. Dylan Thomas's short story develops itself as an entertaining series of erotic fantasies.[72] Most of the other material in this first issue is poetry. There are two reviews, a one-page piece by Glyn Jones on *A Time to Laugh* by Rhys Davies, the other a facetious account of Idris Bell's *Development of Welsh Poetry* by Aneurin ap Gwynn. *Wales* is printed locally in Newtown and published by the editor, Keidrych Rhys. Rhys was a professional journalist who possessed an ebullient personality. He had an appeal to younger writers and was a lively contributor to a wide range of organizations.[73] Indeed, everything about the magazine bespeaks the little magazine genre. The advertisement on the back cover of the first issue refers to Hugh MacDiarmid's advice to avoid aping English mannerisms. It asserts that "there is actually no such thing as 'English' culture" and celebrates Welsh writers as coming from the ordinary people rather than from a literary class.

However, the second issue is already becoming slightly more solemn in tone. There is now an editorial, entitled "As You Know", declaring the intention to "provide a sort of forum where the Anglo-Welsh have their say, as poets, short story writers and critics". It again denies being the product of a literary clique: "[O]nce more we stress that we are with the people".[74] It records some criticism of the first issue it has received, accusing the magazine of "staging an irish [sic] renaissance of violent racial hatred, with a smoke-screen of the resurgent nationalism of 'rural' areas, a bran-dip in the hip-bath of Arthuriana and *Oesau Canol*".[75] The editorial goes on to express a wish to print younger writers, but is wary of being patronizing, displaying a strangely inverted political awareness: "[T]here is something fishy when a commercial, capitalist group hides behind the camouflage of giving the kids a carrot".[76] The contents now have a greater proportion of prose works, both short stories and critical essays. This balance is maintained in subsequent issues, where, over time, financial strains begin to become evident: the magazine becomes slimmer, and the price drops to an even more modest sixpence. Alvin Sullivan notes that, from the fifth issue (Summer 1938) more non-Welsh writers begin to appear.[77] There is a tell-tale "double issue" in March 1939, edited jointly by Keidrych Rhys and Dylan Thomas. The magazine now carries advertisements, for Zwemmers, a respectable London bookshop, and for other little magazines, such as *Seven, Tir Newydd*, and *Life and Letters To-Day*.[78] In August 1939, with Nigel Heseltine now in the editor's chair for the remainder of this series, *Wales* adopts an enlarged format and announces that it will appear in future at quarterly rather than monthly intervals.[79] In what could be construed as a gesture to the Pan Celtic ideal, the editor welcomes Hugh MacDiarmid and Thomas MacGreevey as guest writers. Keidrych Rhys, in an apparently valedictory article, has advice for his successor in the shape of twenty-one numbered sentences (reminiscent of the manifesto in Wyndham Lewis's *Blast*) which includes some rather bitter comments about the beleaguered nature of creative writing in Wales, such as:

> 3. Anthropologically speaking one can, in the end, perhaps, say that this unlovely, soul-destroying and violent Puritanism with its resultant effect on morals didn't even benefit our culture. It doesn't even seem to die a natural death. . . .

> 5. Oxford may have regretted its treatment of Shelley: the Principality has never felt anything like that over Goronwy Owen. Ever heard of a Welshman making a sacrifice for the sake of Art?[80]

However, despite this advice and the new editor's brave front, there are only two further issue of *Wales*, when it closes, probably due to wartime paper restrictions, until 1943.

When the new series starts, once more edited by Keidrych Rhys, there is a conscious and dramatic change of direction and tone. The opening editorial begins thus:

> The policy of *Wales* then, if it needs defining, will be a responsible one *towards* Wales. We are primarily a cultural magazine, cultural in the broadest sense. *Wales* will continue to be non-party, independent and progressive. The only propaganda it will recognise will be the truth. . . . The pioneer work of the old happy-go-lucky pre-war *Wales* is done—the sapping, the literary fireworks, the frontal attack—all that is now *pro-tem.* Our aims have been partially achieved. The era of unfruitful introversion, of the defeated outlook, is gone.[81]

The semantic juggling here with the identity between *Wales* the periodical and Wales the nation starts the process of trying to turn the periodical into the self-conscious voice of the nation. Moreover, the entirely premature claim that the magazine's work has been done and its aims achieved seems, in the light of the actual contents of this issue, to be over-optimistic and ultimately self-defeating. Contributors change in character and the emphasis on creative writing diminishes. Jim Griffiths, M.P., who was to become the first Secretary of State for Wales in 1964, writes about the disillusion of the inter-war years and about the work of the Welsh Council on Reconstruction.[82] There are three articles in this issue analysing the character of Anglo-Welsh writing. In one of them, W. Moelwyn Merchant quotes Saunders Lewis, the leading Welsh Nationalist of his generation, querying whether such a thing exists and saying of Dylan Thomas that he is "obviously an equipped writer but there is nothing Welsh about him. He belongs to the English".[83] The other two articles also query the very idea of Anglo-Welsh writing as a separate literary tradition.[84] This uncertainty is to be replicated continuously in the future, in *Wales* and, indeed, in other publications. The tone contrasts strongly with the sparky confidence of the earlier issues. The link with "the people" is no longer much in evidence. The process of migration towards another genre altogether is now well under way.

The history of *Wales* from now onwards, through its second series up to 1948 and then in its final manifestation in 1958-60, demonstrates a trend which is typical of Welsh little magazines. Steadily it ceases to carry the characteristic marks of the little magazine genre and moves ever closer to the style of the liberal Welsh miscellanies that predominated in the period from 1880 to 1939. It is as if the weight of the expectations bred by the earlier history of the genre in Wales creates an irresistible force towards respectability and solemnity. There are, of course, other credible explanations for these changes, including the ageing of the original editorial group, growing commercialization, pressures from advertisers and the inevitable failures of energy which attend periodicals of longer standing. Ian Hamilton discerns three clear phases in a little magazine's development, from what he calls the "jauntily assertive" opening to a middle phase of "genuine identity" and a closing period he characterizes as typically "wan and mechanical".[85] What appears different about *Wales*, and about some later Welsh magazines, is the relatively rapid transformation from typically irreverent and iconoclastic little magazines into rather weighty miscellanies, journals of record, voices of more conventional opinion.

Whatever the cause, it is demonstrable that, by the summer of 1945, *Wales* has a contents list extraordinarily similar to its Edwardian predecessors. Lord Clwyd writes of "Parliament in my Day"; there are translations from Welsh verse, antiquarian articles by a Welsh landowner and industrialist, economics articles about coal and shipping problems, and an article about the depopulation of the Welsh hill country. Leo Abse writes about Kenya and Lord Tredegar about "Sir Henry Morgan before Panama".[86] The space for new authors, for creative writing and new criticism has largely been usurped by establishment figures. The price has risen to two shillings and sixpence and the magazine seems by now to be directed to a different readership. A year later, in June 1946, *Wales*, like its predecessors of the same name, fifty years or more before, becomes subtitled as "The National Magazine". The paratext now reveals a smart new blue-grey cover, decorated with a harp and a ship in a roundel and there are far more advertisements.[87] The Tenth Year Issue in 1947 carries sixty tributes to *Wales* from a wide range of other journals, including *The Observer*, *The Manchester Guardian*, *Baner ac Amserau Cymru* (the leading Welsh-language periodical, established in 1843) as well as from John Cowper Powys and Jim Griffiths M.P.[88]

In May 1948, near the end of this series, *Wales* prints a list of around eight hundred regular subscribers, running to forty-seven pages of text. This list demonstrates an impressive international reach, with embassies in many European and Commonwealth countries, as well as many major companies, academic institutions and libraries, including those of workers' institutes throughout Wales. After another break, this time an unexplained interval of five years, the magazine's final series appears as *Wales: The National Monthly Magazine* in September 1958. This version is enshrined in a new glossy cover, showing a tourist picture of a little girl in Welsh national costume and with a full page photographic portrait by Anthony Armstrong-Jones of H.R.H. Prince Charles, aged six, listing his full range of titles. An article appears on "Prospects for Rugby" by Wilf Wooller and another entitled "A tory [sic] in Wales" by H. W. J. Edwards, giving an account of his idiosyncratic views linking nationalism with traditional Catholicism.[89] The next month's issue, records the understandable despair of a "reader from Brynmawr" at the transformation of the magazine into something "designed for the London Welsh". The editor is concerned about the degeneration of Anglo-Welsh writing, especially, quoting Cyril Connolly's words, about the "stagy exports" being offered as short stories.[90] This last series ceases publication after two years, apparently because it failed to maintain the publisher's minimum circulation of a thousand subscribers.[91]

There have been many eloquent tributes to the contributions Keidrych Rhys and *Wales* have made to the literary and intellectual life of Wales during the period. Kenneth O. Morgan describes *Wales* as "a landmark in the dawning of Anglo-Welsh literature".[92] Raymond Garlick describes *Wales* as "vigorous, catholic, controversial and colourful".[93] The miscellanies these little magazines quickly became made many valuable contributions to Welsh culture. The point to be emphasized here is, however, to do with the nature of the transformation which takes place, in this particular context, in the genre of the periodical, in the signals transmitted about the kind of material likely to be found and the nature of the audience it solicits. It is about ceasing, quite rapidly, to be "a little magazine". Welsh little magazines do seem unique in this respect; there are few cases elsewhere of similar genre migrations and the difference is something to do with the influence and history of the periodical genre within Welsh society. There are a few exceptions to this rule, one being *The Welsh Anvil: Yr Einion*, published for the Guild of Students of the University of Wales, but this clearly starts life as a publication aimed at a university readership, prioritizing academic issues.[94] The history of *Dock Leaves*, which begins life as a characteristic little magazine but is once again transmuted over a relatively short period of time into something quite different, is far more typical.

Dock Leaves [later subtitled *A National Review in English of Welsh Arts and Letters*] (1949-1957)

This periodical, originally produced in Pembrokeshire at Christmas 1949, as a quarterly, has about it in the first edition all the signifiers of the little magazine genre. Its life cycle, however, like that of *Wales*, illustrates the by now familiar story of the trend of Welsh little magazines towards the serious miscellany. But this could scarcely have been anticipated by the first readers to see its misty green cover, designed and drawn by Keith Cooper, showing symbols of the sun and the sea, with a pattern of trefoil dock leaves and an astronomical instrument, signifying its local origins in Pembroke Dock. The editorial in the second issue, written by the youthful Raymond Garlick (then a twenty-two-year-old schoolmaster working under the direction of Roland Mathias), declares

> Although the purpose of this Review must be to provide, in face of the appalling publishing situation for present-day creative writers, a vehicle for poetry, short stories, essays and criticism of quality—no matter from what direction they may come, it must also be interpreted *as Pembrokeshire speaking to Wales* [my italics].[95]

Dock Leaves's origins are therefore essentially regional and local and the stated objective demonstrates the little magazine's characteristic desire to produce another outlet for writers working against the grain.

There are already, however, one or two signs of the editor harbouring wider ambitions: his description of *Dock Leaves*, in this second editorial, as "a Review" is interesting because, at this stage, it has few of the qualities of the review genre. However, the second issue extends the magazine's length from thirty pages to sixty. There are translations from Mallarmé and from the Swedish of Franc Beningsen. One quite lengthy article comprises a contribution by the magazine to the British national debate on the "two cultures" through an account of Lewis Mumford's *The Condition of Man*. None of these interventions obviously works within the formula of "Pembrokeshire speaking to Wales".[96] However the rest of the issue does contain the work of local writers, such as a poem by Morwyth Rees and short stories on Welsh subjects by Roland Mathias and Olwen Rees. It earns a fraternal expression of solidarity with Irish writers from Austin Clarke, proudly printed on the back cover:

> [*Dock Leaves*] deals with Welsh writing in English, and in Wales, as here, writers have to struggle against many difficulties. . . . [H]ere we have Welsh writers looking to our country for an example of what we might call literary Home Rule.[97]

Austin Clarke, then, appears to see *Dock Leaves* as performing in Wales a similar role to *Irish Writing*, a contemporary little magazine, edited from Cork by David Marcus and so also produced in the western periphery of its country, while seeking a wider national coverage.

The fifth issue of *Dock Leaves*, in May 1951, begins to show even more clearly an ambition to exceed the little magazine genre, now being subtitled, in a way that is becoming familiar, "A National Review in English of Welsh Arts and Letters". Two years later, in Spring 1953, Raymond Garlick has become rather more sententious in his editorial, commenting on the "generally sombre air" of the world in general, the floods in the Netherlands, the Mau-Mau atrocities, and the death of Stalin.[98] Pembrokeshire, far from confining itself to Wales, is now addressing global politics. There are, however, still some more local articles, including one about the history of the Garthewin little theatre, concluding that "much depends on whether Wales can build up a tradition of the drama, as Ireland has done in the last century".[99] Bobi Jones excoriates contemporary English writing for contributing to "a tasteless, merciless and un-premeditated industrialisation and centralisation of society" and claims Anglo-Welsh literature as

> A justified retreat from the cosmopolitan disintegration and proletarian mass-production of London and its fashions, towards a regeneration inside a society which has not yet completely lost its character.[100]

Bobi Jones here echoes Raymond Williams in finding that "literature, in language, material and purpose is social" and he remarks that "cultural regionalism can be a responsible and uncomfortably broad reorientation of energetic purposes".[101] The distinction between region and nation, together with a plea for a wider audience, recalls the rationale behind some Scottish Renaissance periodicals such as Hugh McDiarmid's *Voice of Scotland* or Northern Irish periodicals, such as *Lagan*, *Rann* or the *Honest Ulsterman*. These magazines also make efforts to draw on the energies of regional or national traditions and to dissociate themselves from the perceived weaknesses of fashionable metropolitan writing.

To some extent, then, Bobi Jones is expressing a view that still conforms to *Dock Leaves*'s original prospectus. In many other respects, however, *Dock Leaves* has changed and is becoming further advanced in the process of irretrievably shifting its genre. This issue has far less creative writing, concentrates largely on literary criticism and social commentary and closes with a lengthy and impressive list of over two hundred and fifty current subscribers, including a number of university libraries, in London, Chicago and Harvard, as well as in Wales.[102] This process of movement from the turbulent little magazine of creative writing to the serious-minded miscellany has proceeded still further by the spring of 1954, when *Dock Leaves* produces "A Dylan Thomas Number", in the aftermath of the poet's premature death. Raymond Garlick seeks to link Thomas to the metaphysicals, through Donne, Vaughan and Traherne and also to Gerard Manley Hopkins, in terms of his technical mastery.[103] The tone of the entire issue is uniformly respectful, as well-established writers, Louis MacNeice, Saunders Lewis, Aneirin Talfan Davies, pay tribute to one of their own.[104] In this rather solemn obituary the roaring boy of Dylan Thomas's early short story, "Prologue to an Adventure", celebrated in that first issue of *Wales* in the summer of 1937, stridently walking through the wilderness of the city and celebrating his erotic fantasies, scarcely receives any acknowledgement.[105]

In at least one respect, however, that is in drawing the reader's attention to its continuing financial problems, *Dock Leaves* still belongs to the world of the little magazine. In the summer of 1954 Garlick announces the "annual *Dock Leaves* day" to be held on 22 October. It is to be "an Autumn *Kermesse,* an amalgam of fete, sale-of-work, tea-party, writers' convention and fun-fair, the whole thing strung together upon the cadences of a harp", all designed to raise funds for one of the three issues each year.[106] A year later, while expressing the familiar intertextual anxiety of the little magazine editor about the fate of some of his contemporaries, he urges

> That one must still from time to time sing a dirge for the death of another periodical, great or small, tends to obscure the fact that so many continue to flourish and—in some cases—wax fat and kick.[107]

He notes the existence of four new university college magazines in Wales and also mentions the London-Welsh magazine, *Y Ddinas.* Interestingly, in terms of the ambitions he may now be seen to be pursuing, Raymond Garlick expresses his admiration for the way that Seumas O'Sullivan, in the *Dublin Magazine,* is able "to express so perfectly the rich personality of the urbane and gracious city of its title, and the culture of which it is the capital".[108] There seems to be here a touch of regret that *Dock Leaves* is still essentially seen as a provincial periodical. It is not, as the *Dublin Magazine* is here represented, the product of a capital city of an independent nation, or at least of a cultural centre. Moreover, the *Dublin Magazine* is one of the few examples of the review genre to survive into the twentieth century. As such, it is scarcely a likely model for the quintessential little magazine which *Dock Leaves* originally proclaimed itself to be. The expression of this sentiment by its long-standing editor prepares us for the abandonment of the *Dock Leaves* persona, three years later, and its transformation into a more ambitious and prestigious format.

The Anglo-Welsh Review (1958-1988)

The Anglo-Welsh Review, initially also edited by Raymond Garlick, appears in the spring of 1958, acknowledging its earlier history as *Dock Leaves* by continuing the same numeric series and also by announcing itself as being published by The Dock Leaves Press.[109] Raymond Garlick justifies the change of name by the perceived need to appeal to the "uninitiated" and by his desire to give additional publicity and respectability to the term "Anglo-Welsh".[110] He reports, in some detail, a recent lecture by Professor Gwyn Jones which especially celebrates recent achievements in Anglo-Welsh literature. Lack of official recognition for Welsh literature in English had been a concern of Garlick's at least since 1954, when he wrote an article in the

Dublin Magazine, complaining of the refusal of the University of Wales to allow theses on Anglo-Welsh writing.[111] The magazine, which is now intended for publication twice a year, is a much glossier production than its predecessor, carrying portraits of its contributors and subjects, being printed on better quality paper, and with a preponderance of longer articles. There is a more even balance of creative writing and commentary and there are over twenty pages of book reviews. The whole production is becoming a review in terms of genre, not merely in name, perhaps now even more consciously modelled on the *Dublin Magazine*. For example, the next issue follows the *Dublin Magazine*'s practice, common in the review genre, of dividing the contents into different sections, such as "Literature", "Painting and Music" or "Biography".[112] Raymond Garlick was evidently conscious of the significance of these paratextual shifts. He said later that these first few issues "represent the realisation of what I wanted of the magazine—in terms of typography and format as well as internal structure".[113]

Two years later, in 1960, Raymond Garlick is beginning to worry about the Anglo-Welsh writer becoming extinct, about whether the passing of a "strong, rebellious, idealistic and *kind* generation" between the wars has been marked by the growth of excessive academic influence:

Today, Welsh education appears provincial, academicism is rife. The young man who, twenty years ago, would have tried his hand at poetry or a novel will probably be found trying his hand at a thesis. . . . A society in which people are content that what is daily articulated is not, by and large, their experience of reality, is not a society likely to produce writers.[114]

However, within this issue of *The Anglo-Welsh Review*, the most distinguished article is an account of the poetry of Edward Thomas, which discusses, in some depth, the different evaluations of him by F. R. Leavis and Geoffrey Grigson.[115] The influence of the academics is clearly felt *within The Anglo-Welsh Review* as well as pervading the literary scene outside it. The path from *Dock Leaves*, the little magazine of the 1940s, to *The Anglo-Welsh Review* in the 1960s and 1970s is another story of a trajectory from rebellious iconoclasm towards a measure of respectability. Raymond Garlick goes on to complain that there is no Welsh publishing house and makes an assertion that London publishers shun writing where Welsh influence is dominant. Whilst writers in the Welsh language receive help from their own organizations, and favourable treatment by libraries, the only hope for the Anglo-Welsh writer, he says, lies with the Arts Council.[116] It will be useful to consider briefly at this point the role of Arts Council subsidy in relation to *The Anglo-Welsh Review*.

Wolfgang Gortschacher, in his magisterial study of little magazines, suggests that Arts Council subsidy generally militates against the eccentricity inherent in the little magazine genre and he also points out that the Welsh Arts Council was more generous than its other British equivalents in respect of support for literature.[117] Certainly such institutional support appeared necessary financially. The Welsh Committee of the Arts Council of Great Britain had existed from 1946 but, according to Roland Mathias, endorsed "the convention that literature, unlike opera, music and theatre, was commercial and self-financing".[118] At a later date, Lord Gowrie, when Chairman of the Arts Council of England, reflected on different national attitudes towards cultural subsidy, and remarked that Wales, Scotland and Ireland are closer to Europe in this respect

> England does not have a philosophy of cultural subsidy. Indeed to have one might to some extent violate the philosophical principles which have helped to create a very great culture here. As an Irishman with a Scots title married to a German and living in Wales, I want to identify the English tradition deliberately. Attitudes are different in the smaller countries of the kingdom and in the Irish Republic, which remains closer to the continental mainland in their attachment to principle. The English ethos is empirical, pragmatic and contextual.[119]

The philosophical difference suggested here may also have owed something to the differences between the size and shape of the English audience for cultural productions. Welsh producers not only had a smaller canvas but also a smaller market, one that was, moreover, divided linguistically.

The Welsh Committee did, ultimately, make occasional deficiency grants to *The Anglo-Welsh Review* but little consideration was given to regular financial support for literary magazines until after the separate foundation of the Welsh Arts Council in 1967. In July 1967 Meic Stephens was appointed as Literature Director and established a Literature Committee which took a particular interest in the financing of literary magazines. Roland Mathias, the second editor of *The Anglo-Welsh Review*, was a member of the Literature Committee from 1969-77 and Chairman for three of those years. His later essay on Anglo-Welsh magazines shows that Mathias was personally sharply aware of the administrative problems of editors and the financial burden imposed on volunteers for the task. He points out that, despite all the personal contacts available to its editors, *The Anglo-Welsh Review* never sold more than eight hundred copies, half of them outside Wales.[120] There may well have been a tendency for such heavy reliance upon financial backing to encourage a more conventional approach.

In his interview in *Planet* in 1971 Meic Stephens expresses concern about the sales of the literary and cultural magazines supported by the Arts Council. He says that the Council cannot be expected to go on increasing its subsidies if its support is not matched by sales to the public. In a later interview for

Poetry Wales in 1978 Stephens suggests that the proportion of the Welsh Arts Council's degree of support for literature eventually rises to as much as three times that granted by their Irish and Scottish equivalents. He comments on some of the negative effects of its policy of subsidising existing magazines rather than new publications. Stephens in this interview discounts the alleged dangers of stifling experimentation through subsidy.[121] The interview is immediately followed, however, by a discussion with Peter Hodgkiss, the editor of *Poetry Information*, who criticizes the policy of the Arts Council of Great Britain, saying that "the majority of British poetry in 'approved publications' presents a bland and toothless face".[122] This well-developed institutional support certainly goes some way to explain the relative longevity of Anglo-Welsh magazines as compared with their equivalents elsewhere and it appears likely that it also encourages their migration away from the little magazine genre towards less experimental and more weighty formats.

The Anglo-Welsh Review continues to demonstrate exactly this trend throughout the rest of its thirty years of life. In the 1970s and 1980s, in its "mature" phase, its length can run to as much as two hundred and eighty pages, including more than ninety pages devoted to book reviews. This may have been in part due to its sense of needing to be a comprehensive journal of record in respect of Anglo-Welsh writing.[123] At this weight the magazine begins to approximate to the size of one of the Victorian "thick journals" and the publication has clearly changed in genre terms. It has repeated the history of earlier Welsh periodicals in its almost remorseless passage from a youthful and rebellious little magazine to a mature and maybe over-weight periodical. Shortly before its closure in 1988 a report by Rhodri Williams into the performance of subsidized periodicals, commissioned by the Literature Committee, found that *The Anglo-Welsh Review* "belongs, as it were, to a past age".[124] In a more general comment, Williams remarks that

> the history of magazines is one of ebb and flow, of coming and going. Magazines, like schools of painting or writing have their "big moments". Some of the magazines in question had their moments many years ago.[125]

This process of ebbing and flowing, in the case of *The Anglo-Welsh Review*, is reflected in its generic mutations. First it becomes a miscellany, then it grows into a true review, seeking a national status, performing a stabilizing rather than an innovatory function within the culture. This transformation also represents a more or less conscious shift of genre, similar to that experienced by Keidrych Rhys's *Wales*, towards the prevalent model of the periodical set by its earlier predecessors, the national magazines of Wales in the nineteenth and earlier twentieth centuries.

This paper has tried to show that genre affiliations have had a substantial effect on the form and the substance of periodical writing in Wales. Editors of new productions must inevitably hold in their minds some models of predecessors. This may not always entail a deliberate process of influence and imitation. But editors must start from some concept of what a magazine looks like, how it may be laid out and what is an appropriate form for the kind of material they want to promote. Anglo-Welsh editors in the twentieth century had numbers of such models available to them, both outside Wales in England, Scotland, America, Ireland and also within Wales, derived from historical awareness of their Anglo-Welsh predecessors. The steady drift of so many Anglo-Welsh productions from their beginnings as little magazines to their eventual manifestations as serious miscellanies or reviews is wholly unprecedented in other parts of the British Isles. This must be more than simple coincidence. It is surely linked to their awareness of the genre characteristics of past periodicals proclaiming Anglo-Welsh culture. It can be demonstrated that the successors of these magazines in the later part of the twentieth century were able to maintain considerable stability within the genre patterns they adopted. This may say something further about the nature of the public subsidies that were available to them as well as about the growing confidence of Welsh writing in English during this later period

NOTES

1. Kenneth O. Morgan, *Rebirth of a Nation: A History of Modern Wales* (1981; Oxford: O.U.P., 1998) 33.
2. *Rebirth of a Nation* 92.
3. *Rebirth of a Nation* 258.
4. Glyn Jones, *The Dragon Has Two Tongues: Essays on Anglo-Welsh Writers and Writing* (London: Dent and Sons, 1968) 47.
5. Paul O'Leary, "Accommodation and Resistance: A Comparison of Cultural Identities in Ireland and Wales, c.1880-1914", *Kingdoms United? Great Britain and Ireland since 1500: Integration and Diversity,* ed. S. J. Connolly (Dublin, Four Courts P., 1999) 123, 128.
6. For a more detailed recent discussion of these issues see Malcolm Ballin, "Review Article: The Irish Magazine: 'The Stimulating Power in Ireland'", *Irish Studies Review* 11.2 (August 2003): 199-203.
7. Raymond Williams, *Marxism and Literature* (Oxford, O.U.P., 1977) 166.
8. Mikhail Bakhtin, *Speech Genres and Other Late Essays*, ed. and trans. Vernon W. McGhee, Caryl Emerson and Michael Holquist (Austin, Texas: U. of Texas P., 1986) 98; for a discussion of the link between the miscellany and the contemporary see also his *Problems of Dostoevsky's Poetics*, ed. and trans. Caryl Emerson (1963; Manchester: Manchester U.P., 1984) 107.
9. Malcolm Bradbury, "'Movements, Magazines and Manifestos': The Succession from Naturalism", *Modernism*, ed. Malcolm Bradbury and James MacFarlane (Harmondsworth: Penguin, 1976), 202.

10. T. S. Eliot, "What is Minor Poetry?" [Text of an Address delivered before the Association of Bookmen of Swansea and West Wales, September 26 1944], *Welsh Review*, 3.4 (December 1944); 256.

11. Roland Mathias, *The Lonely Editor: A Glance at Anglo-Welsh Magazines* (Cardiff: University College of Cardiff P., 1984) 3.

12. See Louis James, "The Trouble with Betsy: Periodicals and the Common Reader in Mid-Nineteenth Century England", *The Victorian Periodical Press: Samplings and Soundings*, ed. Joanne Shattock and Michael Woolf (Leicester: Leicester U.P., 1982) 349.

13. See Meic Stephens, ed., *The New Companion to the Literature of Wales* (Cardiff, U. of Wales P., 1998) 84, which describes *The Cambrian* Register (1795, 1796, 1818); *The Cambro-Briton and General Celtic Repository* (1819-22), and *The Cambrian Quarterly Magazine and Celtic Repository* (1829-33). Roland Mathias (*The Lonely Editor* 7) draws attention to *The Cambrian Journal* (1853-c.1863) which was also "distinctively historical in emphasis".

14. In the first issue of *The Welsh Review*, the editor claims that "until *The Welsh Review* appeared, Wales had never possessed a magazine that was not purely and entirely a Welsh production, having for its end a circulation in Wales"; see Ernest Bowen Rowlands, "A Word to the Welsh People", *Welsh Review* 1.1 (November 1891): 2. He therefore seems to discount the earlier *Red Dragon*.

15. *New Companion to the Literature of Wales* 785.

16. *The Red Dragon: The National Magazine of Wales* 1.1 (Feb.-Jul. 1882): "Welsh Poetry in English Dress; The Shake of the Hand" 66; Charles Henry Glascoline, Nestor Williams and Lewis Williams, "Where Ought the Welsh University to be Located?" 83-94.

17. "Gossip from the Welsh Colleges", *Red Dragon* 3.1 (Jan. 1883): 266-71

18. Thomas Henry Ensor, "Notable Men of Wales: Judge Herbert", *Red Dragon* 3.1: 1-13.

19. Charles Gibbon, "Of High Degree", Chapters 44-47, *Red Dragon* 3.1: 14-26.

20. John Howells, "The Cromwell Family and Their Connection with Wales", *Red Dragon* 3.1: 36.

21. Robt. D. Durnie, "A Romance of Pennard-Gower", *Red Dragon* 3.1: 38.

22. "Welsh Poets in English Dress: To the Stars", Dafydd ap Gwilym, trans. A. J. Johns, *Red Dragon* 3.1: 65-67.

23. John Rogers Rees, "In Pembrokeshire with a Sketch Book", *Red Dragon* 3.1: 39-48.

24. I.G., "Welsh Origins of Latin Place-Names", *Red Dragon* 3.1: 49-53.

25. *Red Dragon* 3.1: "Gossip from the Welsh Colleges" 71-77; "A Pendragon", "Our 'Red Dragons' at Westminster" 78-81; "Marginal Notes on Library Books" 82-87.

26. Ap Adda, "Welsh Character Sketches: Women's Clubs", *Red Dragon* 3.1: 68-70.

27. *Red Dragon* 3.1: "Literary and Art Notes of the Month, &c." 90-93; "Draconigenae" 94-96.

28. Ernest Bowen Rowlands, "A Word to the Welsh People", *Welsh Review* 1.1 (November 1891): 2.

29. "A Word to the Welsh People" 1-5.

30. D. Tudor Evans, "Welsh Periodical Literature: Part I", *Welsh Review* 1.1 (November 1891): 74.

31. "Welsh Periodical Literature: Part II", *Welsh Review* 1.2 (Dec. 1891): 179-84.

32. *Welsh Review* 1.7 (May 1892): William Davies-Rowlands, "Sober by Act of Parliament: Part I" 657-69; Nora Phillips, "'A Commonplace Correction' Corrected" 670-79 (referring to Eliza Orme, "A Commonplace Correction", *Welsh Review* 1.5 (March 1891)); James A. Duncan, "Payment of Members" 701-8; The Duchess of Treorky, "Political Notes" 681-700.

33. *Welsh Review* 1.7 (May 1892) : "The Blue Bandit of the Bread Mountains" 732-37; Reef Bedlorme, "The Chaplain's Secret" 709-30; [Anonymous], *Owain Seithenyn*, Book II, Chapter X 755-68; "Liknon", "Studies of the Stage" 746-53; [Anonymous], "Book of the Month" 754.

34. [Editor], "Introduction to Vol. II", *Wales: A National Magazine for the English Speaking Parts of Wales* 2.1 (1895): iii.

35. Harri Webb, *A Militant Muse: Selected Literary Journalism 1948-50*, ed. Meic Stephens (Bridgend: Seren, 1998) 90.

36. Gwilym O. Griffith, "Rural Developments in the New Wales", *Wales* 4 (26 July 1913): 59-64.

37. Mrs. Lees-Popham, "Owen Owen: a tragedy of misunderstanding (continued)" *Wales* 4 (26 July 1913): 78-84.

38. F. E. Hamer, "Twenty-five Years of Welsh Nationalism", *Wales* 4 (26 July 1913): 86-90. Also see Kenneth O. Morgan, *Rebirth of a Nation* 123.

39. *New Companion to the Literature of Wales* 205.

40. J. Hugh Edwards, *From Village Green to Downing Street* (1908). See Kenneth O. Morgan, *Rebirth of a Nation* 140, where he is described as representing Lloyd George's personal history as a symbol of what a "'cottage-bred boy' could achieve and, by extension, of what poor little Wales itself could attain by its own talent and determination". This was the first of three biographies of Lloyd George by J. Hugh Edwards.

41. "Notes", *Cymru Ffydd* 3.1 (Ionawr 1890): 36-41; T. R. Davies, "Bi-lingual Teaching in Schools", *Young Wales* 7.81 (Sept. 1901): 193-98; T. R. Roberts, "Trial by Jury in Wales" 201-3. Also see Kenneth O. Morgan, *Rebirth of a Nation* 95 where he describes these as the products of "a more literate, intellectually lively and sophisticated land than ever before".

42. Thomas Jones was Chairman of the Council for the Encouragement of Music and the Arts (C.E.M.A.) from its foundation and subsequently became Deputy Chairman of the Arts Council of Great Britain from 1939 to 1942. See *New Companion to the Literature of Wales* 407.

43. *New Companion to the Literature of Wales* 407.

44. *The Welsh Outlook* 1.1 (January 1914): Anon., "The Religious Outlook in Wales" 9-13; "The Medical Outlook for Wales" 14-17; T. Gwyn Jones, "Modern Welsh Literature" 19-22; Anon., "Art and the National Life" 25-27.

45. See D. Tecwyn Lloyd, "Welsh Public Opinion and the First World War", *Planet* 10 (Feb/March 1972): 25-37, esp. 28-29, where he outlines a number of articles, mostly commissioned from writers outside Wales, for example an October 1914 article by the Rev. Neville Figgis from Cambridge which developed the anti-Nietzchean argument for seeing the war as a Christian crusade.

46. See the very full treatment of the magazine by Gwyn Jenkins, "*The Welsh Outlook:* 1914-33", *National Library of Wales Journal* 24 (1985-6): 463-92.

47. For a few months before this the magazine was edited by H. J. W. Hetherington with the assistance of Silwyn Roberts and Edgar Jones, "*The Welsh Outlook*: 1914-33": 472.

48. *"The Welsh Outlook*: 1914-33" 474.
49. "R", "Labour Problems V", *Welsh Outlook* 3.1 (January 1916): 22-23; "Observer", "The Mind of the Miner III", *Welsh Outlook* 3.9 (September 1916): 279-82.
50. For a detailed account of the involvement of Lord Davies in the censoring of Chappell's proposed article in the December 1916 issue, see Trevor L. Williams, "Thomas Jones and *The Welsh Outlook*", *Anglo-Welsh Review* 64 (1979): 38-46.
51. *"The Welsh Outlook* 1914-33*"* 477.
52. W. Tudor Davies, "The Economic and Industrial Outlook", *Welsh Outlook* 13 (6 June 1926): 163-64.
53. *"The Welsh Outlook*: 1914-33" 479. Jenkins provides an analysis of circulation and sales figures, suggesting that at the peak in January 1914 these stood at over 4,000, declining to around 2,000-2,500 by 1919 and to 600-700 by 1927. (Appendix I 486).
54. *New Welsh Outlook* 17.1 (January 1930). According to Gwyn Jenkins (Appendix II 487) at this time more than half the subscribers lived outside Wales.
55. *New Welsh Outlook* 20.12 (December 1933): The Editor, "Retrospect" 315-16; T. Gwynn Jones, "Literature" 317-19; J. Morgan Jones, "Religion" 322-24; D. T. Davies, "Drama" 330-33; J. Lloyd-Williams, "Music" 333-35; Dr. D. A. Powell, "Health" 336-38; T. Huws Davies, "Politics" 338-41.
56. Gwyn Jones, "Editorial", *The Welsh Review: A Monthly Journal about Wales, its People and their Activities* 1.1 (Feb.1939): 3-7.
57. Gwyn Jones, "Editorial", *Welsh Review* 2.3 (Oct. 1939): 123-27.
58. Harri Webb, *A Militant Muse* 90.
59. Glyn Jones, "An Afternoon at Uncle Shad's", *Welsh Review* 1 (Feb. 1939): 11.
60. Gwyn Jones, "Editorial", *Welsh Review* 1.6 (July 1939): 303.
61. *Welsh Review* 1.6 (July 1939): 305
62. *Welsh Review* 2.3 (October 1939): 127.
63. "Mulciber", "The Future of the Industrial Novel in Great Britain", *Welsh Review* 2.3: 154-58
64. *Welsh Review* 2.3: Alun Lewis, "The Wanderers" 128-39; Idris Davies, "The Mining Valley" 140; T. A. Redcliffe, "The Dog in the Sky"144-47; Charles Davies, "Pikelets and a Penny" 159-64.
65. Gwyn Jones, "Editorial", *Welsh Review* 3.1 (March 1944): 1-6.
66. Gwyn Jones, "Editorial", *Welsh Review* 4.2 (June 1944): 79-82.
67. *Welsh Review* 4.2 (June 1945): Alun Lewis, "Letters from India" 82-93. The nature of Lewis's relationship to colonial and post-colonial issues has been the subject of recent commentary. See Kirsti Bohata, "Beyond Authenticity? Hybridity and Assimilation in Welsh Writing in English", *Nations and Relations: Writing Across the British Isles*, ed. Tony Brown and Russell Stephens (Cardiff: New Welsh Review, 2000) 89-121, esp. 102-8; also see M. Wynn Thomas and Tony Brown, "Colonial Wales and Fractured Language" in *Nations and Relations* 71-88. The latter article was the subject of further recent discussion in John Pikoulis, Tony Brown and M. Wynn Thomas, "Forum: Alun Lewis and the Politics of Empire", *Welsh Writing in English* 8 (2003): 157-79.
68. *Welsh Review* 4.2: Kate Roberts, "Two Storms", trans. Dafydd Jenkins 94-99; Caradoc Evans, "Excerpts from a Journal" 103-11; Thomas Jones C.B.E., "Old and Young" 135-44.
69. Peter Macdonald Smith, "The Making of the Anglo-Welsh Tradition (1)", *New Welsh Review* 1.1 (Summer 1988): 61-66.

70. *Rebirth of a Nation* 150.
71. *Wales* 1 (Summer 1937) Cover.
72. Dylan Thomas, "Prologue to an Adventure" *Wales* 1: 1-6.
73. Professor Raymond Chapman, Chairman of the Oxford Celtic Society from 1942-45 (currently Chairman of the Irish Literary Society) vividly recalls Keidrych Rhys's visit to the Celtic Society in 1943 as one of the most lively contributions of the period (interview with the present writer, 8 December 2003). Keidrych Rhys was a professional journalist, who later worked for *The People* from 1954-60 and he was also the London editor for *Poetry London-New York* from 1956-60. See *New Companion to the Literature of Wales* 637.
74. Keidrych Rhys, "Editorial: As You Know", *Wales* 2 (August 1937): 35.
75. *Wales* 2: 35.
76. *Wales* 2: 37.
77. Alvin Sullivan, ed., *British Literary Magazines: The Modern Age: 1914-1984* (Westport, Conn.: Greenwood P., 1986) 483.
78. *Wales* 3, 4, 5, double-issue 6 and 7 (Autumn 1937 to March 1939).
79. *Wales* 8 and 9 (August 1939).
80. Keidrych Rhys, "Notes for a New Editor", *Wales* 8 and 9 (August 1939): 246.
81. Keidrych Rhys, "Editorial", *Wales* n.s. 1 (July 1943): 4-6.
82. Jim Griffiths, M.P., "Wales, After the War", *Wales* n.s. 1: 7-10.
83. W. Moelwyn Merchant, "The Relevance of the Anglo-Welsh", *Wales* n.s. 2: 17-19.
84. Wyn Griffiths, "A Note on Anglo-Welsh", *Wales* n.s. 2: 15-16, and Idris Bell, "The Welsh Poetic Tradition" 38-44.
85. Ian Hamilton, *The Little Magazine: A Study of Six Editors* (London: Weidenfield & Nicholson, 1976) 9.
86. *Wales* n.s. 5.7 (Summer 1945): Lord Clwyd, "Parliament in my Day" 7-15; "A Little Anthology: Translations from Welsh Verse" 22-33; Eliot Crawshay-Williams, "The Vale of Glamorgan" 16-21; J. E. Emlyn Jones, "Welsh Industrial Reconstruction: Coal and Shipping Problems" 35-38, R.S. Thomas, "The Depopulation of the Welsh Hill Country" 75-80; Viscount Tredegar, "Sir Henry Morgan before Panama" 94-95; Leo Abse, "We see Kenya" 89-93.
87. *Wales* 6.3 (June 1946) cover and contents page.
88. "Sixty Messages to *Wales*", *Wales* n.s. 7.26 (Summer 1947): 250-259.
89. *Wales: The National Monthly Magazine* third series 1 (September 1958): cover and contents pages.
90. Keidrych Rhys, "Editorial Comment", *Wales: The National Monthly Magazine*, third series 2 (October 1958): 4.
91. Roland Mathias, *The Lonely Editor* 13.
92. *Rebirth of a Nation* 265.
93. Raymond Garlick, "Editorial", *Anglo-Welsh Review* 9.23 (1958): 7
94. *The Welsh Anvil*, aimed "to foster discussion among old students of the Welsh Universities and to provide them with a means of expressing their views upon intellectual and social issues", Alwyn D. Rees, "Editorial Notes", *Welsh Anvil: Yr Einion* 1 (1949): vii. *The Welsh Anvil* published an article by Ioan Bowen Rees, "Wales and the Anglo-Welsh" (4, July 1952, 20-31) followed by a later response from Raymond Garlick, "Seventy Anglo-Welsh Poets" (6 December 1952, 76-84) which initiated a wider debate about the the suggested existence of an Anglo-Welsh tradition that stretched back into the sixteenth and seventeenth centuries.

The Welsh Anvil was briefly revived in 1964, under the title of *The University of Wales Review*, primarily to defend the decision by the Court of the University to remain a single federated institution. See *New Companion to the Literature of Wales* 770.

95. Raymond Garlick, "Editorial", *Dock Leaves* 1.2 (Easter 1950): 1. Raymond Garlick, in an article written twenty-one years later, records his sense of amazement at finding himself in this role at such an early age and the disadvantage he felt in not knowing many of the contributors personally. See "On the Growing of Dock Leaves", *Planet* 9 (December 1971/January 1972): 71-76.

96. L. Alun Page, "Notes on the Dogmas of a Modern Prometheus", *Dock Leaves* 1.2 (Easter 1950): 12-18

97. *Dock Leaves* 1.2: back cover. It continues to appear in future editions, alongside other testimonials.

98. Raymond Garlick, "Editorial", *Dock Leaves* 3.10 (Spring 1953): 1-4.

99. R. O. F. Wynne, "The Garthewin Little Theatre", *Anglo-Welsh Review* 3.10 (Spring 1953): 5.

100. Bobi Jones, "The Anglo-Welsh", *Anglo-Welsh Review* 3.10: 25.

101. *Anglo-Welsh Review* 3.10: 28.

102. *Anglo-Welsh Review* 3.10: 55-60.

103. Raymond Garlick, "Editorial", *Dock Leaves* 5.13 (Spring 1954): "A Dylan Thomas Number" 1-5.

104. *Dock Leaves* 5.13: Louis MacNeice, "A Dylan Thomas Award" 6-7; Saunders Lewis, translation of a BBC Wales Talk from the Welsh, 8-9; Aneirin Talfan Davies, "The Golden Echo" 10-17.

105. Dylan Thomas, "Prologue to an Adventure", *Wales* 1.1 (Summer 1937): 1-6.

106. Raymond Garlick, "Editorial Note", *Dock Leaves* 5.14 (Summer 1954): 1-2.

107. Raymond Garlick, *Dock Leaves* 6.17 (Summer 1955): 1.

108. Raymond Garlick, *Dock Leaves* 6.17 (Summer 1955): 5.

109. Raymond Garlick edited *The Anglo-Welsh Review* up to and including 9.26 (1961), when he handed over to Roland Mathias. Gillian Clarke joined him as co-editor from 22.12 (Spring 1971) and then took over the role herself, with John Davies from 26.57 (1975). Finally Greg Hill and Huw Jones became the editors from February 1984, and the magazine finally closed in 1988.

110. Raymond Garlick, "Editorial", *Anglo-Welsh Review* 9.23 (1958): 3-12.

111. Raymond Garlick, "Editorial", *Anglo-Wesh Review* 9.23: 4. See also his article, "Anglo-Welsh Poetry from 1587 to 1800", *Dublin Magazine*, Jan.-Mar. 1954: 16-23 and his later "Editorial", *Anglo-Welsh Review* 10.26 (1958): 4, where he reports the award of research degrees for studies of Anglo-Welsh writing both in the University of Wales and at the Sorbonne.

112. *Anglo-Welsh Review* 9.24 (1958).

113. Raymond Garlick, "On the Growing of Dock Leaves" 74.

114. Raymond Garlick, "Editorial", *Anglo-Welsh Review* 10.26 (Spring 1960): 5.

115. Roland Mathias, "Edward Thomas", *Anglo-Welsh Review* 10.26 (Spring 1960): 23-27.

116. *Anglo-Welsh Review* 10.26 (Spring 1960): 7.

117. Wolfgang Gortschacher, *Little Magazines Profiles: The Little Magazine in Great Britain: 1939-1993* (Salzburg: Salzburg U.P., 1993) 20-22. Also see the "Literature" sections of each publication of *The Annual Report of the Welsh Arts Council* from 1969-70 onwards up to 1976-77. These show allocations to

periodicals rising from £5,388 in 1969/70 to a figure of £34,800 for seven magazines in Wales during the year 1975-76, including £6,250 for the *Anglo-Welsh Review*.

118. Roland Mathias, "Literature in English", *The Arts in Wales: 1950-75*, ed. Meic Stephens (Cardiff: Welsh Arts Council, 1979) 226.
119. Lord Gowrie, *The Philosophy of Cultural Subsidy* (London: Arts Council of England, 1992).
120. Roland Mathias, *The Lonely Editor* 4 and 17.
121. "Interview with Meic Stephens", *Poetry Wales* 14.2 (Autumn 1978): 19-49.
122. "Interview with Peter Hodgkiss", *Poetry Wales* 14.2: 49-50.
123. An example is 22.50 (1973), which has 288 pages, including 92 pages of book reviews. Roland Mathias records Gillian Clarke's joking comment that "she took over just in time to prevent me from having reviewed a book on snails because it was written by a Welshman" (*The Lonely Editor* 14).
124. Rhodri Williams, "Review of Subsidised Periodicals", Welsh Arts Council, January 1987, 26. (Welsh Arts Council Archive, National Library of Wales, Vol. II, DIR/286. "Director's Files, 1986/7", quoted with the permission of the Chief Executive, Arts Council of Wales.)
125. "Review of Subsidised Periodicals" 107.

Margiad Evans's *The Wooden Doctor*: Illness and Sexuality

Sue Asbee
The Open University

Margiad Evans's *The Wooden Doctor* (1933) is a fictionalized autobiography, a first-person account of a young woman's unrequited love for a doctor old enough to be her father.[1] This love begins as Arabella approaches puberty and endures into her early twenties—the time span of the novel—along with persistent undiagnosed abdominal pains requiring medical attention. Arabella's developing sexuality is not straightforward and in some way is bound up with her illness. The discovery of perverse androgyny and sly sexuality in Aubrey Beardsley's drawings arouses her passionate response, perhaps among other things signalling a latent attraction to other women. At the end of the novel a brief love affair with Oliver, a young man of her own age, is consummated and the couple vow to marry, but Arabella's devotion to Dr Flaherty overrides her decision and the narrative ends surprisingly and abruptly, her love for the doctor rekindled by a meeting in the street. "I cannot understand myself", Arabella says towards the end of the novel and this admission seems to have less to do with sophisticated use of a limited first-person narrative technique, than with intensely close identification of author and narrator. In spite of the frank, confessional tone of the narrative, Arabella is no better able to interpret her story at the end than she was at the beginning. One might say that the author isn't either, but that raises sensitive issues of correspondence between other fictional characters and their real-life counterparts, and remains a step too far. The method of the present paper has been to use biographical material to establish parallels between Evans's life and Arabella's story, but not to rely on extrapolations from textual analysis to make deductions about events in the author's life.

"I have conveyed my misery", Margiad Evans wrote in her journal after *The Wooden Doctor* was published. "I have wrought bones, muscles, a beating heart; my book's *alive* and it was worth it' (7 March 1933).[2] The published book becomes a body in its own right, and a vital one at that. But images of illness, pervasive in the novel, feature in Peggy Whistler / Margiad Evans's journals for years to come:

> I have a tumour that will not burst. I will struggle. I will not [indecipherable] and sicken away. If I must I'll take a knife to myself—*you* Arabella know that I will. I'll cut away thought, tear my books and burn all I've written and write never again. I'll curse . . . and show I *can* live on the scar of what cruelly hurt me.
>
> (12 September 1935)

The tone is typical of the journal writing at its most intense, and not only is the act of writing identified here with sickness, but the real Peggy Whistler refers to *The Wooden Doctor*'s Arabella as a kind of alter ego. It is the first entry in a new journal, tellingly entitled "Arabella's Voice".[3] It is not entirely clear to what crisis the "tumour" refers, but by 1935 Whistler has got over her obsession with Dr. Dunlop—Flaherty in the novel—so may defer to "Arabella" here as representing a triumph of endurance. "I'm in flames and burning. Run Arabella, run", she writes on 26 April 1934, but she also calls herself "Margiad Evans" (14 September 1933), and she is pleased that "nobody knows I did that too" (17 March 1933) referring to the frontispiece of *The Wooden Doctor* which she drew, and initialled "P.W." Discrimination between author and narrator blurs, for the pen name, which might function as a distancing device, is used in the private writing too. In the manuscript of *The Wooden Doctor* the narrator sometimes refers to herself as "Peggy", as if, as Ceridwen Lloyd-Morgan says, she had "temporarily forgotten that she was ostensibly writing a novel, and had to correct herself".[4] Multiple identities might suggest a writer who takes for granted fragmentation, dissociation of experience and, equally important and practically the opposite, the overlapping of different aspects of the self.

Whistler / Evans suffered severe, persistent, and debilitating attacks of cystitis.[5] The fictional Arabella's suffering is not so straightforward. A confident initial diagnosis is undermined, and repeated medical examinations reveal no physical cause. Her mother is dismissive: "It just bears out what I have thought all the time. . . . It's nothing but nerves" (119). Arabella herself believes she is "sick in body and mind" (79) while her beloved doctor also considers a psychosomatic root to her problem. Discussing hysteria from a medical point of view, J. Jureidini and D. C. Taylor raise the issue of parental responsibility in the condition, arguing that it is "the one serious psychiatric disorder that might indeed be, as parents often fear and deny, 'all in the mind'. The problem must therefore be 'psychological', but what does that mean?" They go on to say that the word "psychological" is used "as a euphemism for non-structural, marginally volitional, possibly contrived, or even dissembled" illnesses and, significantly for Evans's narrative, suggest that hysteria "carries moral connotations and negative implications about parenting".[6] It is clear that Arabella lacks parental nurture; either parent, for different reasons, might be at least partly responsible for her illness. It is equally clear that whatever the cause, Arabella herself is unaware of it, and her pain is physically crippling.

Elaine Showalter defines hysteria as "a form of expression, a body language for people who otherwise might not be able to speak or even to admit what they feel".[7] Whereas Mark Micale asserts that it is not a disease, but "an alternative physical, verbal, and gestural language, an iconic social communication".[8] These are useful definitions for discussing a text which is ostensibly open about painful emotional issues, and yet which maintains many silences. Showalter says that according to Freud, hysterics were "unable to tell a complete, 'smooth and exact' story about themselves; they left out, distorted, and rearranged information because of sexual repression". The analyst's task was to "edit or construct" a complete narrative for the patient, who would then be cured.[9] Textual analysis of *The Wooden Doctor* corresponds with the analyst's task, although Arabella's narrative resists any single sustained interpretation. The text suggests that Arabella could be suffering repression of sexual feelings, or of sexual trauma, for reasons connected with her father, her mother, or even the beloved doctor himself. In addition she might feel guilt at a sexuality that is hinted at but barely developed in relation to the Beardsley drawings. Each of these suggestions will be discussed below.

Arabella is graphic about the medical procedures she undergoes, and eloquent about her dysfunctional family life: "[W]e sharpened our claws in one another's flesh" (xviii); her love for the doctor: "I could not attract the man I loved: henceforth I should walk in utter humiliation" (145); and her abdominal pains: "I felt as though I were transfixed by a fiery sword; at each breath it twisted like a corkscrew" (113). Each of those quotations has a biblical ring, histrionic, compelling and intense, not untypical of the register of the narrative as a whole. Arabella has little reticence about painful topics, but the narrative still maintains some silences: there is no obvious cause for her illness, no diagnosis, and no cure for her abdominal pains. Caged canaries are prized for their singing, yet Arabella's own canary is mute (76).

Hallucinating in hospital after painful tests, she sees Hans Anderson's Sea Witch and the Little Mermaid who has traded her voice for legs, at the cost of pain equal to walking on knives for ever more.[10] The Mermaid's love for the Prince remains unrequited and, inevitably, unspoken. The "grotesque, fantastic shapes" of the Little Mermaid and her tormentor that writhe on the wall by Arabella's hospital bed (114) recall her bedroom walls that "wavered in and out as though they were paper" (xiv) in her first childhood illness, linking these later hallucinations with her first meeting with Dr Flaherty. Significant revisions were made to this key passage, which in an early draft reads like this:

> ". . . lie still. I want to sound ye're chest."
> "May I listen?"
> "No. Don't talk."
> I stared at the thoughtful face bent above me. I had never seen him before.
> "Have you finished?"
> "Yes."
> "Why does mother's face look so funny?"
> "Because ye're ill."
> "I began to feel ill at school this afternoon and they let me come home. My head *does* ache. Can you stop it?" (mss of *The Wooden Doctor* 238)[11]

There is no suggestion here of an incomplete—hysterical—narrative: the account is simply brief and factual. It comes, however, right at the end of the bound book in which the manuscript was written, not at the chronological beginning of the narrative, which is where, in its revised form, it appears in the published work:

> ". . . lie still. I want to sound ye're chest."
> "May I listen?"
> "No, don't talk."
> I stared at the thoughtful face above me. I had never seen him before. He unbuttoned my nightgown, pushed it open. My chest was glistening. As the stethoscope moved I suddenly knew terror, not of him nor his machine—no, indeed—but of a dreadful, indescribable nightmare, a nightmare that came to us when we were wide-eyed, a nightmare Esther shared with me and which we spoke about to each other and to nobody else. Everything glided smoothly, swiftly, flowing like the road beneath a car, then, oh, awful, oh, horror—chaos, weltering, tangled confusion.
>
> The room whirled and straightened for its spinning rush; my mother vanished into a void; I saw the doctor at the end of a long, long tunnel and sobbed at what was coming. From infinite distance he stretched out his hand, sliding it between my head and the pillow, and gathered my hair from my burning face. In the same moment the room swung back into focus. His touch had cheated the terror. "My head does ache!" (xiv-xv)

This expanded version is pivotal to whatever we make of Arabella's later illness, pain, and hospitalization. The "wide-eyed . . . nightmare" that the sisters share and which they keep secret begins for Arabella at the moment the doctor performs the intimate act of unbuttoning her nightgown and exposing her "glistening"—and developing—twelve- year-old chest. It is not the doctor she fears, but the act that will lead to horror like the scene of an accident, frightening, chaotic, a "weltering, tangled confusion". From experience, then, intimate touching leads to nightmare, while the mother who should protect her vanishes. The implication, suggested through imagery but never articulated, is one of sexual abuse by her father. This time the "terror" is averted because it is the doctor who touches. In her fevered state, Arabella sees him "at the end of a long, long tunnel, and sobbed at what was coming"—but what she expects is spoken only through the imagery. Chaos and "weltering . . . confusion" result when normal roles and relationships are transgressed, but a medical examination is sanctioned, and safe; the doctor is kind and compassionate. The two experiences become fused, however, establishing a pattern of confusion between pain, sexuality, and desire. The imagery in that extract can be variously interpreted as a result of consciously-imposed censorship buckling under the weight of what cannot be named, the narrator's failure to interpret pathology, or indeed the text itself suggesting far more than the author intended. In the fiction, silence on the subject of sexual trauma results in an illness which makes Arabella's body the focus of medical attention.

This early passage establishes the twin themes of pain and Arabella's dependence on Flaherty. The suffering she endures becomes a punishment as well as a perverse reward for her desire for the doctor—when pain cripples her, he attends. Even if we reject the notion of past sexual abuse, Arabella's emotional deprivation and the physical and verbal abuse she certainly receives from her father would offer reason enough for her attachment to Flaherty, who becomes her "Papa doctor", her "father confessor"; medical, religious, and paternal roles are conflated in his "divine image". Silently addressing him, she begs "Let me in, Papa, this is my home" (127). "He thought me a child", she says when he has rejected her, "and as a child he had treated me, my Papa-doctor, a tender and indulgent father" (134). But she views him with more than filial feelings, perhaps suffering attendant—if unacknowledged—guilt as a result. The structure of the narrative works to contrast Arabella's father's drunken and abusive behaviour with the doctor's calm, professional presence. The "bad" father and the "good' father are juxtaposed.

At sixteen she is to leave for France as a pupil teacher. In the early hours of the day of her departure, she goes to her father's aid when he returns home drunk and incapable. Her mother is in the kitchen, lamp in hand, as Arabella helps him in:

> She did not speak; after one glance she turned it low and I blew out the lantern that we might not see. One gleam shone still upon her face and his, and mine reflected in a mirror until I bent my head. (3)

Degradation is to be hidden, but the three family members, inextricably bound together and lit by the gleam of a candle, Arabella's face reflected (not for the first or last time) in a looking glass, make a striking portrait of conspiracy and concealment. "[W]arning and imploring", her mother tells her to go to bed, but her father screams and

> What happened then was, as always, like a play which must be acted as it is written, words and gestures repeated, actors inscrutably elected, audience as God ordained it.
> High heaven, but, played by such a ghastly clown! it was horrible!
> Desperately, wearily, sternly, with all her heart my mother cried:
> "See the horrors of a drunken man!" (4)

With telling ambiguity Arabella remarks "I looked for all my life". The theatrical metaphor emphasizes the relentless inevitability of events, but it also implies a learned detachment from the reality of the domestic drama. While "No power on earth" will make Arabella go to her father during the night, nevertheless, obscurely, she is too ill to travel the next day and the doctor is called. Exhaustion would be realistic after a night of such incident, but no symptoms are described: she simply seems to need the comfort of the "other", sympathetic father. Arabella "had been in pain—it was over: I had longed for him—he was there. My bare arm lay along my side. His hand rested on it' (5). Those three oppositions moving from pain to sensuality—pain/no pain, absence/presence, her bare arm/his touch—contrive in her perception to bring her and Flaherty together in a way that is just slightly uncomfortable for a patient/doctor relationship. Arabella's idealization may simply stem from her father's inadequacies. However, the love she has for Flaherty is not simply filial, nor is it an uncomplicated love a young girl might conceive for an older man; instead the two are fused.

This is the case even at the very end of the novel. On her journey home from Wales Arabella thinks of Oliver, the young man to whom she has lost her virginity, and whom she has agreed to marry. "We should be happy", she thinks, remembering herself in his arms:

> The Wooden Doctor had been right; autumn could not mate with spring. I had loved him because I had met no other man who stirred my blood. He knew it, my wise Irishman. I acknowledged the truth of his consolations now. How well he understood the human mind, how far he could see! Everything ended so quickly, so quickly. Pain and the cause of it alike forgotten, years of growth obliterated in a few months. (219)

But this is not the narrative's resting place, nor is it Arabella's:

> I was in a hurry to be home, until I met the Wooden Doctor face to face. He was walking. He put out his hand:
> "Arabella, are ye back again?"
> "Oh, Papa—" I stammered.
> It looks absurd written down, the conviction that I could not marry any other man. Yet it came upon me just as suddenly.
> It only remained to tell Oliver. (219)

If Arabella looked on Flaherty only as an idealized father-figure, there would be no need to break off her conventional and sexual relationship with Oliver. But she addresses Flaherty as "Papa". (Never, even in her imagination, does Arabella ever refer to Flaherty by his first name.) By implication "[p]ain and the cause of it" is not over. Love for the doctor is the cause, and unacknowledged guilt at regarding a father-figure with sexual feelings might be sufficient in itself to generate the hysterical pain that brings him to her side.

An even earlier episode in the Prelude seems to be sexually formative; it is concerned with the transitional world of puberty and leads to Arabella's first feverish illness. At the opening of the novel, set in 1921, she is twelve years old, her sister Esther nine. They are curious about the physical changes that have transformed their older sister when she returns from boarding school; their own bodies are "so slight, that [they] looked like insects" (ix). Later, when "faint curves of flesh" appear on Arabella's frame, she observes them "angrily"; while other changes a servant warns her about are awaited with "fearful curiosity" (xii).

Between those descriptions of her skinny and her developing body, Arabella has a significant encounter. She meets the tenant of the house her parents are buying:

> She sat on a green and gold striped sofa and a green parakeet sidled up her shoulder. The woman's long silk-covered legs, contrasting strangely with our brown shins and our aunt's stumps, ended in green shoes. Her face was a flower drooping from a dry stalk, a strange, painted flower, or a mask. (xi)

The description foreshadows the Beardsley prints Arabella discovers when she is seventeen, in a magazine article on his work: exotic, luxurious, and compelling (75). The scene is presented as a static visual image—an illustration—and the woman plays no part in the action of the novel. She is present in the text as a symbol of otherness and attraction at a crucial moment in Arabella's sexual development. The rooms are empty next time they visit the house. In contrasting vivid visual images, Esther blows the yolk from a finch's egg "on the red tiles" of the veranda while Arabella "peered through the glass door into the long bare room where we had sat near the fantastic, bedizened lady" (xii). The scene presents a dramatic juxtaposition of colour/lack of colour, presence/absence; equally important is the separation between the sisters' interests: while both remain outside the house, Arabella, looking into it, is aware that she has "entered into a region where as yet [Esther] could not follow" (xii).

Arabella's interest in other women's appearances is established with the description of the tenant. Other exotic women fascinate her later: Agnes Sorel, Madame de Pompadour, and Jezebel, all powerful, compelling, and sexually potent. Arabella's sharp appreciation of beauty and well-developed sense of the grotesque are fundamental in her response to Beardsley at the beginning of Part Two. Recognizing aspects of herself in his work, she is fierce and passionate:

> I was pierced by delight, my imagination leapt. . . . Those ordered fantasies, those formal visions, these fairy things cased in whalebone, queer figures in cold blood cast from white-hot fancy . . . this curbed riot, this dammed river, how it bore me away! The Elizabethan explorer who climbed a palm tree and from thence espied the Pacific Ocean was not more aghast at his discovery than I at mine. (75)

She is at once passive in the face of this onslaught of sensuality: "*pierced* by delight", and "*born away* by the overflow", and also galvanized into action: Beardsley's sensual decadence communicates itself across the decades and unsuspected new realms are indicated with the implicit reference to Keats's sonnet "On First Looking into Chapman's Homer" where with "eagle eyes" Cortez first "stared at the Pacific—and all his men / Look'd at each other with a wild surmise— / Silent, upon a peak in Darien". Arabella's use of the word "aghast" is interesting. She picks up on Keats's speechless sailors, imputing dismay or consternation to them rather than delight. Like a shock of recognition, the drawings articulate previously unformed or unacknowledged feelings latent within her, and there is a sense in which she finds the discovery as appalling as it is exciting and compelling.

Her immediate response is imitation; using Indian ink she chooses the Old Testament figure of Jezabel as her subject. In Hebrew the name means "chaste", but Jezabel is synonymous with female depravity: her "harlotries and sourceries" are manifold.[12] In the context of Arabella's family life Jezabel is, perhaps, a less extraordinary subject for a seventeen-year old girl than one might at first think. She and Esther have grown up hearing their father call their mother names "that would have shamed a harlot, not below the breath, but as one might sing praises" (xvi). They have shivered behind bolted doors with "hands over our ears that we might not hear him scream of the horrors that he saw, and shut our eyes to those that were not delirious fancy" (xvi), so the cruel power and intensity of her drawing comes from experience as well as imagination. But Arabella's Jezabel, inspired by Beardsley, sounds exactly like his work: "a striped shawl, her breasts naked, her black hair gathered up above her gloomy forehead, two dogs licking their chops in her shadow" (75). The lasciviousness of the dogs anticipating their feast on her blood is particularly relished, a sharp counterpoint to the luxury of Jezabel's depiction, foreshadowing her end. The detail represents a wish-fulfilment for the death of a tyrant, for the sisters have wished their father "dead, drowned, buried, or for ourselves that freedom" (xvi).

Arabella becomes—like her creator—an artist and a writer, intensifying the narrative's complex web of intertextuality, and the Beardsley reproductions form a significant part of this. It is Arabella's father, "a most inconsequential reader" who owns the volume of *The Idler* where the Beardsley article actually appears.[13] The article begins with the quotation "'*L'Art decadent, c'est moi*'", and the comment "whether that utterance is to be taken as a proud boast, or a humble confession, there is no evidence to show"[14]; the second paragraph refers to Beardsley's youth—he is twenty-three—and the fact that "he has not long to live". Arabella's illness is not tubercular, but in the text its appearance follows very swiftly after her discovery of Beardsley. Eleven illustrations appear in *The Idler* article,[15] presenting a variety of Beardsley's strong and unconventional female characters: Madame Rejane with her feet up, wealthy and petulant; a New Woman; prostitutes in *Les Passades*, and the almost-bare-breasted androgynous figure of Atalanta hunting, her dog thrusting forward from between her striding legs. Each carries a strong undercurrent of sexuality, while decadence and perversity are pervasive.

Beardsley was popular with the public, but many contemporary reviewers disapproved of his work. It was "vulgar in idea and offensive" (*Daily Chronicle* 12 July 1894); "thoroughly morbid" (*The Academy* 28 July 1894); "freakish" (*Saturday Review* 22 October 1894); "repulsive" (*Times* 8 March 1894); and "ugly" (*Times* 13 June 1896).[16] His drawings were scrutinized by his publishers, anxious to avoid prosecution for obscenity, but Beardsley cultivated a range of sexual emblems as a means of displacing overt sexuality, while ensuring that it remained firmly within the frame. Erect or guttering candles, tight or full-blown roses, and sly concupiscent expressions slipped past the vigilance of John Lane. Linda Zatlin suggests that only a viewer "familiar with Rowlandson would readily comprehend the sexual significance of the dog running beside Atalanta . . . as she strides clutching her bow, an equally phallic referent".[17] The language in which the reviewers reviled Beardsley's work suggests that they certainly responded to implicit sexual references; Arabella does too, consolidating her just-prepubescent encounter with the exotic tenant. Esther's childlike preoccupation with her birds' egg collection while her sister enters a new realm no longer seems quite so innocent. The observation, recalled by Arabella's subsequently Beardsley-trained eye, of her sister absorbed in her task and of yellow yolk on red tile can be read in this context as abortive and perverse. Chronologically the fascination with the tenant predates Arabella's first fevered meeting with Flaherty, a fascination which sews seeds of sexual awareness and provides a potentially unstable and unhealthy context for that meeting.

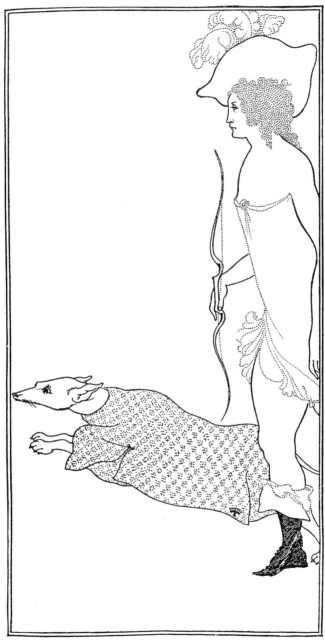

Atalanta. By Aubrey Beardsley.

The sisters grow up accepting their father "at first with terror and disgust, finally with bitter resignation" (xvi). The family have no friends for the father, an "habitual and incurable drunkard" (xvi), alienates all neighbours:

> One and all, year in, year out, as we grew up or old, we nursed the prospect of escape. We quarrelled among ourselves; fretted, isolated by our eccentricities, we sharpened our claws in one another's flesh. Our home among the quiet fields became a cage of savagery. (xviii).

"Cage" is a repeated image in Evans's writing, different here from its appearance in so many other women's work, for the whole family suffer, inflicting violence on each other behind their common bars. Even more unusual, however, is the violence of claws in flesh, for it foreshadows imagery Arabella repeatedly uses later to describe her crippling pains, locating family violence within the body itself. Significantly, this first appearance of the image roots her illness in the isolation of family life where conventional rules of society, unobserved, are transgressed. The metaphor is extended much later in the novel —"I thought of the Wooden Doctor who had grown into my miserable heart as my very flesh" (156)—love and violence are uncomfortably close companions.

The pain that dominates Part Two begins after Arabella completes a commission to illustrate a collection of fables. She takes the mute canary out to the garden and lays beneath the trees: "I did not move for hours. I ceased to question myself what was the matter with me. I put my face to the earth and forgot pain; it passed me by, the fear left me" (77). There is no account of the origin of this pain:

> I *had* suffered, I was afraid to admit how severely. I was afraid to confess even to my mother, to make it concrete. I had hidden it within my mind. And now suddenly, inexplicably, the oppression lifted. Twisting on the grass I could not recall the sensation which had frightened me into strict economy of movement. I leapt up, the bird fluttered, and I went to find groundsel for him, searching among the flowers. It was July: the blood-red poppies had shed their petals, the lilies were dashed and draggled, the delphiniums were losing their colour, and their skeletons showed through their blooms. (77)

Readers might be forgiven for believing the pain to be metaphorical: "I *had* suffered" might refer to the misery of being misunderstood, accused of shameless conduct at school in France after spending an afternoon talking to Julian Mannel, a young Englishman, unchaperoned in the garden (41), but this is by no means clear. Arabella had hidden her suffering "in her mind". Speaking of it would make it real: "I was afraid to confess to my mother, to make it concrete". "Confess" implies guilt, suggesting perhaps that the pain is in some way deserved as part of a victim's irrational sense of complicity in forbidden acts. Or guilt may simply be about sexual awareness which a child conceals from parents.

The passage moves from stillness ("I did not move for hours") to movement ("Twisting . . . I leapt up"), and back to stillness, but not before another oddity: "The garden was so deep in leaves that I took off all my clothes" (77); then she feeds the birds and eats raspberries and milk before lying down again. While the narrative offers visual detail, it offers little motivation. Do the leaves provide a reason for the removal of her clothes, or simply a screen from prying eyes? Whichever it is, the descriptive language that follows tellingly suggests spoiled beauty and desecration. Blood-red petals are shed on the ground, lilies—symbols of purity—are "dashed and draggled", while blue delphiniums are losing their colour: these are compounded as images of the body with the remark: "their skeletons showed through their blooms". Later, in Clystow Royal Infirmary Arabella notices that she has begun to grow thin "this pleased me". Looking at her "protruding bones" she says "How do you do? I haven't seen you since I was thirteen" (101). On this occasion the skeleton suggests a welcome return to pre-pubescence, to sexual immaturity, rather than age and decay. Nakedness and flowers are associated in this later hospital episode too: immediately after noticing her bones, Arabella continues:

> I was obliged to leave the bathroom door open so that the nurses could fetch what they wanted; at first they were very apologetic and turned their eyes in other directions, but when they discovered that I did not mind in the least, they scrubbed my back for me.
> During the night all the flowers were put in the bathroom in buckets so that I bathed in a perfect bower. Once I found the bath itself full of red and yellow chrysanthemums. I jumped in among them. (101-2)

She has exhibitionist tendencies and is curiously uninhibited about nakedness, while the bath of flowers implies something other than a concern for hygiene. Other patients tell her that bathing night and morning she will "wash [herself] away" (101). Practically this may simply represent sheer pleasure in hot running water, a luxury that her home, lit by candles and lamps, is unlikely to provide. But like confession, the relentless action suggests sin and guilt, a contradictory impulse to that of exhibitionism. The two are thus confusingly compounded.

Any female figure naked in a garden is loaded with cultural implications of guilt, pain, and loss of innocence. Arabella's nakedness follows almost immediately after her discovery of the Beardsley illustrations and her own drawing of Jezabel; in this context the scene looks positively Beardsleyesque.

The details of milk and raspberries (nipples?), bird, cage, flowers, naked girl and foliage reads like a description of one of his drawings, and far from removing any idea of sexuality, lends a layer of decadence to the passage. The pain returns: "like a fox in a bag scratching and rending to get out. My spirits trailed in the dust. The claws penetrated my sleep, dragging me awake and I sat up in bed. I knew that I was ill" (77-78). At first the explanation is crisp: "The Wooden Doctor said I had cystitis" (78) but his certainty is in doubt for recovery is not quick. The fox "withdrew", then with "hideous cunning" returns, the doctor can do no more than "cut its claws" (78). While cystitis has a number of causes, including masturbation, it has been commonly known as the "honeymoon complaint", so called because unaccustomed sexual activity can bruise the urethra and surrounding tissue resulting in a bacterial infection. Either might result in guilt at acknowledging sexual feelings. Three weeks of bed rest brings no improvement and the Doctor, puzzled, changes her medicine and advises her to "go away". Seeing some of her drawings, however, he remarks "What an imagination ye must have!" (78) and she reads in his eyes the thought that it was her "nerves that were wrong". Psychosoma is in her mother's mind too: "At last, one day he said it, and my mother echoed him. A flavour of dankness in her remarks made me think that they had been a long time submerged" (79). The drawings are disturbing, suggesting an unhealthy turn of mind, an interest in sex that is associated not with free, natural feelings but with unwholesomeness and guilt, and the possibility that the imagination that produced them could also produce psychosomatic—or hysterical—pain. Arabella's self-diagnosis is that she "was sick in body and mind", unable to "fight the terrible beast that ravaged" her (79); interestingly she is able to countenance a mental cause even as she gives it physical substance in her metaphor. The penetrative male fox cannot be avoided.

Between the manuscript and the published version pain has been foregrounded once again. The manuscript says merely: "some obscure internal complaint caused me acute suffering. Distracted I implored [the Doctor] to operate: he refused and sent me to a specialist. There was no money for the nursing home. He paid" (mss of *Wooden Doctor* 143). In the revised text, medical procedures are described in some detail. The account of an x-ray Flaherty carries out is one example: "He began the preparations. I lost my desperation lying on the floor half naked. My wandering glance came to rest on his intent face while his deft hands did their work" (81). We may account for any oddities here by recollecting the very basic conditions in a rural GP's surgery at the time, but there is remarkable frankness in what follows: "He stretched me on a couch and stuck all kinds of instruments up me. They hurt very much, and I should have hated anybody else to do it" (82).

Her pain is not alleviated by this procedure, but there is a sense of satisfaction—quite possibly with attendant guilt—from this kind of medical intimacy from the man she loves. At the end of this examination his conclusion is "there is nothing wrong. Ye are an enigma" (82). Her body presents a problem which cannot be named, and no amount of examination or reading interprets the signs conclusively.

The tension between Arabella and her mother may also have its part to play in Arabella's illness. One of the patients in hospital reminds her of her mother "with painful vividness". She thinks of the "old devotion to each other, lying dead between us, killed by cruel words, senseless misunderstandings, wild and wicked recriminations" (105). Christopher Bollas argues that mother / child rejection is at the heart of hysteria. When hysterics present themselves to hospitals, they are actually presenting a false body ailment "in order to use the body as the occasion for love":

> All along the body suffered no intrinsic illness; it was purely a matter of the mother's rejection of the self's sexuality. When he or she is pleased to have an ailment confirmed as real, possibly even to have some small surgery, the hysteric feels that he or she will be the recipient of the doctor's intelligent love.[18]

The doctor's love is sought as a substitute for the mother's, for the doctor "tends to bodies out of love"[19] as once the mother tended to the infant's body. After Arabella's return from her first exploratory operation, the house resounds with her mother's "shrill, passionate voice" as she "began to abuse Esther in the kitchen" (91). Esther and her mother have been arguing again when Arabella returns from a second hospital visit with the news that she is unlikely to have an operation. Her mother is dismissive: "It just bears out what I have thought all the time . . . that it's nothing but nerves" (119). But later, contrite, she throws her arms around Arabella passionately declaring her love while Esther yawns and the sisters' eyes meet "with deep understanding" (119), cynical and unconvinced.

Dysfunctional family dynamics are illustrated in a brief condensed episode occurring between hospital episodes. The mother has influenza, "our father had a roaring drinking bout," and Arabella has another attack:

> To quench the stream of abuse we [the sisters] pretended to have hysterics and yelled and laughed till our father sat down in his armchair. Crossing his legs, and holding a sodden cigarette stump, he ejaculated softly:
> "You little bitches, you *bloody* little bitches."
> I banged on the piano with my fists. Esther's enormous eyes were wide and black. . . . Our mother wept. (93)

Sometimes a cigar is only a cigar—or a sodden cigarette stump—but the emotional heat and language in this scene is intense and suggestive, while no family member behaves with any sense of responsibility.

In the context of Bollas's argument, we may comprehend the hysteric's "constant visits to hospital as a continual call to the mother to take the self back into care", something which Arabella's mother is not prepared to do. Neither, in spite of the protestation of love, is she disposed to "rediscover the infant's body as something now desirable".[20] This background of rejection and loss may help to account for sensual and sexual language Arabella uses to describe her arrival at the nursing home in Clystow, and her observation of other women. Delivered by taxi, she notices "a servant who had the most beautiful legs" standing on the steps "taking a tip from a wan woman with violets pinned to her breast. Another taxi throbbed for her" (83). Even in distress Arabella notices women, often with a strong undercurrent of sexual attraction: the young school mistress with appendicitis who twice a day combs and tends her dark curling hair "which fell over her shoulders to her waist" (108), and the nurse with close-cropped hair who "swung her hips as she moved like a person dancing a slow, sensual tango". She takes an interest in Arabella too:

> "I say, you're a mystery, aren't you? Nobody can find out what's the matter with you. Wouldn't it be *lovely* if I could? You don't mind me taking a look, do you. . . . I really should be most grateful if you'd let me examine you! You will?"
> I lay down on my bed, stripped. Of course she found nothing. (109)

The nurse's sense of excitement, the compliance with which Arabella turns herself into an object for examination, and the ambiguity of the comment "of course she found nothing" (because there is nothing to find, or because the nurse is inexperienced?) invite attention. When Mr Maitland pours water into her bladder through a funnel and catheter to gauge Arabella's reactions, the same nurse is present, smiling at Arabella "on the sly and [running] her fingers through her hair" (111). While an encouraging or sympathetic smile might be expected, "sly", together with the gesture, implies a sexual conspiracy; meanwhile "the fox, tracked to the very source of its being, twisted and turned within me" suggests a perverse penetration by proxy. Even other patients stare at her "as though they would penetrate my flesh and discover what ill it concealed" (100). But the illness, like the cause, remains hidden while the symptoms are only too painful.

Patriarchal authority in the person of the consultant says "This must be stopped . . . it can't go on", and repeats "it can't go on". Arabella finds his examination "quite bearable" unless "the instruments actually touch the fox's stranglehold", then "it scratched and bit" (84). But as Mr Maitland peers and bends he murmurs "Perfectly normal, perfectly normal". Later, learning that Flaherty has paid her bill, she leans back against her pillow "burning with thoughts of the Wooden Doctor. The idea that he was doing so much for me thrilled me with delight. What should I do without him; at any time, well or ill, what should I have done without him?" (86-87). The financial transaction gives great satisfaction—if you are poor, then of course there is relief at having bills paid. But the context here, sore from invasive procedures, *burning* with thoughts of the doctor, *thrilled with delight*, is disturbing. Of this, the manuscript has only the terse comment, "he paid" (mss of *The Wooden Doctor* 143). Significantly in the published version, after a row of asterisks, which here signify the end of a train of thought but which equally conventionally draw a veil over a sexual encounter, the narrative resumes with the repeated words "This must be stopped" (87). The words belong to the consultant, but also apply to feelings Arabella has just expressed. The narrative supplies its own censorship, while the ambiguities multiply, for tests discover nothing: "I could go home in the afternoon. They no longer said 'It must be stopped'" (89).

Flaherty's response to the inconclusive report he receives provides a quixotic double message: "[I]t's the nature of youth to recover", he says, adding "be brave Arabella, and fight it yourself", which leaves open to interpretation whether he refers to a medical condition, an hysterical illness, her love for him, or each of those. Later, characteristically using images of sickness and anatomy to give shape and substance to her feelings, Arabella says it is "possible to be happy before loving, perhaps after, but never while that *diabolical poison* coursed through the veins" (152, my emphasis).

In describing her illness Arabella insists on what cannot otherwise be named or represented, whatever that might be. While the text hints at a number of possible reasons for her physical pain, no single suggestion offers a sustained or coherent rationale for the narrative as a whole. This is almost certainly because author and narrator are so closely identified that the novel derives as much from self-expression as it does artistic detachment. Exhaustive textual analysis does not "explain" *The Wooden Doctor*; the text retains more than enough gaps and silences for further critical exploration.

NOTES

1. Margiad Evans, *The Wooden Doctor* (Oxford: Basil Blackwell, 1933). Further references are to this edition and will be given in the text.
2. Margiad Evans, Journal 1933-4, National Library of Wales 23366D.
3. Margiad Evans, Journal 1935, National Library of Wales 23577C.
4. Ceridwen Lloyd-Morgan, *Margiad Evans* (Bridgend: Seren, 1998) 35.
5. Lloyd-Morgan 44.

6. J. Jureidini and D. C. Taylor, "Hysteria: Pretending to be sick and its consequences", *European Child and Adolescent Psychiatry* 11 (2001): 123.
7. Elaine Showalter, *Hystories: Hysterical Epidemics and Modern Culture* (London: Picador, 1997) 7.
8. Showalter 7.
9. Showalter 84.
10. Hans Anderson, *Fairy Stories: A Selection* (Oxford: Blackwell, 1998).
11. Early manuscript version of *The Wooden Doctor* in the National Library of Wales 23357B.
12. 2 Kings 10:23.
13. Arthur H. Lawrence, "Mr. Aubrey Beardsley and his Work", *The Idler* Vol. XI, No. 11 (March 1897): 189-202.
14. *The Idler* 190.
15. The illustrations are as follows: the headpiece from "Le Morte Darthur"; *The Moska* (*Savoy* No. 1); *Portrait of Madame Rejane*; the frontispiece to *A Book of Bargains* by Vincent O'Sullivan; *The Battle of the Beaux and the Belles* (from "The Rape of the Lock"); *Merlin* (from "Le Morte Darthur"; "The Coiffing" (*Savoy* No. 3), Avenue Theatre Poster for *A Comedy of Sighs*; *Les Passades*; *La Femme Incomprise*; and *Atalanta*.
16. Quoted in L. G. Zatlin, *Aubrey Beardsley and Victorian Sexual Politics* (Oxford: Clarendon Press, 1990) 5.
17. Zatlin 161.
18. Christopher Bollas, *Hysteria* (London: Routledge, 2000) 59.
19. Bollas 59.
20. Bollas 59.

Misrule in Milk Wood:
A Bakhtinian Reading of
Dylan Thomas's "Play for Voices"

Jackie Benjamin

University of Wales, Swansea

In *A Reference Companion to Dylan Thomas*, James A. Davies writes that "Welsh criticism of Dylan Thomas has not yet brought to bear on its subject the full force of modern literary theory".[1] While this paper does not attempt to bring "the full force" of literary theory to Thomas's work, it will, however, examine Thomas's poetry and prose from a single theoretical perspective. The application of literary theory to Thomas's work has been hindered by the legends surrounding his life which have dominated writing about Thomas and have tended to cloud criticism of his work. This intertwining of life and literature can, however, be used constructively; for instance, Thomas, the irreverent "young dog", can be seen as being analogous to the mischievous trickster of Bakhtinian carnival. This paper will examine *Under Milk Wood* alongside Thomas's other writing in order to identify elements of carnival present in his work; it will also explore the progress of Thomas's subversive carnival, from the radical stance of his early poetry and short stories, through the comic realism of *Portrait of the Artist as a Young Dog*, to the comic anarchy of the "domesticated" carnival that is *Under Milk Wood*.

Mikhail Bakhtin believed that carnivalization was a process of inversion and disruption, where folk, or "lower", culture erupted into forms of "higher" culture. As well as humour, the other carnivalesque elements which Bakhtin identified as crucial to carnival's inversion of hierarchy include the multiple discourses and registers of "heteroglossia" and its resultant ambivalence; the elevation of the clown/joker figure into a Lord of Misrule and the subsequent chaos, parody and masking; grotesque realism with its emphasis on the body and all its processes; and the irreverent treatment of life, death and renewal. For Bakhtin, carnival is a subversive and liberating force which allows alternative voices to challenge social and literary hierarchy. This gives rise to polyphonic texts, with a mixture of the sacred and profane, the sublime and ridiculous, where irreverent humour erodes the distinctions between social strata. Bakhtin believed that this subversive aspect of the carnivalesque was most pronounced in periods of transition and unrest and he developed his theory of carnival in *Problems of Dostoevsky's Poetics* and *Rabelais and His World*.[2] The application of Bakhtin's theory to texts from revolutionary Russia and Renaissance France suggests that literature is carnivalized in periods of social turbulence and, although *Under Milk Wood* was not written during revolution or at the intersection of social systems, the society which informed Thomas's writing was indeed in a period of tension and flux. As M. Wynn Thomas points out, "[c]ataclysmic change, of an unmistakably cultural, social, economic and political kind, was the dominant reality of south Wales life between the Wars".[3] *Under Milk Wood* was conceived during this troubled inter-war period and completed after two World Wars had accelerated the movement towards a more egalitarian society where social boundaries and hierarchies were relaxing, precisely the requirements for the eruption of carnival into "serious" literature.

Llareggub is both Welsh and English (Mog Edwards, for example, lives in "Manchester House"), typical and atypical, everywhere and nowhere and its position on the geographical divide between land and sea perhaps symbolizes the position of the Anglo-Welsh at the intersection of cultures which Bakhtin identified as the scene of carnival. This makes carnival theory an ideal tool for the analysis of Welsh writing in English for, in addition to the manifestations of carnival in Thomas's work, Bakhtinian theory might account for grotesque realism in writers such as Caradoc Evans and Glyn Jones and, also, for the high incidence of fantasy and fable in the "first flowering" of Welsh writing in English. Modern Welsh society might be viewed as a carnivalesque version of English society, the strict social hierarchies of English society being promiscuously mixed in Welsh society and this social mix becomes inscribed in Welsh-English society, resulting in the carnivalized way in which writers of Thomas's generation used the English language to produce a literature which carnivalized both Welsh and English literary traditions and the societies which produced them. Thomas's position seems more ambiguous than most; Saunders Lewis notoriously said, "he belongs to the English",[4] and this is echoed by David Holbrook who believes that "his Welshness is without true roots".[5] In his carnivalized revelation of social tensions and hypocrisies, Thomas reacts both to the ideologies of Welsh culture, encapsulated in Welsh literature and Nonconformity, and to English ideology imposed on Wales, encapsulated in the social hierarchies of capitalism.

In his essay, "'An insult to the brain?': how criticism fails Dylan Thomas",[6] John Goodby takes a similar view to that of James A. Davies and comments on the lack of the application of recent theoretical literary criticism to Thomas's work. Goodby notes Thomas's "taste for Gothic and the grotesque" and, although he links this to Thomas's Modernist tendencies, Goodby believes this to be "a subversive literary strategy with a serious purpose". Whether it is related to Modernism or carnival, the "subversive glory" of Thomas's use of the grotesque represents a challenge to the literary status quo and, despite Thomas's relegation to an apolitical position because of his apparent personal and social irresponsibility,[7] his writings show that he was politically aware.[8] Throughout his career, Thomas wrote against social realism and his subversive writing strategies, such as the inclusion of gothic and grotesque, point to the implicit socio-political content of his work. His most explicitly political work, however, is his most realist, particularly the comic realism of *Portrait of the Artist as a Young Dog* where Thomas, the bourgeois bohemian, explores the social strata of suburbia, and where social awareness and seriousness undercut the humour to produce a tragi-comic medium full of explicit class imagery and political references. The application of Bakhtinian theory does have political implications for Thomas's work as the Marxist Bakhtin used literary criticism to voice an implicit protest against Stalin's ugly parody of Marxism; his subversive carnival was a critique of the political status quo.

At the exposition of *Under Milk Wood* the carnival has already begun, for the lack of an omniscient narrator produces a polyphonic text which allows all voices to be heard—of whatever social status, prose or rhyme, anonymous or named. This reflects the liberating force of carnival, where unofficial discourse challenges and mocks all that official discourse takes seriously. The *Play for Voices* is the ideal vehicle for carnival; it is fluid and amorphous, reflecting its medium of radio, its sea-town setting and its subject matter of dreams and reality, while the multiplicity of voices is typical of the heteroglossia and polyphony of carnival theory where no one voice is given precedence. In this context, one would have to argue that *The Definitive Edition* of Walford Davies and Ralph Maud, which conflates First Voice and Second Voice without serious justification, is anti-carnival as, by introducing one omniscient narrator, it makes the text more realist and, therefore, more conservative. The conflation of these voices is compounded by choosing to present the resulting single voice in italicized text, attributed only once, at the beginning of the play as "First Voice". This completes the transformation of Thomas's intended play between First and Second Voice, often hierarchically indistinct from other competing voices, into a single omniscient narrative voice which imposes a privileged metalanguage. The justification for this unwarranted editorial interference is given as a desire to make the play more reader-friendly by avoiding textual signifiers for the separate voices: "[b]y relieving the reader of the 187 switches that the eye had formerly to pay attention to, the present edition frees the reading ear to hear what is in reality one narrative guide".[9] Davies and Maud dismiss any difference in the language, register and material which Thomas gives to First Voice and Second Voice: "[i]t is not as if Thomas had made the First and Second Voices distinguishable through traits of speech patterns, imagery, personality, or depth of soul". However, in his review of this edition of *Under Milk Wood*, James A. Davies points out that "the reader is entitled to read what Thomas wrote and not what he might (or might not) have written had he lived to supervise publication" and Davies dismisses the easy-reading justification: "it is simply not true that 'there is really no separate role for the Second Voice'".[10] He also identifies some of the distinctions between First Voice and Second Voice: "First Voice sets the scene and introduces the characters, Second Voice describes their dreams . . . the two voices reflect, respectively, the general and particular nature of the material". This distinction between First Voice and Second Voice is particularly noticeable at the outset, with Second Voice breaking into the informative dialogue of First Voice on the cue of "dreams of".[11] The reduction of First Voice and Second Voice to one italicized narratorial voice destroys Thomas's concept of unmediated voices with no hierarchical structure and reduces the carnival heteroglossia of competing discourses.[12]

For Bakhtin, carnival represents the liberation of the individual from authority, for the discourse of carnival is democratic and permeated with humour which undermines all forms of authority. The subsequent free play of unrepressed voices in subversive discourses which challenge official discourse results in the struggle for dialogic ascendancy which Bakhtin terms "heteroglossia". This is explored by Bakhtin in *Problems of Dostoevsky's Poetics*, where he first outlines his theory of carnival. Bakhtin recognizes that, in order to speak to those imprisoned in ideology, a writer must use the language with which they, the proletarian and, possibly, plebeian folk, identify and this is why the language of the ordinary "folk" is so crucial to carnivalized literature; as folk culture infiltrates higher forms of culture, the language of the folk allows them to identify with the resultant carnival impulse.

Although it can be argued that much of the folk culture had vanished from Thomas's Wales, residual traces, such as that promoted in Romantic literature, remained. M. Wynn Thomas describes this Romantic construct as "the 'wild Wales' of a semi-pagan people who retained something of an ancient Celtic magic".[13] *Under Milk Wood* alludes to this Celtic inheritance: "Llareggub Hill, that mystic tumulus, the memorial of peoples that dwelt in the region of Llareggub before the Celts left the Land of Summer and where the old wizards made themselves a wife out of flowers" (*UMW* 86). These words are given to the Rev. Eli Jenkins who, as the allusion to the tale of Blodeuedd from the *Mabinogion*[14] suggests, is keeping alive the folk culture of Llareggub by recording its history in "The White Book of Llareggub" (*UMW*

79). Thomas is alluding here, of course, to mediaeval manuscripts, such as The Black Book of Carmarthen and The White Book of Rhydderch, which preserved Welsh literature and history; it is an allusion first used in "The Orchards" where reference is made to "The Black Book of Llareggub".[15] By choosing the Christian Eli Jenkins as the keeper of the pagan past, is Thomas replicating the transformation of pagan festivals into the carnivals of Mediaeval Christianity? On one level, Thomas may be reproducing this transition while, on another level, with his depiction of the Christian preacher who cherishes the pagan past, he is reversing the progression from pagan to Christian, thereby tapping into the energies of the pagan past, and, on yet another level, the figure of the preacher-poet allows Thomas to parody both pagan, bardic inheritance and contemporary, Christian religion, poking gentle fun at Nonconformist ministers who also donned the robes of the Gorsedd and engaged in its "pagan" ceremonies. This exemplifies the complex dimensions of *Under Milk Wood* where subversion is itself subverted and disguised by comedy in a typically carnivalesque manner.

In *Corresponding Cultures*, M. Wynn Thomas notes Thomas's attraction to this pagan, "pre-Nonconformist, 'Celtic' Wales"[16] and points out that Thomas, in "The Poets of Swansea", a series of articles in the *Herald of Wales*, had urged Welsh writers in English to quarry "the wonders of Celtic mythology".[17] Dylan Thomas describes:

> the inexplicable fascination that Welsh legends are bound to exercise upon whoever takes enough trouble to become acquainted with them. W. H. Davies could have made something very great out of the legends of his own country. He could have recreated the fantastic world of the Mabinogion, surrounded the folk lore with his own fancies. . . . (*EPW* 118)

A letter to John Bell of the Oxford University Press shows that Thomas had been approached with a proposal for a collection of "Welsh Fairy Tales" for children and was "very interested indeed . . . especially on such themes" (*CL* 852). In an essay on Rhys Davies, M. Wynn Thomas notes the attractiveness of this pre-Christian Wales for writers who wanted to subvert Welsh Nonconformity and believes that one of Rhys Davies's strategies for escaping the confines of socially-constructed gender roles was to utilize the pagan past. Thomas also notes the significance of Davies's "vision" of Dr. William Price who "offers Davies a means of connecting himself with an alternative, autochthonous Wales, of supposedly pagan Celtic (or even Iberian) freedoms".[18] Dylan Thomas was also aware of William Price and he inspired the character of Rhys Rhys in the early short story, "The Burning Baby".[19] Glyn Jones recalls how Thomas was fascinated by the story of Price's notorious cremation of his baby son:

It was new to him, and he was enthralled by it, because the matter, the substance, of what I was saying was such he immediately and instinctively recognized, as would supply the material for one of his own short stories—the poetic-fantastic type he was writing then. The story was the true one, well known in Wales, about Dr. William Price, the druidical Chartist of Llantrisant, the nudist mountain chanter and wearer of hieratical comms who at eighty-four burned the body of his little illegitimate son Jesus Christ on the hilltop.[20]

This has several elements of carnival: the telling of folk-tales; the grotesque image of the nude on the mountain-top; and the pagan ritual which immolates the symbol of Christianity, the child called Jesus Christ.

David Daiches believes that "Thomas was by instinct a popular poet . . . he drew on universal folk themes"[21] and Thomas utilizes folk themes in other early stories. For example, in "The Orchards", Thomas's protagonist, Marlais, is a "folk man walking" (*CS* 47) through Aberbabel, a polyglossic[22] reference to the Tower of Babel, a symbol which itself epitomizes multiple discourses. The burning trees of "The Orchards" evoke another important image of Celtic folk-tale; the magical tree that burns, yet remains alive and green, is used by Gwyn Williams to symbolize the ambivalent juxtaposition in Welsh poetry of "love and war, of summer and winter, of holy sacrament and adulterous love".[23] M. Wynn Thomas links Thomas's symbolic use of orchards to Afallon, the place of apples, later transformed into the Arthurian Avalon.[24] Such images relate easily to the symbol of The Garden of Eden which is used by Thomas both in his poetry, culminating in the idyllic pre-lapsarian imagery of "Fern Hill",[25] where the subject is "prince of the apple towns" and "young and easy under the apple boughs" (*CP* 134), and in his prose, from early short stories such as "The Tree" and "The Orchards" to the Edenic evocation of Llareggub as a "God-built garden" (*UMW* 89). Thomas's utilization of Biblical tales, imagery and language, which would have been familiar to his readers, extends the range of material which he can draw upon in order to encourage identification with his carnival. He draws upon other possible points of shared reference by utilizing myths, folk-tales and legends: the speaker of "Over Sir John's hill" (*CP* 142) is "young Aesop fabling"; "Ballad of the Long-legged Bait" and "How shall my animal" draw on Ovidian metamorphosis; Marlais, protagonist of "The Orchards" walks towards "the wine-coloured sea" (*CS* 46), an epithet drawn from Homer's *Odyssey*; and "A Winter's Tale" inverts the classical tale of Leda and the Swan while playing with Yeatsian and Shakespearean allusions. "In Country Sleep" (*CP* 139), itself an elaborate bedtime story, draws upon many systems of stories, "hearthstone tales", "hobnail tales" and sagas "from mermen to seraphim" and Thomas's diverse allusions include the Bible, Shakespeare and Father Christmas. In addition to these tales and legends, Thomas evokes the pre-history of Wales in "A Child's Christmas in Wales":

> Years and years and years ago, when I was a boy, when there were wolves in Wales, and birds the colour of red-flannel petticoats whisked past the harp-shaped hills, when we sang and wallowed all night and day in caves that smelt like Sunday afternoons in damp front farmhouse parlours, and we chased, with the jawbones of deacons, the English and the bears, before the motor-car, before the wheel, before the duchess-faced horse . . . (*CS* 305)

Thomas's tongue-in-cheek narrative takes the reader back through the evolutionary process to the beginnings of Welsh culture while playing with stereotypical preconceptions of Wales and the Welsh. Interestingly, the Welsh translation of *Under Milk Wood*, T. James Jones's *Dan y Wenallt*,[26] moves closer to the folk carnival as it circumvents the anglicization of Welsh culture prevalent in south-west Wales and returns to the roots of Welsh folk culture. Jones's "purpose from the first in translating the play had been to restore to Dylan Thomas the Welsh-language heritage of which he had been deprived".[27] Despite this deprivation, it is clear that Thomas's allusions to Welsh folk culture can be identified in his earliest short stories and added to his wide-ranging use of folk-references from many cultures.

This Bakhtinian concept of residual folk culture which erupts into literature also translates into an inclusion in *Under Milk Wood* of popular culture. Examples include: the social life of the pub, the Welfare Hall and the Mothers' Union "Dance of The World" (*UMW* 85); references to Dr. Crippen (*UMW* 70) and film stars called "Dolores" (*UMW* 20); and Sinding's popular classic "The Rustle of Spring" (*UMW* 54; *DM-UMW* 75). This inclusion of popular culture is very relevant to Thomas's work as a whole. Cinema, for example, is an important metaphor in both poetry and prose: "Our eunuch dreams" (*CP* 17) uses cinematic imagery for its theme of illusion and reality and alludes to both horror and gangster films; the third stanza of "Then was my neophyte" (*CP* 57) is full of cinematic imagery; "The Orchards" includes the "high noon" showdown of popular Westerns (*CS* 46) and this Western imagery extends to the incongruous and carnivalesque depiction of the archangel Gabriel as a cowboy, "from the windy West came two-gunned Gabriel" (*CP* 60), while "Old Garbo" is a tragi-comic parody of Hollywood legend, Greta Garbo. C. J. Rawson notes Thomas's letter to Vernon Watkins discussing "The tombstone told", where Thomas writes of "the winding cinematic works of the womb",[28] and Rawson goes on to compare Thomas's techniques to those of Walt Disney: "[i]n Thomas's importations from cinema, a corresponding point of encounter between wit and fantasy is provided by the longer Disney films of children's fairy tales. *Under Milk Wood* is the completest inheritor of this mode of vision". Rawson relates such lines as "bridesmaided by glow-worms down the aisles of the organplaying wood" (*UMW* 1) to the world of Disney and believes that such connections are also identifiable in Thomas's poetry; for example, for Rawson, in "A Winter's Tale",[29] "the dead oak walks for love" (*CP* 101) in a Disneyesque landscape. In a letter to Henry Treece in July 1938, Thomas writes, "quite a good number of my images come from the cinema & the gramophone and the newspaper, while I use contemporary slang, cliché and pun" (*CL* 310). As Ken Hirschkop states, Bakhtin is "the only major contributor to Marxist cultural theory for whom popular culture is the privileged bearer of democratic and progressive values"[30] and Thomas's modern carnival includes many symbols of both folk and popular culture.

Dylan Thomas was fascinated from a young age by the nature and potentialities of the English language; in a letter to Pamela Hansford Johnson he writes that "[t]he greatest single word I know is 'drome' which, for some reason, nearly opens the doors of heaven for me" (*CL* 73) and Glyn Jones, equally fascinated by the English language, describes Thomas's reaction to the seemingly ordinary word 'huddled':

> He stopped and began repeating it over to himself, remarking on its strangeness, savouring it as though it were as outlandish as Chimborazo or Cotopaxi and not an ordinary English vocable in common use. . . . Dylan was not just interested in words but was obsessed by them.[31]

This delight in words lends itself to the carnivalization of language, the heteroglossic jostle of words, as does Thomas's self-proclaimed liking for all forms of wordplay:

> I use everything and anything . . . old tricks, new tricks, puns, portmanteau-words, paradox, allusion, paranomasia, paragram, catachresis, slang. . . . Every device there is in language is there to be used if you will. Poets have got to enjoy themselves sometimes. (*EPW* 158)

There are conflicting theories and evidence as to the exact nature of Thomas's writing process. Thomas described his writing as an organic process:

> Each image holds within it the seed of its own destruction, and my dialectical method, as I understand it, is a constant building up and breaking down of the images that come out of the central seed . . . any sequence of my images must be a sequence of creations, recreations, destructions, contradictions. (*CL* 281)

This seems the essence of carnival. However, he also describes the process as laborious, "I have written hundreds of poems & each one has taken me a great many painful, brain-racking & sweaty hours" (*CL* 51), and his work-sheets with their revisions, word-lists and thesaurus references are evidence of this. While the two processes are not necessarily mutually exclusive, it is possible to suggest that Thomas may have adopted two styles of writing; the writing process for his "serious" poetry was a laborious "craft and sullen art" where he shed "syllabic blood" (*CP* 18), while the writing process for his prose was more spontaneous and playful. Daniel Jones suggests such a pattern in Thomas's writing: "Thomas's work inhabits two different worlds: the private introspective world of his most concentrated and meticulously constructed poems, and the public extrovert world of his broadly humorous and highly coloured 'prose'" (*UMW* xi). Although aspects of carnivalized language are distinguishable in both poetry and prose, the comic elements of the latter, more public and more spontaneous, lend themselves more easily to the carnivalesque.

Language is a key area of Bakhtin's theory; believing language to be socially-constructed, he thus saw it as a medium of social control and, potentially, a source of social conflict. The possible pertinence of carnival theory to *Under Milk Wood* is highlighted by R. B. Kershner who believes that "for Bakhtin the model of language is spoken, rather than written".[32] Bakhtin believed that polyphony occurs when the multiplicity of voices in a text are allowed to speak without authorial comment, thereby breaking down the "unified monologic world of the author's consciousness" (*PDP* 43).[33] This breakdown of the monologic text allows unmediated dialogic exchange between voices. The polyphonic resonance of *Under Milk Wood*'s voices, presented without authorial or unified narratorial comment, creates the conditions for heteroglossia, where conflicting discourses compete for ascendancy. Heteroglossia depends on these competing discourses being identifiable one from another and so Thomas's variations of syntax, language, diction and register are crucial. His use of internal monologue and dramatic irony to see "inside" the characters is also important as this reveals the conflict between the private language of individuals and the public language of monologic officialdom. *Under Milk Wood* also contains several examples of polyglossia, which Bakhtin identified as occurring when a text is bilingual or multilingual. Thomas uses Welsh to create humour and play word games: most obviously, the disguised carnival profanity of "Llareggub"; Mog Edwards is "late of Twll" and advertizes in *The Twll Bugle* (*UMW* 52); Jack Black shouts "Ach y fi" in his sleep (*UMW* 8); "Bach, fach" (*UMW* 88) plays with a third language; and in Rev. Eli Jenkins's morning poem (*UMW* 26), the Welsh pronunciation of "Nedd" does not fit the ballad rhyme scheme while an English one might. Thomas utilized Welsh to create humour in other works: in the short stories we find the villages of Cathmarw and Aberbabel; characters called Tom Twp and Dai Twice; on their annual outing, the "boys" of "A Story" visit a pub called "The Twll in the Wall". This polyglossic bilingualism again illustrates the carnivalesque in Thomas's use of language and contradicts assertions that he is simply "an English poet".[34] Although Ralph Maud notes Thomas's description, in "A Child's Christmas in Wales", of the sea as "two-tongued" (*CS* 304), he does not believe that this is a reference to bilingualism. An earlier version, in "Memories of Christmas", however, makes the bilingual reference more explicit, since here the sea is "Welsh-speaking"[35], while "Quite Early One Morning" has "the bilingual sea" (*CS* 301).

Thomas's democratic vocabulary combines colloquialism with the formal and archaic; slang is juxtaposed with biblical imagery; foreign borrowings with reworked clichés. These are all evidence of the language of lower social strata carnivalizing the language of "high" culture. Bakhtin believed that "where high and low registers of language dialogize each other in the historical context of folk humour, we can detect the presence of the carnivalesque"[36] and, in line with this Bakhtinian emphasis on diversity, *Under Milk Wood* has a complex range of registers working on both social and individual levels to create different discourses. The unofficial discourse of the "natives" of Llareggub is a subversive challenge to official discourse, parodied in the Voice of a Guidebook:

> Less than five hundred souls inhabit the three quaint streets and the few narrow by-lanes and scattered farmsteads that constitute this small, decaying watering-place which may, indeed, be called a "backwater of life" without disrespect to its natives . . . (*UMW* 24)

Thomas uses this Received Pronunciation of English, redolent of Holbrookian élitism, to expose the hidden agenda of officialdom for, while the voice is supposedly objective and, like the anthropological tourist guides which it also parodies, gives statistics and facts, Thomas's parody exposes the implicit metropolitan subjectivity contained in its language. The whole speech subtly criticizes Llareggub, for there is nothing to do, nothing to see, nothing of interest, while "natives" suggests a primitive culture. This device of an official discourse contradicted by "reality" had in fact already been used by Thomas in other broadcasts; "Margate—Past and Present" (*B* 104-19), includes the Voice of Information which is intertwined, interrupted, and annoyed by Rick, voice of American democracy, while "The Londoner" has the Voice of an Expert contradicted by the Voice of an Old Resident who gives the folk perspective (*B* 76). Such examples point to the way in which radio, broadcasting to a popular audience, facilitates a carnivalesque play of voices. These broadcasts have other techniques which anticipate *Under Milk Wood*; "Margate" has a pair of narrative guides, 1st Voice and 2nd Voice, who introduce, but do not interact with, other voices, while the Narrator of "The Londoner" leads us into characters' dreams (*B* 77-78) in another cyclical text which ends as it begins, with "The Jacksons are dreaming" (*B* 91). The stichomythic dialogue of 1st, 2nd and 3rd Shopper (*B* 83) parallels the dialogue of the women in Mrs. Organ Morgan's shop and a more vicious version of the broadcasts' stichomythic dialogue appears in "Old Garbo":

> In low voices the women reviled Mrs. Prothero, liar adulteress, mother of bastards, thief.
> "She got you know what."
> "Never cured it."
> "Got Charlie tattooed on her."
> "Three and eight she owes me." (*CS* 221)

Under Milk Wood appears to be the culmination of Thomas's "radio prose" but is also an extension of his prose writing, for the qualities which Peter Lewis identifies as particular to his "radio prose"—"transferred epithets, invented and compound adjectives, personification, unusual metaphorical identifications, departures from normal word-order . . . comic incongruities, zany flights of fantasy, grotesque comparisons and surrealist humour"[37]—are also present in Thomas's other writings.

The voice of officialdom is further parodied by Gossamer Beynon's comic efforts to teach her pupils to speak, and sing, with a "proper" accent:

> CHILDREN'S VOICES
> It was a luvver and his lars
> With a a and a o and a a nonino . . .
>
> GOSSAMER BEYNON
> Naow, naow, naow, your eccents, children!
> It was a lover and his less
> With a hey and a hao and a hey nonino . . .[38]

Gossamer Beynon's social aspiration is also registered in her ambivalent distaste for Sinbad Sailors' dropping of "his aitches" (*UMW* 64), a sign of being "common". Their respective registers represent the social boundaries which keep them apart, Thomas highlighting the hierarchies inherent in language and its function as marker and divider of social strata. This distinction of registers is typical of the play, for most characters have a recognizably individual voice and vocabulary, for example, the voice of Mrs. Ogmore-Pritchard is easily distinguished from that of Mary Ann Sailors.[39]

First and Second Voice use a second person narrative to induce their auditors to join the carnival and a third person narrative to guide the auditors around Llareggub and introduce the townsfolk. They do not speak directly to other characters, although dialogues are interwoven and some of their narrative descriptions are interrupted by the dialogue of the townsfolk. Characters see, hear and comment on each other but interaction is limited and this creates the impression that, although Llareggub is a community, it is full of isolated individuals like Lily Smalls whose dialogue is with herself.

> Oh there's a face!
> Where you get that hair from?
> Got it from a old tom cat. (*UMW* 27)[40]

This complements Thomas's vision of "a community of individual people", freed from normal social constraints and each with "the right of the individual to lead his own life in his own way" (*DM-UMW* xxii). Apart from such brief interaction of characters as occurs when Willy Nilly "delivers" his letters ("delivers" usually in the sense of oral expression), most of the interactive dialogue takes place at mealtimes or in the pub, shop and village square, in line with Bakhtinian emphasis on the feast and the market-place as the site of carnival.

Thomas's carnivalized differentiation of registers is not confined to dialogue; his prose is interspersed with verse and songs and Thomas's projected plan for additional songs in the evening section would have heightened the carnival.[41] Thomas uses a ballad form, rhyming *abcb*, complete with refrain, for Mr. Waldo's song (*UMW* 86-87) which combines folk song and popular ribaldry. The Rev. Eli Jenkins's morning and evening prayers are also ballads. His morning prayer, composed of alternating octosyllabic and heptasyllabic lines rhyming *abab*, parodies the high art forms of both Welsh praise poetry, with its sustained use of assonantal and alliterative "cynghanedd", and the Romanticism of the Celtic twilight.

> Dear Gwalia! I know there **are**
> Towns **lovelier** than ours,
> And **fairer** hills and **loftier** far
> And groves more full of **flowers** . . . (*UMW* 26)

In the first line alone, Thomas has four assonantal rhymes on "are" which continue through the quatrain and are echoed by the polysyndeton of "and". The alliterative progression of "lovelier" / "loftier" and "fairer" / "far" / "flowers" reinforces Thomas's version of cynghanedd. The allusion to Grongar in Rev. Jenkins's evening prayer (*UMW* 82) allows Thomas to conjure an image of Golden Grove, stereotypical of Celtic Romanticism, and it is also a reference to John Dyer's "Grongar Hill", humorously reviewed by Thomas in his 1945 broadcast "Welsh Poetry" (*B* 35).[42] Eli Jenkins's evening prayer has many carnivalized features: it is another folk ballad; its use of apostrophe creates a dialogue between the poet-preacher and his God; "all poor creatures born to die" evokes the carnival juxtaposition of life and death; and it contains a carnival mixture of registers as the colloquial "just for now" and "touch and go" are mixed with the biblical and archaic "Thy" and "Thou wilt".

Polly Garter's morning song (*UMW* 57) is set out in stanzas which alternate eight lines and four lines of rhyming couplets. These can be broken down into a ballad quatrain of *aabb*, every third quatrain forming a refrain which reverberates throughout the play with the repeated couplet of:

> But I always think as we tumble into bed
> Of little Willy Wee who is dead, dead, dead . . . (*UMW* 69 and 89)

This reflects the tragi-comic juxtaposition of life and death in the character of Polly Garter, while the repetition of "dead" links *Under Milk Wood* to the final words of "Return Journey" and the Park-keeper's six-fold repetition of "Dead . . ." (*B* 189). The allusion to "Wee Willy Winkie" is one of several allusions to popular nursery rhymes; Mr. Waldo's Mother recites "This little piggy . . . " (*UMW* 9) and Second Woman sings a version of "Rockabye Baby" (*UMW* 84). In his "Poetic Manifesto", Thomas cites "nursery rhymes and folk tales" (*EPW* 157) as where he first discovered his fascination with words and he claims that nursery rhymes and ballads carry "the common fun of the earth" (*EPW* 155). Llareggub's "Rockabye Grandpa" links the beginning and end of life, consistent with Bakhtinian emphasis on the young and the old where "the body stands on the threshold of the grave and the crib" (*RW* 26), one life merging into another in carnivalesque renewal. In Llareggub, "babies and old men are cleaned and put into their broken prams and wheeled onto the sunlit cockled cobbles" (*UMW* 39). Then, as the cycle of the play moves back towards night, "babies and old men are bribed and lullabied to sleep" (*UMW* 84). Thomas recognizes, and poignantly evokes, the cyclical movement of life where the very young and the very old are alike helplessly dependent, the play once again evoking carnival's linking of "both poles of transformation, the old and the new, the dying and the procreating, the beginning and the end of the metamorphosis" (*RW* 24). This carnivalized juxtaposition of life and death is also present in Captain Cat's emotive dialogue with his dead love, Rosie Probert (*UMW* 72-73); the question and answer form epitomizing Bakhtinian dialogics, linking tragic and comic, living and dead.

In *Reading Dialogics*, Lynne Pearce identifies a concept of carnival, present in Bakhtin's writings on Rabelais, which is not dealt with in *Problems of Dostoevsky's Poetics*. In his further exploration of discourse, Bakhtin defines "double-voicedness" as "the dialogue of the people against authority"[43] and Pearce describes this as an ambivalent voice for "the voices of carnival are exceptional in that they are addressed both explicitly to their allies (the people of the market-place) and implicitly to the absent authorities".[44] Thomas's "double-voicedness" uses radio, the voice of authority addressed to the people, as a medium for his implicit critique of authority; in other words, he subverts the use of radio as a perpetuating agent of the status quo by delivering a double-voiced dialogue which critiques officialdom from the inside. This "double-voiced" ambivalence is a feature of oxymoronic carnival language where praise and abuse are intertwined for, as Pearce points out, "carnival uses its double-voiced language simultaneously to honour and deride".[45] This praise/abuse dichotomy is apparent in the reception of *Under Milk Wood* and Peter Lewis tellingly points out that "*Under Milk Wood* is probably Thomas's most maligned work, but paradoxically it is still his most popular".[46] Lewis defends the play from hostile literary criticism by stressing the importance of its medium; he believes that *Under Milk Wood* cannot be adequately discussed without acknowledging the role of radio.

As Geoffrey Moore suggests, "B.B.C. patronage . . . introduced a vivid histrionic and comic talent to a large and varied audience"[47] and Douglas Cleverdon believes that "Thomas was indubitably a master of radio" and that "radio is *par excellence* a poet's medium . . . free from the visual element that constricts theatre, television and even films, with a few evocative words it can send the imagination ranging through time and space".[48] While Thomas's "double-voicedness" may be considered subversive, he clearly had to stay within the bounds of accepted B.B.C. decorums. For its first broadcast in January 1954, *Under Milk Wood* underwent minor censorship with the removal of "wriggle her roly poly bum" (*UMW* 46) and any mention of "nipples" (*UMW* 63). This is similar to the 1954 publication of the play where the carnival profanity, "Llareggub" was sanitized to "Llaregyb" against the wishes of the editor, Daniel Jones.[49] Moreover, as Daphne Watson points out, "the original 1954 broadcast omitted the guidebook description of Llaregyb";[50] the Received English register of the Voice of a Guidebook was, presumably, too close to the voice of the B.B.C. to allow a parody. In 1954 B.B.C. Radio was still very much the voice of officialdom, a role which had become more pronounced during wartime when radio relayed information and broadcast propaganda in order to unify and encourage the population. Thomas was required to adopt this official voice in public information films and broadcasts and his own voice with its "cut-glass accent" (*CS* 336) is typical of the voices of "Reithean" radio. Equally, Thomas was aware that not all his listeners were middle-class, sharing establishment values and hence, perhaps, his "double-voiced" undermining of officialdom.

Radio thus can be a carnivalized medium, making every listener simultaneously actor, director and auditor, a site where subversive and conservative come together, high and low cultures merge and sensory perception is prioritized but dislocated in synaesthetic confusion. Captain Cat's blindness places him in the position of auditors who "hear and see behind the eyes of the sleepers" (*UMW* 3). Paradoxically, his blindness allows him to observe with particular insight and, as he knows Llareggub by sound, he is, as Daniel Jones writes, "a natural bridge between eye and ear for the radio listener" (*UMW* viii). Thomas's onomatopoeic language adds to the synaesthesia: for example, First Voice's description of Llareggub at midday where "[t]here's the clip clop of horses on the sunhoneyed cobbles of the humming streets . . . tomtit twitter from the bird-ounced boughs . . . crow caw, pigeon coo, clock strike, bull bellow . . ." (*UMW* 46-47). Paradoxically, the "play for voices" rises out of the sound of "Silence" and Thomas frequently crosses phonic and graphic boundaries to foreground the senses, "[y]ou can hear the dew falling . . . hear the houses sleeping . . . hear and see, behind the eyes of the sleepers . . . (*UMW* 2-3). Carnival emphasizes and prioritizes the sensory world over the spiritual world as it prioritizes body over mind and the medium of radio contributes to sensory dislocation as we visualize through our ears. Bakhtin describes carnival as "a pageant without footlights" for "everyone is an active participant, everyone communes in the carnival act" (*PDP* 122) and "the people in it are both actors and spectators simultaneously".[51] While such a view is manifestly relevant to most radio drama, it is particularly relevant to *Under Milk Wood* where auditors are explicitly drawn into the world of the play: "only *your* eyes are unclosed to see the black and folded town . . . you alone can hear the invisible starfall . . . from where you are, you can hear their dreams" (*UMW* 2-3). The second-person present tense address is part of carnival dialogics where the characters of carnival "act and speak in a zone of familiar contact with the open-ended present . . . the living present, often even the very day" (*PDP* 108). The Sailors Arms is not only in this "living present" but outside time for "[t]he hands of the clock have stayed still at half past eleven for fifty years. It is always opening time in the Sailors Arms" (*UMW* 38). In "A Dearth of Comic Writers", Thomas states that "[a] truly comic, invented world must live *at the same time* as the world we live in" (*B* 194); this "living present" encourages spectators to join the carnival. The concept that people are both spectators of and actors in carnival gives rise to much of its ambivalence.

This is but one of carnival's ambivalences; indeed carnival personifies the opposition of order and disorder into the Rabelaisian characters of Lent and Carnival. Bakhtin himself emphasizes carnival's ambivalence and writes:

> All the images of carnival are dualistic; they unite within themselves both poles
> of change and crisis: birth and death, blessing and curse, praise and abuse, youth

and old age, top and bottom, face and backside, stupidity and wisdom. Very characteristic for carnival thinking is paired images, chosen for their contrast or their similarity . . . (*PDP* 126).

This dualistic pattern is pronounced in *Under Milk Wood*: in the contrasting pair of Mrs. Dai Bread One and Two, "one for the daytime one for the night" (*UMW* 49), or Cherry Owen's double existence, "sober as Sunday as he is every day of the week . . . happy as Saturday to get drunk as a deacon as he does every night" (*UMW* 83). Specifically, the personification of order and disorder into the Rabelaisian characters of Lent and Carnival are echoed in Thomas's play: Mrs. Pugh is clearly a candidate for the role of Lent, as is Mrs. Ogmore-Pritchard whose attempts to keep order involve the repression of natural process—"before you let the sun in, mind it wipes its shoes" (*UMW* 17)—and who does not "want persons in my nice clean rooms breathing all over the chairs" (*UMW* 42). Mrs. Ogmore-Pritchard, however, while by day a repressor, afraid of the processes of nature and time, by night becomes a sinister siren who instructs her ghostly husbands to put on their "pyjamas from the drawer marked pyjamas" and then to "take them off" (*UMW* 81).

For John Ackerman, the eponymous milk is emblematic of another central duality, "the paradox of innocence and sexuality sustained throughout the play", and symbolizes "copulation, birth and growth, semen and mother's milk".[52] Ackerman extends the associations to the cosmic energies of the Milky Way, an image used by Thomas to describe the omniscient being who presides over his projected sequence of poems, "In Country Heaven", as "the milky-way farmer".[53] Indeed, Thomas foregrounds the ambivalent symbolism of milk: the innocence of Bessie Bighead is linked to milk through the cows of Salt Lake Farm while the experience of Polly Garter is highlighted by her breast-feeding of her "poor little milky creature" (*UMW* 32); the virginal Bessie is "alone until she dies" (*UMW* 20) while Polly is as fertile as Spring, figured by Thomas as a nursing mother with "breasts full of rivering May-milk" (*UMW* 68). The ambivalent juxtaposition of innocence and experience is appropriate for a town whose inhabitants "are not wholly bad or good" (*UMW* 82). Mary Ann Sailors represents the goodness of a pre-lapsarian Garden of Eden but neither Polly Garter's post-lapsarian experience nor the "sin" of Sinbad Sailors or Nogood Boyo is represented as evil for Thomas presents his characters without judgement. The closing speech reflects the play's ambivalence as God and Devil are implicitly juxtaposed in an eternal landscape, peopled by transient individuals who are offered eternal regeneration through Thomas's optimistic pantheism.

In *Rabelais and his World*, Bakhtin distinguishes between Romantic carnival, "in most cases nocturnal", and Renaissance carnival, in which, "on the contrary, light characterizes folk grotesque . . . it is a festival of spring, of sunrise, of morning" (*RW* 41). Thomas's carnival opens on a "spring, moonless night",[54] subverting the moonlight of Romanticism but fulfilling its nocturnal setting, enters folk carnival proper at sunrise, then returns to the nocturnal Romantic carnival at sunset to begin the cycle of night and day, life and death once again. In *Under Milk Wood*, darkness is a time of freedom from social constructs while daylight means the townsfolk must hide their inner thoughts and conform to social norms. Gossamer Beynon, for instance, personifies the ambivalent duality of public and private and Thomas's writing moves seamlessly between exterior and interior: "Gossamer Beynon high-heels out of school. The sun hums down through the cotton-flowers of her dress . . . She blazes naked past the Sailors Arms" (*UMW* 63). Michael Bristol argues that "carnival personae reveal by a cogent mimicry that both rule and misrule are equivocal, unstable qualities"[55] and this is emphasized in Thomas's play by the repeated patterns of contradictions as dreams and daydreams belie outward respectability; insight into the minds of characters allows multi-faceted perspectives. Characters are fragmented and doubled and much of the ambivalence comes from the many candidates for key carnival roles, such as Lent and Carnival, the Lord of Misrule and the Jester.

Does *Under Milk Wood* contain a Lord of Misrule who has usurped power and released the subversive forces of carnival? Interestingly, Thomas was familiar with a west-Walian example of carnival ritual still extant when he and Glyn Jones visited Llansteffan in the 1930s. This was "a ceremony and carnival involving a mock election which was held in 'The Sticks', a magnificent beech wood".[56] Thomas alludes to such a mock mayor-making in "A Visit to Grandpa's" when the story's protagonists stand "on the concert platform in the middle of the wood where visitors sang on midsummer nights and, year by year, the innocent of the village was elected mayor" (*CS* 145). Elevation of a Lord of Misrule is mirrored by the descent of authority and, in *Under Milk Wood*, the character most representative of authority has descended to the bottom of the social scale. Lord Cut Glass, in his "old frock-coat belonged to Eli Jenkins", is reduced to buying "postman's trousers from Bethesda jumble" (*UMW* 31) and eats "peppery fish-scraps" from "a dogdish, marked Fido" (*UMW* 68). Carnival laughter calls authority into question and Thomas's carnival humour obliterates the authority of the aristocracy, the church and the law with his comic portrayals of Lord Cut-Glass, Rev. Eli Jenkins and P.C. Attila Rees. Captain Cat, elevated above the town at his window in Schooner House, might be considered a candidate for Lord of Misrule, presiding over Llareggub's carnival. First Voice and Second Voice, who introduce the carnival and command the auditors' participation with the imperative "Look" and "Listen", might also be considered for this role, but are, ultimately, commentators rather than instigators of events. It seems that the carnival inversion of order and disorder, sanity and insanity, reality and fantasy is already in progress "behind the eyes of the sleepers" (*UMW* 3) as night allows the sleepers to escape the social constructs of daylight. Imagination then becomes the Lord of Misrule as fantasy takes over from reality and the private, interior world takes precedence over the public, exterior world.

While the significance of the story-teller in carnivalized literature is not explored in Bakhtin's writings, it is implied by his focus on folk culture, for the story-teller is necessary for the oral transmission of knowledge and culture carried by folk-tales. Thomas returns to the vocal roots of story-telling in his early short stories; the gardener in "The Tree" and Sam Rib in "The Map of Love" function as the keepers of knowledge that must be handed down through the generations by means of stories. While these are transmitted orally, the story-teller protagonist of "The Mouse and The Woman", a genesis story, uses the written word to create his world. In this story, Thomas highlights both the power of the omniscient story-teller, who functions as a god-like figure with the power to create and destroy worlds, and the power of the written word, a recurring theme throughout his poetry and prose. In the "Jarvis Valley" stories, Thomas creates his own folk-lore, much as Caradoc Evans does with Manteg. Thomas creates complex levels of story-telling: for instance, in "A Prospect of the Sea", the boy protagonist switches between being a boy in Thomas's story to being a boy in a story within a story, "Now he was riding on the sea, in seven-league boots he was springing over the fields. . . . Now he was a boy again" (*CS* 89). The boy then makes up his own story, a version of Thomas's later poem "Ballad of the Long-Legged Bait", which he then enters. In addition to these story-tellers within stories, Thomas's characteristic, self-reflexive metafiction foregrounds the story-telling artist. In his self-referential Künstlerroman, *Portrait of the Artist as a Young Dog*, writer, narrator, protagonist and reader are conflated in an interpenetration of fiction and reality. The semi-autobiographical protagonist of "The Peaches" is "a snub-nosed story-teller . . . in the snug centre of [his] stories" (*CS* 30). The narrator of "Old Garbo" steps out of the story with an afterword: "When I showed this story to Mr. Farr, he said: 'You got it all wrong'" (*CS* 223); this semi-autobiographical narrator, who wants to "put them all in a story by and by" is corrected by one of his prospective characters. Thomas's *Portrait* stories about writing stories are comparable to his self-reflexive poems about writing poetry where, paradoxically, the "dumb to tell" poet produces a poem which tells of his failure to produce a poem. Ann Mayer believes that the semi-autobiographical *Portrait* stories with their "increased use of dialogue and an insertion of other voices, especially as story-tellers . . . may be seen as steps toward the play for voices, *Under Milk Wood*".[57] In stories such as "Where Tawe Flows", Thomas allows other story-tellers, such as Mr. Evans, to speak in a Dostoevskian[58] model of polyphony, similar to that of *Under Milk Wood*, where characters are allowed to present their own stories. Story-telling has its roots in the vocal transmission of folk culture and the play returns to these roots, confirming the importance of the story-teller in Bakhtinian carnival.

The introductory pages of this paper referred to Thomas's reaction, in *Under Milk Wood*, to both Welsh Nonconformity and the hierarchies and values of English bourgeois life. Thomas's response to Welsh society is apparent in his affectionate parody of the preacher-poet Eli Jenkins which allows him to critique both religious and literary traditions. In addition to the parody of Welsh praise poetry already discussed, Thomas caricatures the figure of the bard: Eli Jenkins has "bard's white hair" (*UMW* 25), keeps "portraits of famous bards and preachers, all fur and wool from the squint to the kneecaps" (*UMW* 77) and shouts "Eisteddfodau" (*UMW* 21) in his sleep. Thomas's humour extends to the pagan culture of the druids: "from this small circle of stones, made not by druids but by Mrs. Beynon's Billy" (*UMW* 24) might also carry a critique of the essential artifice of the Gorsedd ceremonies, instigated by Iolo Morganwg. This humour at the expense of Welsh cultural heritage is also present in "The Peaches"; Uncle Jim is a rural Lord of Misrule whose grotesque eating and drinking contribute to the disorder at Gorsehill and his favourite chair is "the broken throne of a bankrupt bard" (*CS* 130). Ironically, this jibe at Thomas's Welsh literary heritage is couched in the complicated assonantal and alliterative language for which the poetic tradition is renowned and Thomas reveals further knowledge of this tradition when Eli Jenkins "intricately rhymes, to the music of crwth and pibgorn . . ." but, then the image characteristically turns to caricature with: " . . . all night long in his druid's seedy nightie in a beer-tent black with parchs" (*UMW* 22). Thomas never misses an opportunity to challenge the authority of "blaspheming chapels" (*CS* 230) and puns on both "parchedig" (reverend) and "parch" (respect) when, in "After the funeral", he refers to "the parched worlds of Wales" (*CP* 73) in a portrayal of the arid world of his aunt's Nonconformist culture.[59] This punning extends to his letters and a letter of 1944 to Tommy Earp contains an attack on "parchs", in comic verse (*CL* 524). Eli Jenkins, his father, Esau, "undogcollared because of his little weakness" (*UMW* 77), is the last in this line of mocking challenges.

Recent commentary on Dylan Thomas has finally challenged the myth of his being an apolitical writer. Not only was Thomas active in left-wing politics in the Swansea of the 1930s, but his socio-political awareness is much more visible in his writing than critics have usually acknowledged.[60] Thomas considered himself a socialist, "though a very unconventional one" (*CL* 97) and the subsequent tensions of middle-class life emerge in his work. This political aspect of Thomas's work is at its most explicit in the comic realism of *Portrait of the Artist as a Young Dog* where Thomas explores life "at home with the *bourgeoisie*" (*CS* 87); for example, "Where Tawe Flows" is full of intrinsic and extrinsic class imagery as Thomas exposes class division and hypocrisy, even making direct reference to contemporary politics with his condemnation of Mosleyite characters as "Thugs" (*CS* 189). Although Thomas's voice was aligned with the establishment in his wartime work with the B.B.C. and the Ministry of Information, the post-war broadcast, "The Londoner", is explicit in its critique of government policy, as Ted Jackson voices his concerns over democracy and atomic warfare:

> We're the Government, aren't we. It's we who got to say . . .
> "We don't want atom bombs." (*B* 82)

Apocalyptical images of atomic warfare become increasingly common in Thomas's work as he worries that capitalism is on the road to total annihilation. In 1946, he writes of "this apparently hell-bent earth" (*B* 62) and his unfinished project, "In Country Heaven", deals with post-apocalypse memories of a vanished Earth. Walford Davies believes that "the legend of the irresponsible bohemian surrounding Thomas has obscured the sense of moral shock at the heart of his late work" (*DM-UMW* xxi). Thomas's response to the fears, raised by the atomic age, of total annihilation, what became known as "Mutually Assured Destruction" ("MAD"), is to invert socially-constructed meanings of sanity and madness. Madness, like carnival, is a release from the rationality of officialdom and Thomas's working title of *The Town That Was Mad* is a carnivalized inversion, for the town perceived as mad is "Thomas's bastion of sanity in an insane world".[61] If the technology of atomic warfare represents the "sane" world, then the naïve and childish "madness" of Llareggub is preferable.

Carnival frees individuals from social norms and carnival humour can engage with deviant social behaviour such as bigamy and adultery, bringing these taboo topics of society's underworld to the surface. As the monogamous family is the base unit of capitalism, any deviance is a challenge to the legitimized system and Polly Garter is, therefore, a subversive threat to monogamous patriarchy: "Polly Garter has many illegitimate babies because she loves babies but does not want only one man's" (*CL* 814). Thomas captures the social stigmatization of her illegitimate pregnancies but he makes the Christian imagery of the townswomen's criticism backfire; the ironic voice of Mrs. Pugh, a member of the Mothers' Union, which describes "Saint

Polly Garter" as being "martyred" in Milk Wood (*UMW* 67), ultimately adds to Thomas's sympathetic portrait of Polly Garter as well as adding to Thomas's critique of religion as a perpetuating force of dominant ideology. Willy Nilly's delivery of "another paternity summons" (*UMW* 44) to Mr. Waldo represents the establishment's efforts to enforce social norms. While the sexual freedom of Polly Garter and Mr. Waldo challenges the monogamous family, the bigamous household of the Dai Breads also contradicts social norms, although Dai Bread's wives represent the poles of socially-constructed female roles—Mrs. Dai Bread One as "The Angel in the House", and Mrs. Dai Bread Two as "The Whore". Subversive humour encompasses everything that society keeps hidden and brings the private into the public domain, just as Thomas does with the exposure of his characters' dreams and desires. The exposure of the social underworld can bring a dark side to carnival and this is implicit in *Under Milk Wood*: Jack Black "grimly, joyfully" seeks out lovers in the woods in what amounts to voyeurism, Bessie Bighead is an abandoned baby and Nogood Boyo offers money to children for implicitly sinister reasons: "Nogood Boyo gave me three pennies yesterday but I wouldn't" (*UMW* 75). Apart from these most "deviant" examples, Llareggub includes a number of characters not "properly" fulfilling their social roles, such as the postman who reads the mail. Bakhtin believes that "[c]arnival makes familiar relations strange"[62] and this is echoed by Thomas's own comments on the voices of *Under Milk Wood* which "never judge nor condemn but explain and make strangely simple and simply strange" (*CL* 814). The carnival created by Thomas disrupts relationships and questions social norms by foregrounding the underworld of social deviance.

If the underworld is part of carnival then so is the otherworld. Ghosts in the text add to the process of carnivalization, highlighting the tensions between normal, the realm of officialdom, and paranormal, the realm of carnival. The drowned sailors and Mrs. Ogmore-Pritchard's ghostly husbands play a crucial role in "the downward movement . . . inherent in all forms of popular-festive merriment and grotesque realism".[63] Thomas describes his writing style as having "one syllable in the grave" (*EPW* 162) and believes that "death plays a great part in our lives. Only tax and unhappiness are as inevitable" (*EPW* 161). Life and death are intertwined in Llareggub; death-in-life and life-in-death reflecting Bakhtin's belief that "the beginning and end of life are closely linked and interwoven" (*RW* 317). The carnival of *Under Milk Wood* blurs the boundaries of life and death as the voices of the Drowned speak in Captain Cat's consciousness, Rosie Probert's descent to death retains speech and memory, and Mrs. Ogmore-Pritchard's dead husbands remain a part of her life. Bakhtinian carnival recognizes the inevitable death of the individual but includes a celebration of the continuing regeneration of human life. Both

Bakhtin and Thomas adopt "the life cycle that transcends the individual"[64] for carnival, like life, never ends and life, death and renewal are key concepts of carnival found in all of Thomas's work.

Rabelaisian grotesque realism, with its emphasis on the body and the feast, comic distortion and hyperbole, is probably the most widely recognized element of carnival. The grotesque body is open to the world and endlessly reproducing it:

> The grotesque body is cosmic and universal. It stresses elements common to the entire cosmos: earth, water, fire, air; it is directly related to the sun, to the stars. It contains the signs of the zodiac. It reflects the cosmic hierarchy. This body can merge with mountains, rivers, seas, islands and continents. It can fill the entire universe.[65]

The work by Thomas which most conforms to this macrocosm/microcosm analogy has become known as the "process" poems and, in an early letter, Thomas famously defends and describes his techniques:

> What you call ugly in my poetry is, in reality, nothing but the strong stressing of the physical . . . of course, all these contrasting things are equally beautiful and equally ugly. Only by association is the refuse of the body more to be abhorred than the body itself. Standards have been set for us . . . It is polite to be seen at one's dining table and impolite to be seen in one's lavatory . . . it is little wonder that any poetry dealing impartially with the parts of the anatomy, and with the functions of the body, should be considered as something rather hideous, unnecessary, and, to say the least, indelicate. But I fail to see how the emphasising of the body can, in any way, be regarded as hideous . . . All thoughts and actions emanate from the body. Therefore the description of a thought or action can be beaten home by bringing it onto a physical level. Every idea, intuitive or intellectual, can be imagined and translated in terms of the body, its flesh, skin, blood, sinews, veins, glands, organs, cells, or senses. (*CL* 39)

This emphasis on the physical body and its processes, especially those usually considered "unmentionable", is characteristic of Bakhtin's subversive carnival, as indeed is the juxtaposition of that physical body with the sacramental. Marshall Stearns, in a perceptive essay, "Unsex the Skeleton", written while Thomas was still alive, emphasizes how "sex and religion often interpenetrate" in Thomas's poetry, citing the "Crucifixion" sonnet of "Altarwise by owl-light" as where "[t]he fusion of the two reaches perhaps its highest pitch".[66] This is echoed by Ralph Maud who cites the same sonnet as an example of where the "religious is expressed in sexual terms".[67] This carnivalesque mix of sacred and profane is present in *Under Milk Wood*, Polly Garter's sexual activity being expressed in terms of her being "martyred" (*UMW* 67).

The focus of grotesque realism falls upon all the processes of the body, "copulation, pregnancy, childbirth, the throes of death, eating, drinking, or defecation" (*RW* 26). Eating and drinking, then, are central to carnival theory; feasting was a time when social boundaries might be relaxed for, while "rank was especially evident during official feasts, all were considered equal during carnival . . . the true feast of time" (*RW* 10). Carnival is especially manifest in the body's processes of eating, drinking and digesting, where the body acts on the world and is in turn acted upon: "[I]t is as if the carnivalesque body politic had ingested the entire corpus and in its bloated and irrepressible state released it in all manner of recombination, inversion, mockery and degradation".[68] Grotesque ingestion is a prominent feature of the play: the abnormal eating of Mrs. Organ Morgan "with her mouth full of fish as a pelican's" (*UMW* 67), Lord Cut-Glass, "that lordly fish-head nibbler" (*UMW* 69) and Butcher Beynon's dreams of "owlmeat, dogs' eyes, manchop" (*UMW* 20) all foreground the carnival feast. Marty Roth believes that intoxication is an aspect of Bakhtinian carnival which is often overlooked or downplayed,[69] but, in a town in which "it is always opening time", there is plenty of alcoholic consumption, manifesting itself most graphically in the drunken promiscuity of Mr. Waldo and Cherry Owen's drunken behaviour which, despite being condoned by Mrs. Cherry Owen, carries undertones of domestic violence (*UMW* 34). Beyond eating and drinking,

> [t]he stress is laid on those parts of the body that are open to the outside world, that is, the parts through which the world enters the body or emerges from it, or through which the body itself goes out to meet the world. This means that the emphasis is on the apertures or the convexities, or on various ramifications and offshoots: the open mouth, the genital organs, the breasts, the phallus, the potbelly, the nose. (*RW* 26)

The physically grotesque is not as prominent in Thomas's writing as, for example, in that of Glyn Jones, but elements of grotesque realism are present in *Under Milk Wood*: Dai Bread is "a hairy little man with big pink lips [and] a wall eye" (*UMW* 55); Mae Rose Cottage "draws circles of lipstick round her nipples" (*UMW* 81); Mrs. Ogmore-Pritchard sits "erect as a dry dream" (*UMW* 80); and the perpetually pregnant Polly Garter "can't say no even to midgets" (*UMW* 67). Thomas's sensual and sexual imagery certainly stretched the accepted decorum of 1950s Britain, though his humorous exposure of personal habits frowned upon by "nice" society, such as Mrs. Ogmore-Pritchard who "belches in a teeny hanky" (*UMW* 54), P.C. Attila Rees who urinates in his helmet and fishermen who "gob at gulls" (*UMW* 53), is tame when compared to his early poetry and prose but is, nevertheless, part of carnival which liberates the populace "from norms of etiquette and decency" (*RW* 10).

Daphne Watson believes that *Under Milk Wood* is redolent of the licensed "naughtiness" of "sea-side postcards"[70] and Thomas alludes to this sanctioned ribaldry in "One Warm Saturday". This carnivalesque story portrays a "holiday Saturday" where "the eccentric ordinary people came bursting and crawling, with noise and colours, out of their houses" (*CS* 230) to recreate the "comic coloured postcards of mountain-buttocked women on the beach and hen-pecked, pin-legged men with telescopes" (*CS* 229). The comically rude sea-side postcard encapsulates aspects of carnival apparent in *Under Milk Wood*, but it is sanctioned subversion of etiquette and represents Llareggub's carnival as licensed and limited, a tame version of Rabelaisian carnival.

In his discussion of grotesque realism, Bakhtin emphasizes the female body and relates his theory to an analogy of earth as mother: "earth is an element that devours swallows up (the grave, the womb) and at the same time an element of birth, of renascence (the maternal breasts)" (*RW* 21). The process of renewal vital to carnival is also described in female terms of "conception, pregnancy and birth" and, like Polly Garter, "[i]t is always conceiving" (*RW* 21). Bakhtin identifies the female body, particularly when pregnant or ageing, as crucial for grotesque realism's creation and destruction: " . . . in living carnival images, death itself is pregnant and gives birth, and the mother's womb giving birth becomes a grave" (*PDP* 164). Polly Garter is a fecund and liberated example of female sexuality in contrast to the barren dust of Rosie Probert who has more in common with the "barren as boulders women" of "In the White Giant's Thigh" (*CP* 150). These "daughters of darkness" also speak from the other side of death as they lament their lack of fertility from the site of a gigantic and carnivalesque image of male sexuality. Through the repetition of "throats", "tongues" and "mouths", Thomas emphasizes the "deathless" voices of the women who have become part of the earth. The tomb and womb of Bakhtinian regeneration is a major theme in Thomas's work and in *Under Milk Wood* the townsfolk are, like all humans, "poor creatures born to die" (*UMW* 82). However, Thomas's awareness of death-in-life is countered with his optimistic and pantheistic vision of regeneration through the eternal cycle of Nature.

Carnival arises out of bodily energies and the introduction of female sexuality contributes to the process of carnivalization, but the presence of women in carnival is "quintessentially dangerous"[71] as women and their bodies are potentially transgressive and unruly, in or out of carnival, and female sexuality is a threat to monogamous, patriarchal society and primogeniture. James A. Davies notes that "the more overt sexual innuendo was eliminated"[72] during Thomas's revision of the play, but Polly Garter, Mae Rose Cottage, Gossamer Beynon and Myfanwy Price remain to represent female sexuality, in varying degrees of repression and expression. Carnival celebrates Polly Garter's pregnancies but the anti-carnival component of the play, epitomized by the Lentian figures of Mrs. Pugh and Mrs. Ogmore-Pritchard, censures their illegitimacy. In sensual language, full of Freudian imagery, Second Voice reveals the sexual repression of both Myfanwy Price who dreams of "her lover, tall as the town clock tower, Samson-syrup-gold-maned, whacking thighed and piping hot" (*UMW* 6), and Gossamer Beynon who daydreams that "Sinbad Sailors places on her thighs still dewdamp from the first mangrowing cock-crow garden his reverent goat-bearded hands" (*UMW* 63). The "otherness" of female sexuality and madness have often been linked by patriarchal society, female sexuality being associated in the past with erotomania—the madness of unfulfilled desire. Thomas's synopsis of *The Town That Was Mad* demonstrates his awareness of madness as a social construct and, in *Under Milk Wood*, Thomas counters any hints of madness in female expressions of sexuality with the madness of Jack Black's repression of sexuality. Thomas allows his female characters to proclaim their sexuality and, in so doing, subverts a social system which believes that female sexuality represents a subversive discourse against social hierarchy and must, therefore, be constructed as social deviance. Female sexuality is a significant element of carnival contributing to its subversive nature and Bakhtin's emphasis on the female body and its processes acknowledges the importance of women's role in carnival.

The "sub-textual seriousness"[73] which James A. Davies identifies in *Under Milk Wood* links the play to the serious explorations of Thomas's poetry and the tragi-comic content of Thomas's writing makes his work an ideal medium for carnival ambivalence. This exploration of carnival in *Under Milk Wood* places Thomas nearer to the Dostoevskian model of carnival, with its emphasis on language, than to the Rabelaisian model, with its emphasis on grotesque realism. Bakhtin writes that "carnivalization allows Dostoevsky to glimpse and bring to life aspects in the character and behaviour of people which in the normal course of life could not have revealed themselves" (*PDP* 163) and the relevance to Thomas's play is clear. Thomas's carnival impulse is apparent throughout his canon and, while it remains subversive, its progression is from an explicit Rabelaisian position towards an implicit Dostoevskian position.

As Philip A. Lahey writes "A certain type of critical approach to the work of Dylan Thomas, based for the most part on the events of his seemingly chaotic and irresponsible life, has tended to dismiss him as an immature bohemian, incapable of producing poetry which would have any lasting value." Lahey acknowledges that, despite this destructive overshadowing of the work by the life, "a biographical approach to a poet's work can give us certain insights which are of use in interpreting the poetry and understanding it more fully . . . but the work of Dylan Thomas, assessed on these principles, is placed in a narrower perspective than that justified by a more comprehensive approach to his work".[74] While Thomas's work refuses to be limited to any single specific meaning, the application of carnival theory exposes the rich layers of subversive humour and points to the socio-political content of the work. In a circular movement, typical of carnival, a Bakhtinian assessment of the writing leads to a reassessment of the legends surrounding Thomas, the "popular" poet whose life and work personifies carnival ambivalence. Thomas's quest in *Under Milk Wood* to give a voice to the populace is the essence of carnival where the polyphonic text is an expression of liberty and equality. Thomas presides over Llareggub's carnival as a benign Lord of Misrule who sees the everyday carnival of common life as a liberating force in both literature and society. In *Under Milk Wood*, Thomas creates and celebrates an egalitarian community where all the voices of carnival are heard; he seeks to liberate and empower the populace, releasing their potential as Bakhtinian theory releases the potential of the text.

NOTES

1. James A. Davies, *A Reference Companion to Dylan Thomas* (London & Westport: Greenwood P., 1998) 286.
2. Mikhail Bakhtin, *Rabelais and His World*, trans. Helene Iswolsky (Bloomington: Indiana U.P., 1984), *Problems of Dostoevsky's Poetics*, ed. and trans. Caryl Emerson, Theory and History of Literature Series, Vol. 8 (Minneapolis: Minnesota U.P., 1987). Although *Rabelais and his World*, published in 1965 but written as a doctoral thesis in the 1940s, is more widely recognized as the source of Bakhtinian carnival theory, *Problems of Dostoevsky's Poetics* (1929) initially sets out Bakhtin's theory of carnival which was subsequently developed with more emphasis on grotesque realism in *Rabelais and his World*. Further refernces will be included in the text (*RW* and *PDP*).
3. M. Wynn Thomas, *Internal Difference* (Cardiff: U. of Wales P., 1992) 32.
4. Saunders Lewis, "Is there an Anglo-Welsh literature?", quoted in M. Wynn Thomas, *Corresponding Cultures: The Two Literatures of Wales* (Cardiff: U. of Wales P., 1999) 48.
5. David Holbrook, *Llareggub Revisited* (London: Bowes & Bowes, 1962) 197.
6. *Poetry Wales* 34.2 (1998): 45-49. This article is extended and elaborated upon in John Goodby and Chris Wigginton, "'Shut, too, in a tower of words': Dylan Thomas' modernism", *Locations of Literary Modernism*, ed. Alex Davis and Lee M. Jenkins (Cambridge: C.U.P., 2000).
7. Roland Mathias in "A Niche for Dylan Thomas", *Poetry Wales*, Dylan Thomas Special Issue, 9.2 (1973): 57, writes: "[h]is inability to write politically-motivated or socially conscious poems is well-known".
8. In addition to the explicit markers of class in his work, Thomas's letters and interviews demonstrate social and political awareness; see, for example, his letter of July 1938 to Henry Treece [Dylan Thomas, *The Collected Letters*, ed. P. Ferris (New York: Macmillan, 1985) 309-11 (*CL*)] or "Answers to an Enquiry" and "The

Cost of Letters" [Dylan Thomas, *Early Prose Writings*, ed. Walford Davies (London: Dent, 1971) 149-153 (*EPW*)]. Ralph Maud believes that the Notebook poems of July 1932-January 1933 show a growing socio-political awareness: "They exhibit a new social awareness, an expansion into political consciousness". See Ralph Maud, *Poet in the Making: The Notebooks of Dylan Thomas* (London: Dent, 1968) 115.

9. *Under Milk Wood,* The Definitive Edition, ed. Walford Davies and Ralph Maud (London: Dent, 1998) Introduction xi-xii. Further references are included in the text (*DM-UMW*). It should be noted that Walford Davies has recently edited a Penguin edition of *Under Milk Wood* where he restores First Voice and Second Voice. (Harmondsworth: Penguin, 2000).

10. *New Welsh Review* 33 (Summer 1996): 98-99.

11. This happens four times in quick succession; see *Under Milk Wood: A Play for Voices*, ed. Daniel Jones (London: Dent, 1974, rept. 1992) 3-9.

12. Due to this anti-carnival editorial emendation, all references to *Under Milk Wood* will be to the Daniel Jones edition (*UMW*) unless otherwise stated. Douglas Cleverdon had previously conflated these voices for a 1956 stage production.

13. *Internal Difference* 177.

14. Although "Blodeuedd" and "Blodeuwedd" are often treated as interchangeable, Blodeuedd (Flowers) is the name of the woman protagonist while Blodeuwedd (Flowerface) refers to the owl into which Blodeuedd is changed as punishment for infidelity; see Gwyn Jones, *Welsh Legends and Folk-Tales* (Harmondsworth: Penguin, 1979) 80-81. Blodeuwedd is an important symbol in Welsh writing in English; R. S. Thomas, Gillian Clarke, Glyn Jones, Saunders Lewis, Emyr Humphreys and Tony Conran are amongst those who have used this folk-tale in their writing. *DM-UMW* 77-78, has informative notes on this quotation, the most relevant here being that Thomas, in addition to the *Mabinogion* allusion, is quoting from Arthur Machen's *Far off Things* (1912) and alluding to the Celtic Romanticism of Arthur Machen's writing.

15. Dylan Thomas, *Collected Stories*, ed. Walford Davies (London: Dent, 1998) 42. Further references are included in the text (*CS*).

16. *Corresponding Cultures* 93.

17. Quoted in *Corresponding Cultures* 93. For "The Poets of Swansea, see *EPW* 97-121.

18. M. Wynn Thomas, "'Never seek to tell thy love': Rhys Davies's Fiction", *Welsh Writing in English* 4 (1998): 17.

19. M. Wynn Thomas also recognizes this significance in *Corresponding Cultures*. 93.

20. Glyn Jones, *The Dragon Has Two Tongues: Essays on Anglo-Welsh Writers and Writing* (London: Dent, 1968)190.

21. David Daiches, "The Poetry of Dylan Thomas", *Dylan Thomas*, ed. C. B. Cox. (New Jersey: Prentice-Hall, 1966) 24. Further references are included in the text (*Cox*).

22. Thomas's use of Welsh and English in bilingual wordplay fulfils Bakhtin's definition of polyglossia—a bilingual or multilingual aspect of heteroglossia.

23. Gwyn Williams, Foreword to *The Burning Tree*, quoted by John Ackerman (*Cox* 30). Williams is in turn quoting Matthew Arnold quoting the *Mabinogion*.

24. *Corresponding Cultures* 93. Glyn Jones also draws upon this Celtic and Arthurian imagery for *The Island of Apples*.

25. Dylan Thomas, *Collected Poems*, ed. Walford Davies (London: Dent, 1993) 134. Further references are included in the text (*CP*).
26. *Dan y Wenallt*, trans. T. James Jones (Llandysul: Gwasg Gomer, 1968).
27. M. Wynn Thomas. "'He belongs to the English': Welsh Dylan and Welsh-language culture", *Swansea Review* No. 20 (2000): 130.
28. C. J. Rawson, "Randy Dandy in the Cave of Spleen", *Dylan Thomas: New Critical Essays*, ed. Walford Davies (London: Dent, 1972) 73-106.
29. This 1945 poem has other resemblances to *UMW*, e.g., in stanzas 12, 13, 15, and 16, the imperatives "Listen" and "Look" directly address and involve the reader.
30. Ken Hirschkop, "Bakhtin, Discourse and Democracy", *New Left Review* 160 (1986): 92-113.
31. *The Dragon has Two Tongues* 194.
32. R. B. Kershner, *Joyce, Bakhtin and Popular Literature* (Chapel Hill: North Carolina U.P., 1989) 19. Kershner also mentions "a play of voices". Kershner is discussing Bakhtin in relation to Joyce's *Ulysses*, not *Under Milk Wood*, and there are many instances of comparison between these two texts, mostly uncomplimentary to Thomas.
33. Author and narrator are interchangeable in Bakhtin's writing. It is not always possible to decide which he means or, indeed, if the terms are differentiated.
34. Ralph Maud, *Entrances to Dylan Thomas' Poetry* (Pittsburgh: Pittsburgh U.P., 1966) 2.
35. Dylan Thomas, *The Broadcasts*, ed. Ralph Maud (London: Dent, 1991) 22. Further references are included in the text (*B*).
36. Michael Holquist, *Dialogism: Bakhtin and his World* (London: Routledge, 1996) 50.
37. John Drakakis, ed., *British Radio Drama* (Cambridge: C.U.P., 1981) 81-83.
38. *DM-UMW* 42. This section is omitted from *UMW* and this removes most of the comedy created by the Shakespearean allusion (*As You Like It*, V.3 ll.15-38), although the refrain is retained, interlaced with Polly Garter's song and emphasizing the spring-time setting of the play (*UMW* 59). See *DM-UMW* 97 for details.
39. *DM-UMW* has "Mary Ann the Sailors" to reflect her communal identity as landlady of the pub, The Sailors' Arms; this is in line with Tom the Sailors (*UMW* 52) but as Sinbad Sailors is retained there is no consistency. Although Davies and Maud quote Thomas's intended change of name in "Tom [later Sinbad] the Sailor's" (*DM-UMW* xxxvii), Tom the Sailors remains in both editions (*UMW* 52 and *DM-UMW* 38).
40. cf. Lily Jackson's soliloquy in "The Londoner" (*B* 82-83).
41. Thomas's plans to extend the evening section of the play are discussed in *DM-UMW* xl. Davies and Maud note that "[t]he main plan for extending the evening of the play was to expand the section in the Sailors Arms by writing songs for Nogood Boyo, Mary Ann the Sailors, Evans the Death and Lily Smalls". David Higham quotes Thomas's intention of developing the play from "midnight to midnight" and expanding "the day after dusk" to balance the movement of the play (*CL* 904).
42. In his 1945 broadcast "Welsh Poetry" (*B* 31), Thomas describes the term "Anglo-Welsh poetry" as "an ambiguous compromise" and proceeds to discuss a selection of Welsh poems written in English. He declares that "[a]fter Vaughan, there is no other considerable Welsh poet . . . until the 20th century" and then proceeds to cite the 18th century Dyer. "There was John Dyer (1700-1758) of Carmarthenshire,

whose "Grongar Hill", an irregular Pindaric ode, is still remembered, if only as a name, by those who read poetry for a degree and by those who live near Grongar Hill . . . We must read it together one day" (*B* 35).

43. Lynne Pearce, *Reading Dialogics* (London: Arnold, 1994) 59.
44. Pearce 59.
45. Pearce 60.
46. Peter Elfed Lewis, "Return Journey to Milk Wood", *Poetry Wales* 9.2 (1973): 27.
47. Geoffrey Moore. "Dylan Thomas", *Dylan Thomas: The Legend and the Poet*, ed. E.W. Tedlock (London: Heinemann, 1960) 249.
48. Douglas Cleverdon, *The Growth of Milk Wood* (London: Dent, 1969) 85. Thomas described the B.B.C. as the place "poets run away to, to-day's equivalent of the sea" (*EPW* 161).
49. Daniel Jones, in his 1974 Preface, writes: "At the time of first publication I was obliged against my will to change the name Llareggub to Llaregyb" (*UMW* xiv).
50. Daphne Watson, "Voices Still Singing", *Dylan Thomas: Craft or Sullen Art*, ed. Alan Bold (London: Vision P., 1990) 151.
51. J. Lechte, *Fifty Key Contemporary Thinkers* (London: Routledge, 1996) 8.
52. John Ackerman, *A Dylan Thomas Companion: Life, Poetry and Prose* (Basingstoke: Macmillan, 1991) 263, 261.
53. Ackerman 261.
54. Caradog Prichard's *One Moonlit Night* is set in winter moonlight in contrast to *UMW*'s "spring moonless night" and more akin to the winter setting of "Quite Early One Morning".
55. Michael D. Bristol, *Carnival and Theater* (London: Methuen, 1985) 67.
56. D. Tudor Bevan, *Glyn Jones: The Background to his Writings*, M.A. dissertation, University of Wales [Swansea], 1989, 66. Glyn Jons also uses this subversive "mayor-making" ritual in his novel, *The Valley, The City, The Village* (1956; London: Severn House, 1980) 289-98.
57. Ann E. Mayer, *Artists in Dylan Thomas's Prose Works: Adam Naming and Aesop Fabling* (Montreal: McGill-Queen's U.P., 1995) 86.
58. Bakhtin's analysis of Dostoevsky's work gives greater attention to the aspects of carnival, such as heteroglossia, polyphony, discourse, which demonstrate a multiplicity of democratic voices and narratives within a text, than to the grotesque realism which he addresses in his later analysis of Rabelais.
59. On Thomas's punning on "parchedig", see also Ralph Maud's comments in his recent study, *Where have the Old Words Got Me?: Explications of Dylan Thomas's* Collected Poems (Cardiff: U. of Wales P., 2003) 8.
60. For two recent considerations of Thomas's polticical vision, see Victor N. Paananen, "The Social Vison of Dylan Thomas" and Victor Golightly, "'Writing with dreams and blood': Dylan Thomas, Marxism and 1930s Swansea", in *Welsh Writing in English: A Yearbook of Critcal Essays* 8 (2003): 46-66, 67-91.
61. Peter Elfed Lewis, "Return Journey to Milk Wood" 27.
62. *Dialogism: Bakhtin and his World* 89.
63. Pam Morris, ed., *The Bakhtin Reader: Selected Writings of Bakhtin, Medvedev, Voloshinov* (London: Arnold, 1994) 238.
64. Sue Vice, *Introducing Bakhtin* (Manchester: Manchester U.P., 1997) 154.
65. Mikhail Bakhtin quoted in *The Bakhtin Reader* 234.
66. Marshall Stearns, "Unsex the Skeleton: Notes on the Poetry of Dylan Thomas", Tedlock 120.

67. *Entrances to Dylan Thomas' Poetry* 98.
68. Mary Russo, *The Female Grotesque* (London: Routledge, 1994) 62.
69. Marty Roth, "Carnival, creativity, and the sublimation of drunkenness", *Mosaic: A Journal for the Interdisciplinary Study of Literature* 30.2 (1997): 1-18. Roth quotes critics who have charged Bakhtin "with robbing carnival of its dark potency and rendering it a sanitized Utopia". On one level, *Under Milk Wood* might project an atmosphere of "sanitized Utopia" but beneath the surface of the text, Thomas portrays the darkness beneath the surface of society.
70. A concept of *UMW*'s "licensed" carnival first suggested to me by M. Wynn Thomas. See Daphne Watson, Bold 150.
71. *The Female Grotesque* 60.
72. *A Reference Companion to Dylan Thomas* 236.
73. *A Reference Companion to Dylan Thomas* 238.
74. Philip A. Lahey, "Dylan Thomas: a reappraisal", *Critical Survey* 5.1 (1993): 53-65.

"Life's miraculous poise between light and dark": Ceri Richards and the Poetry of Vernon Watkins

Tony Curtis
University of Glamorgan

Ceri Richards and Vernon Watkins have both suffered from a lack of critical interest since their deaths. Both shared commitments to and a love of the Gower, the tradition of European culture and the poetry of Dylan Thomas. The relationship between Ceri Richards and the work of Dylan Thomas, then the relationship Richards built with Vernon Watkins and their mutual friend the Italian poet and art critic, Roberto Sanesi, informs the work of all three artists and rewards further consideration.[1]

Critical and personal responses to the work of Ceri Richards often make reference to qualities which one associates with poetry—his mature series of paintings and lithographs based on the Debussy *Cathédrale engloutie* Prelude were described by Mel Gooding as being underpinned by the principles of pattern and resolution like "a villanelle".[2] In response to Mel Gooding's monograph on Richards[3] and the "Selective Retrospective" of Richards's work which Gooding organized in 2002-2003, *The Western Mail* noted that "in the late 1940s Richards developed an intensely lyrical vision".[4]

In fact, the organizing principle of Mel Gooding's exhibition was that of Poetry and Music. Richards's work, experimental and aware of the possibilities of the surreal in the 1930s, in the following four decades rarely excludes the lyrical and the metaphorical. An important early work from 1937 *The Female Contains All Qualities* took its title from lines found in Walt Whitman's "I Sing the Body Electric" which, in a story quoted by Mel Gooding, Richards came upon while conducting a surrealist game of chance reading.[5] In many cases the works, usually in series or sequences, reference poets and composers—Dylan Thomas, Vernon Watkins, Beethoven, Debussy—and often clearly acknowledge specific poems and compositions—"The force that through the green fuse", "Music of Colours: White Blossom" and "La Cathédrale engloutie".

The first such influence on Richards, and the most important for his work was, of course, Dylan Thomas whose poetry informed the art of Ceri Richards for over thirty years and who was at the centre of the triangular relationship of Watkins, Richards and Sanesi. It may be argued that the work of the artist reflects back upon that major and often daunting poet. The sense of reciprocity, a dialogue between the poet's work and the artist's, is most fully and usefully explored by the poet Richard Burns in his *Ceri Richards and Dylan Thomas—Keys to Transformation* in which he convincingly argues that Ceri Richards's drawings on four copies of Thomas's *Collected Poems* in 1953 offer insights and clear approaches to those challenging poems.[6]

It is the painting and lithograph of Dylan's "Do not go gentle" which most profoundly express Richards's feelings of loss at Dylan's untimely death. In a letter to Moelwyn Merchant, Richards attempts to recreate the circumstances of these works:

> I felt I could see the isolated and pathetic passivity of man on the thresholds of Eternity—I hope very deeply that I say those last words with deep reverence and seriousness—but I think this (is) what I conveyed in my drawing—the body of man is tossed out of the shroud into the void—his resistance quietened.[7]

Evidently, Richards had approached the poem and its theme with awe, "reverence", and not entirely a convinced quietude in the face of oblivion. Ceri Richards seems more likely to "rage" than Dylan's friend Vernon Watkins, whose life's work was to construct edifices of words to render irrelevant the erosions of time. The "Do not go gentle" drawing, lithograph and painting depict an awkwardness in the tumbling corpse, a distressed face, while the owl and the manuscript-shroud flies overhead and onwards.

The importance of Dylan Thomas to Ceri Richards from the 1940s until his death in 1971 is paramount. Richards was born in Dunvant in 1903, Thomas in Swansea in 1914. Both men moved to London for professional reasons, Richards living exclusively there for most of his life, apart from a period of teaching at Cardiff College of Art during the war[8] and his visits back to the Gower where he had bought a cottage. That cottage made him a near neighbour of Vernon Watkins and the poet Roberto Sanesi was a visitor there too.

Ceri Richards was the most truly European artist to have grown from Wales, but his roots remained in the Gower. It was almost inevitable that he would pay attention to, find resonances in and then meet Dylan Thomas. Their meeting was, however, singular and late. In the early 1950s Ceri Richards had been ill and was spending time in his rented cottage near Pennard, close to Vernon Watkins. One day in October 1953 Ceri and Frances Richards were taken down to the Boathouse at Laugharne by the painter Alfred Janes, one of the "Kardomah boys" and a "wonderful friend" of Richards's in London.[9] (This was, according to Gwen Watkins, at the suggestion of Vernon.) Janes

Do not go gentle into that good night, 1965.

considered Richards to be "the most creative and inventive British painter of this century", though he thought that Dylan had not known of Ceri's work:

> We saw him two or three days before he left for America that last time. He'd never met Ceri, so Mary and I took him down to Dylan in the Boathouse in Laugharne. I had a lovely little Sunbeam Talbot drop-head coupe at that time. . . . I don't think Dylan was terribly well acquainted with Ceri's work. Dylan's was very much a word-mind, one track brain. He was like the average person when it came to painting and other things.[10]

Of course, Dylan died shortly after in New York; but it is intriguing to speculate what his reaction might have been to working with Richards. Ironically, it was the death of Dylan Thomas which impacted dramatically on the painter. Ceri Richards, hearing of Dylan's collapse and coma, bought four copies of *Collected Poems* and began to re-read the poems, drawing copiously on the pages of the books in the days before Dylan's death. Three copies survive and it is from these that Richard Burns has re-constructed *Ceri Richards—Drawings to Poems by Dylan Thomas* and written the accompanying monograph.[11] Burns explains that he discovered, with great surprise and excitement the existence of the drawings when collaborating with Frances Richards on a separate publishing project.

Central to Burns's study is *The Black Apple of Gower*. This painting deals more specifically with the Gower-genesis of the poet and artist, rather than the war-nightmares of the poet's "I dreamed my genesis". There is an ambiguity in the Gower-mandala's darkness—seed, womb, tunnel, the "rotating shell" even—and of the presence of the owl, bringer of death and conveyer of souls. As Jung wrote to Richards, "It is pure black substance, which the old alchemists called *nigredo*, that is: blackness, and understood as night, chaos, evil and the essence of corruption, yet the *prima material* of gold, sun and eternal incorruptibility". He added, "I understand your picture as a confession of the secret of our time".[12] John Ormond said of this drawing, "Richards is touching on and making a design out of what Vernon Watkins called "life's miraculous poise between light and dark'".[13] Thomas, Richards and Jung are working through language, paint and science towards the same appreciation of the duality, the deep ambiguity of human existence: we are rooted in the world, but may only completely occupy it and fulfil ourselves through the imagination.

It was Ceri Richards who designed the set for the memorial reading in London in the February following Dylan's death. He wrote a report of the event to Vernon Watkins.[14] He was less than impressed by the contributions of some others: "Betty Lutyens doesn't possess the appropriate spirit for it. . . . Edith Evans as a reader was completely out her depth—Emlyn W was good

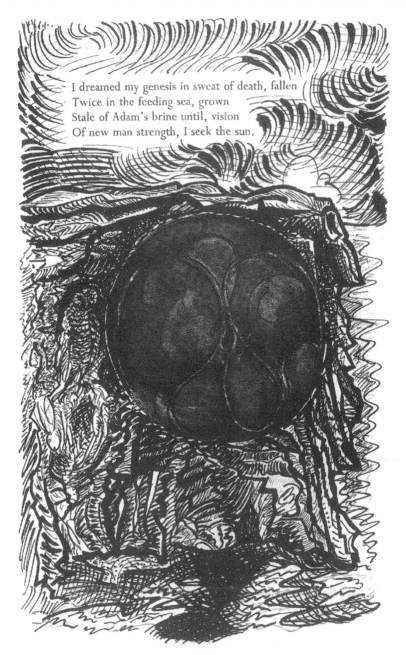

I dreamed my genesis in sweat of death, fallen
Twice in the feeding sea, grown
Stale of Adam's brine until, vision
Of new man strength, I seek the sun.

From Ceri Richards's drawings to Dylan Thomas's *Collected Poems*, 1953.

but not so good as in the rehearsal. . . ." However, "R. Burton read Fern Hill very well, obviously he loved this poem and knew it inside out so to speak and that is very important". He ends with the P.S., "Whatever would Dylan say or think if he was able to see what is happening—he would perhaps blow the froth off his celestial beer at us and say we blasphemed—and that we took his name in vain—but he would like it if he feels we do it for love". But the commission of love was clearly important for Richards and signified a sad culmination of the concern to interpret and respond to a poet who had driven much of his art over the previous decade: "My curtain was in glorification of Dylan and my stage décor more seriously suggesting his passing and flight away from us". Sadly, he was to perform the same elegiac role for Dylan's fellow Swansea poet and their mutual friend Vernon Watkins.

Vernon Watkins has not sustained the critical attention and the wide readership one might have assumed three decades ago. John Berger's view of Ceri Richards's comparatively low reputation in the 1950s might well apply to Watkins: "He is the kind of artist who suffers most from our lack of any collective mythology or symbolism. There is no framework in which he can set his instinctive intimations".[15] Watkins aligned himself alongside his younger friend Dylan Thomas, but had no fireworks of a personal life, no dangerous legend to buoy up his readership and intrigue biographers. Instead, he ploughed a rather solitary furrow, a neo-platonist who became a Christian visionary; his cyclical poetry constantly polished the jewel of itself, aimed at the defeat of time, immortality achieved through an appropriation of traditional forms of language and myth.

Vernon Watkins's love of, and location on, the Gower was shared by Richards, the Watkinses' near neighbour. Richards's contribution to Leslie Norris's Faber collection of tributes after Watkins's death is sincere and lyrical:

> To be with Vernon when he wished to show the Gower to you, which meant the immediate and familiar Gower round him, was a special experience. He took you straight to his personal vantage points. He was remarkably sure-footed. Far down on the foreshore, when you called to see him, and the tide was right—you saw him from aloft—and he was master with the prawns, crabs and lobsters, striding through pools, over rocks slippery with seaweed, up rocky faces and sand dunes, and through acres of bracken and gorse, in his own natural diversity of ways.[16]

Watkins would, no doubt, have been delighted at this characterization. He was Taliesin, occupying the landscape, at ease among the rocks and pools, agile as any of the denizens of that shore. He would have been pleased too that Ceri Richards should witness a sign as propitious as this—"Owls and hawks were flying, and the heron often seen beside the river in Castle Valley alighted one day on his lawn".[17] The Gower was still Dylan-priested. Ceri Richards and Vernon Watkins were kindred spirits under the shadow of Dylan; each was changed profoundly in his respective art by Thomas.[18] For Ceri Richards, whose image hoard had been filled in the 1940s and 1950s by Dylan's *Collected Poems*, Vernon Watkins carried the torch on:

> His poetry, sensitive and beautifully wrought, was in his conversation too, and there were many unexpected and illuminating moments when it surfaced from the deeper recesses of his sensibility. For me and for my painting, it was a privilege to listen to him, and to what was really an affirmation of the creative processes although the character of our work was very different. I have paid him homage in drawings and paintings over the years.[19]

That contribution is preceded by a line drawing *The Gower Coast from Pennard*. It is no more than a sketch, but has a sad, celebratory freedom of line which contrasts with the sonorous weight of the *Black Apple of Gower* painting. The sea's edges, the sun, the cliffs are held in tensions of lines which plunge towards the arabesque. It is an idea of a landscape energized by loss.

Watkins and Richards met also in London; on occasions they visited the poet and artist David Jones together, as Gwen Watkins recalled: "I remember watching aghast from an ascending escalator as Vernon and Ceri Richards, northbound to see David (Jones) at Harrow, became so deeply absorbed in conversation that they stepped into a southbound train, probably not to emerge until the end of the line".[20] The two visionaries were so deep in discussion that their pilgrimage to the most important poet-painter since Blake left on the wrong track. Ruth Pryor claims that Frances and Ceri Richards were friends of David Jones,[21] though there seems to have been no extensive study of the relationship in artistic terms. Perhaps there was no direct artistic exchange between the two men. In letters to Vernon Watkins, David Jones apologizes for missing Ceri Richards's exhibitions at the Redfern Gallery in Cork Street, and at the White Chapel Gallery in the East End, both recommended by Watkins. However, David Jones was a virtual recluse in Harrow and little can be read into his not attending.[22]

Vernon Watkins had a serious interest in the contemporary painters of Wales; he knew many of them and was supportive of their work in the sense that he agreed to speak at the openings of a number of exhibitions, including that initiated by Kingsley Amis in Cambridge in 1963 at which all the leading Welsh artists exhibited except for David Jones and Ceri Richards.[23] This support by Amis of Welsh culture is indeed intriguing, as was the return of Watkins to his old university. He also opened the 56 Group exhibition at the Dillwyn Gallery in Swansea in that May and playfully ended his speech of welcome with a punning list of the participants:

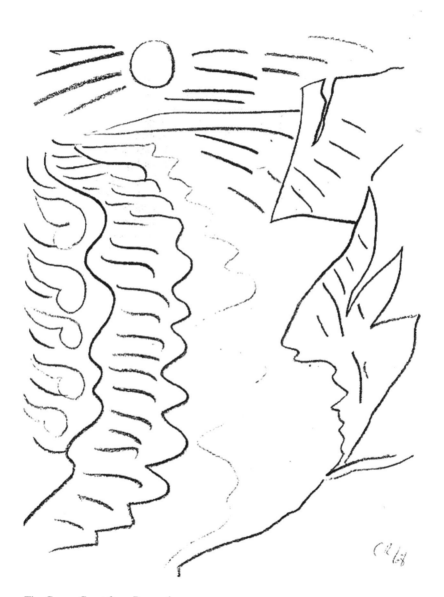

The Gower Coast from Pennard.

This is a FAIRLEY comprehensive exhibition, ZOBOL(D)LE I HUNTER ound for something to say about it, before you STEELE yourselves to look at the pictures. The artists have done their job, and what WRIGHT have I to TINKER with it? I'm shaking like a GIARDELLI as it is. What with a KOPPEL at the MALTHOUSE, I'm like a fish out of water.

Now, you other fish, look at these attractive BATES. Snap them up. WILL ROBERTS be yours, or which? It mu STEVEN Sem I can't talk properly, but I know them all, and they're all here.

I declare the exhibition open.[24]

The wit may be schoolboy stuff, but it does indicate that Watkins was familiar with the artists and relaxed in his approach to them. In the previous year, 1962, Vernon Watkins had opened the two-man show by Alfred Janes[25] and Will Roberts at Parc Howard, Llanelli, and in 1964 he opened the Glynn Vivian Gallery's Ceri Richards exhibition which featured the *Cathédrale engloutie* series of paintings; Watkins's Introduction to the catalogue underlines the common intent of the painter and poet:

> The mystery of these paintings must remain inexhaustible, which is always the mark of great art. Just as a supreme composition in music has the secret of self-renewal, of endlessly beginning afresh, so these pictures hold the attention through a multiplicity of images and then return it to their imaginative source where it is confronted with them again. It is this secret that makes the effect of these works a continually changing one, like a fountain which renews its identity through exuberance, and remains sudden and fresh.
>
> There is a bond between all the arts, and his response to music and poetry is an integral part of Ceri Richards's painting.

The relationship between Richards and Watkins was obviously a warm and supportive one, but Richards was in London during the Kardomah years and their friendship dates from their middle age. In 1964 Watkins wrote specifically of the *Cathédrale engloutie* series:

> At the 1962 Venice Biennale people from all over the world were astonished by his subtle harnessing of lyric mobility to sculptural strength, of exhilaration to profound feeling, of movement to repose. The line itself sings, less from appreciation than from praise. Where does sensuousness end and thought begin, when both give such immediate pleasure, and project so instantly the mystery at the heart of painting, poetry and music? And who better understands tragedy than one who has joy at his fingertips?[26]

Praise is elevated above appreciation by Watkins; the wonderment in the world, natural and projected through art, leads to, and is supportive of faith. Both men, one feels, had a clear faith in life-affirming creativity, though the work of Vernon Watkins was not directly to influence the art of Ceri Richards as had that of Dylan Thomas, especially in the sense that Dylan's "Force that through the green fuse" image had powered much of the mature work of the painter. In 1967, the year of his death, Watkins again wrote, "But the favourite word of today's artist, 'breakthrough', is irrelevant. Breakthrough to what? Is there a suggestion that art has progress? Tradition has no progress, but it is always roving to its youth; it is always manifesting what does not change, except in its material aspect." Watkins, perhaps rather surprisingly, enthuses about these late, semi-abstract, quite challenging "Cathédrale" works because they are rooted in music, myth and faith. Gwen Watkins characterized it thus: "They both responded to the miraculous and eternal and sacred, in contrast to Auden and Spender and Orwell at the time".[27]

Watkins's first collection, *Ballad of the Mari Lwyd*,[28] explored in the title poem the custom of processing a horse's skull, held aloft by a man from beneath a sheet, around the local houses at Christmas to engage in a challenge of versifying. It is perhaps surprising that through his long friendship with the poet Ceri Richards was never fully drawn to this custom as an image-source. There is a Mari Lwyd horse's head in the drawing Richards offered to Watkins for the cover of his collection *Cypress and Acacia*, published in 1959. The image was not, however, used, though it was reproduced in the Vernon Watkins Special Issue of *Poetry Wales* in 1977.[29] The image appears to be an unresolved sketch for a larger work: there are couples in Sabine-rape congress in the upper left corner and the Sabine-theme horseman in the bottom right is bending down to what is clearly a Mari Lwyd horse's skull. Richards did, however, "illustrate the whole of *Cypress and Acacia* every page of it, in the manner of his 1953 illumination of Dylan Thomas's *Collected Poems*", and Watkins loved it.[30] In a letter to Watkins[31] Ceri Richards thought that his drawing might be suitable to accompany Watkins's poem "The Immortal in Nature", published in the same collection, a poem in which the poet again rehearses his belief in the cycle of nature as the key to our acceptance of the world:

> Where time is not, all nature is undone,
> For nature grows in grandeur of decay.
> These royal colours that the leaves put on
> Mark the year living in his kingly way;
> Yet, when he dies, not he but time is gone.
>
> Beethoven's music nature could not stun.
> Light rushed from Milton.
> > > > See the Sistine ray.
> There burns the form eternally begun.
> That soul whose very hand made marble pray,
> The untempted, mightiest master, holds in sway

Facsimile of Ceri Richards' design for cover of *Cypress and Acacia*.

The wrestling sinews death had seemed to own
And might have owned, but that they were not clay.[32]

Beethoven, Milton, Michelangelo's Sistine Chapel, and Ceri Richards who, as Watkins appreciated, all dealt with "the form eternally begun" and their art was, for Watkins, the answer to the erosions of time, and death's finality. For him, art survived, actually and Platonically; both Watkins and Richards worked between the two energies of painting and poetry.

According to Gwen Watkins,[33] Richards also praised "The Tributary Seasons" in which all four seasons converge to form the river of life. The poem begins and ends with Autumn:

Tree of beginning, Autumn tree:
Divine imagination's tree.

God has *imagined* the world into being and the artist—poet and painter—is the priest handling the sacraments. "The Tributary Seasons" is not the strongest poem in *Cypress and Acacia*; its rhyming couplets are achieved at the expense of both music and syntax; inversions and infelicities weaken its conviction—

To robins crusts and crumbs are tossed,
Yellow against the white of frost.   (*Cypress and Acacia* 70)

But Richards recognized that Watkins was again dealing with the cycle of nature, as the painter had done constantly in his mature work in that decade of the 1950s.

In his posthumous collection *Fidelities*[34] Watkins included "Deposition (on the painting by Ceri Richards)". Although there was a version in St. Edmund's Hall, Oxford, Watkins almost certainly refers to the work which now hangs in St. Mary's Church, Swansea. The poet responds in detail to the specific figuration of the painting: "These giant, dilated / Hands and feet." The "Swift, clasped fingers / Complete the Cross" in the sense that the hands clasped in prayer to the left of the painting are locking fingers together in a prayer which is empowered by Christ's crucifixion and sacrifice. Watkins notes the matter-of-fact depiction of the dead Christ, fragile, distorted, brought down to the brown earth: for "In the eye of the world / Resurrection fails" and faith is undercut by "speculation". When "One reaches the clasp / For the bag of nails", the poet's eyes are drawn to the carpenter's bag held by an unseen man at the top right of the painting. The nails are both the means of a cruel death and the pinning of flesh to the tree of our world. They are both the tools of execution and the relics of the faith.[35]

Although there are few instances when Richards worked on specific poems by Watkins, the two men were drawn into a close friendship and admiration through their common love of the work of Dylan Thomas and the Gower peninsula. After Watkins's early death at sixty-one, Ceri Richards responded to that sadness with a number of elegiac works. The lithographs in the Roberto Sanesi portfolio *Journey Toward the North*[36] were among the final works of the artist's own life and appeared posthumously in 1971. In 1970 Richards had directed the publication of two lithographs inspired by an unpublished Watkins poem, the "Elegiac Sonnet" which the poet had sent to him in manuscript years before, after the death of Dylan Thomas.[37] It is not the strongest of Vernon Watkins's works, failing to lift off from the Petrachan form:

> Over this universal grave the sky
> Brings to the grieving earth its great reward,

The poem rests too heavily on unrealized images, the abstract, with sound occasionally swamping meaning—

> This body sleeping where the dead leaves lie
> Gives back to trees the colours they discard
> The patient light of its own penury

It ends with a flat, platitudinous image that aims for the sonority of a Victorian graveyard inscription—

> It is the shade the sun no longer flings
> Of one who touched the humble and the proud.

Ceri Richards, however, was clearly moved to celebrate the life and work of his friend Vernon Watkins, but this was not to be the most fitting remembrance.

The first of the Richards lithographs[38] has the swallows "turning in their own cloud" above landscape / leaf shapes that were to be developed in the later "Information Report XVI" in *Journey Toward the North* and which occur in drawings in memory of Watkins. The second has a fallen figure which is more at rest than the tumbling corpse of Dylan Thomas in the 1966 lithograph *Do not go gentle*. The stark black lines of this figure are working in a similar vein to the white-lined horses of the "Homage to Beethoven" (1953) and the black swan which lies beneath the white blossoms in the large, memorable canvas "Music of Colours: White Blossom", executed in the months after Vernon Watkins's death (and much later given by Frances Richards to the Glynn Vivian Gallery in Swansea for their Ceri Richards room). This painting,

Elegiac Sonnet (1) 1970.

Elegiac Sonnet (2) 1970.

in response to the Watkins poem of the same name, owes everything to the poem and closes the circle of mutual empathy and understanding: "The bud of the apple is already forming there".[39] The poem is one of Watkins's strongest, bringing together his concerns with the nature of immortality and the necessary tensions between the light and dark forces. The white is the white of blossom and of "the Nazarene", also "Of Leda, the swan, whitest of his loves"; but it is, too, the colour of decay—white gives meaning to black

> The mound of dust is nearer, white of mute dust that dies
> In the soundfall's great light, the music in the eyes,
> Transfiguring whiteness into shadows gone,
> Utterly secret. I know you, black swan.

Much of the work of both Watkins and Richards is concerned with closing the circle from white to black, life to death, blossom to decay and back to fruiting blossom again. The wordplay of the Swansea poets resonated in the studio of the London artist who travelled regularly to Pennard to refresh himself with sea air and visions. As early as 1940 he had painted *Blossoms*, a portent of the coming Blitz that would force him out of London when the art schools closed and to Cardiff, a teaching post at the School of Art and anti-aircraft and fire-watching duties. That painting is an ironic flowering of exploding shells, based on a description he had read of the Italian bombing campaign in their conquest of Abyssinia. The following year came the *Target Blossom* painting and drawings and *Desolate Landscape*; other paintings of the war period included *Falling Forms* (1944). In all these works bio-morphic forms explode and re-form into the energy forces of growth. Destruction prefigures re-birth, growth, development: white and black give meaning to each other. What the painter found, heard in the poetry of Dylan Thomas and later Vernon Watkins, was an articulation of the cyclical forces which he came to see as the driving force of the world, the driving force of his art.[40] Ceri Richards wrote of his admiration for Watkins's "The Mare", which he thought "a lovely poem"[41]:

> Do not pass her too close. It is easy to break the circle
> And lose that indolent fullness rounded under the ray
> Falling on light-eared grasses your footstep must not yet wake.
> It is easy to darken the sun of her unborn foal at play.
>
> (Cypress and Acacia 24)

The horses that roamed throughout the Gower would have been well-known to both men. Watkins saw the foal as a manifestation of another spirit, "Looking for that other, the foal no longer there".[42] Birth pulls one away from another life. Of course, the poet had imagined (in "Taliesin in Gower"): "My country is here. I am foal and violet. / Hawthorn breaks from my hands".[43] And "Foal" ends with an image of the complete cycle of existence through the life of the horses:

> . . . Startled he stands
> Dazzled, where darkness is green, where the sunlight is black,
> While his mother, grazing, is moving away
> From the lagging star of those stars, the unrisen wonder
> In the path of the dead, fallen from the sun in her hooves,
> And eluding the dead hands, begging him to play.

In Watkins's "Ballad of the Mari Lwyd", the grey mare of legend and custom, paraded at the cusp of the year on 31 December, is the haunting prospect of mortality which Vernon Watkins worked all through his writing to oppose. For

> 'None can look out and bear that sight,
> None can bear that shock.
> The Mari's shadow is too bright,
> Her brilliance is too black.
> None can bear that terror
> When the pendulum swings back
> Of the stiff and stuffed and stifled thing
> Gleaming in the sack.'
>
> Midnight. Midnight. Midnight. Midnight.
> Hark at the hands of the clock.[44]

and it is the hands of the clock that the poet works to stop. It is the two-spirited foal that the mare must carry, the new life imprinted with an ancient, eternal form.

Horses in the work of Ceri Richards carry the Romans to their Sabine prey in the series of works from the 1940s. In the 1953 works horses prance, *sgraffito* white lines against the blackness behind the figure in *Beethoven and St. Cecilia*, and in the background of *Beethoven and St. Cecilia II* horses and lions clash. Then, in the 1960s paintings after Delacroix's *La Chasse aux lions,* they tangle in a dance of death. Though it is in Dylan Thomas's "Fern Hill" that the horse as an originator of life is most memorably envisioned –

> So must it have been after the birth of the simple light
> In the first, spinning place, the spellbound horses walking warm
> > Out of the whinnying green stable
> > On to the fields of praise.

In the drawing Richards did in the space after the poem on that page in one of the copies of *Collected Poems* the horses charge away into the sky, becoming muscular cloud forms. The poet rides to sleep, "huntsman and herdsman"; they are the horses of the life-force, the ponies of Pennard which Thomas saw, as Watkins clearly did, as an exuberantly free-spirited life force.

Vernon Watkins directly returned the admiration that Ceri Richards had for his work and his visionary re-ordering of the world. In "The Forge of the Solstice" he describes the work of the artist. Firstly, David Jones who

> . . . scrawls on rock the names of hallowed things,
> Letters and hieroglyphs that yet shall last
> When darkness measures with a martyr's eye
> The glories shed by life's unchanging tree.

And then Richards who was

> Another, curbing vigour on his page
> To movement, makes the abounding life his own
> And rhythmic finds in a discordant age,
> Singing like living fountains sprung from stone,
> Those unifying harmonies of line
> Torn from creative nature.[45]

Vernon Watkins responds warmly to these two quite different artists because, for him, each is also working to build on ancient truths, honouring the traditions of the culture, working within the aesthetics of European high culture. This is the artist as martyr in the face of a darkness that will weight his achievements against his mortality. These artists, living in "a discordant age", find direction and purpose in the "unifying harmonies" of the graphic line and the poetry line, though that must be hard won, "torn" from the toil of the creative discipline.

At the poem's end "Love gives their art a body in which thought / Draws, not from time, but wisdom . . .": the artist's vision arms his bow with stars to strike at the heart of time itself. Of course, what the reader cannot find in such writing is the objective correlative, the location of life as we live it, daily life as we know it. Watkins believed that, "Cold craftsmanship is the best container of fire".[46] In a letter to Watkins in 1963, David Jones commiserated with him about unsympathetic reviewers, " . . . it's no good taking any notice of what chaps say. They say the exact opposite a year or so after!"[47] Unsympathetic critics, poets without strict form—"the prose-idiom boys" Watkins calls them—are irrelevant to Watkins and Jones.[48] And, Watkins would have claimed, for Ceri Richards too. Certainly Richards's art moved more securely into that shared high culture of Europe as he matured—the sequins and feathers of the early works of costers of the streets of London were always going to become decorative, semi-abstract arabesques of eternal energy, the life force. Watkins's Taliesin asks, "How shall I loosen this music to the listening, eavesdropping sea?".[49] Much of the work of both men addresses that challenge.

The Italian poet, critic and novelist Roberto Sanesi first met Ceri Richards in 1948 when he was visiting Vernon Watkins at his house "The Garth" in Pennard. Sanesi had translated the poetry of Dylan Thomas, then much later would translate that of Watkins himself. He was also friendly with Alfred Janes, but it was his admiration for the art of Ceri Richards which engaged most fully his own poetry and art criticism. "I got to know Vernon Watkins, and through Vernon I got to know Ceri Richards. Even though there are many linguistic differences between their works, the triangle was perfect, in a series of internal connections which gave me a lasting key to a culture".[50] Sanesi regarded the connections between the poetry of Watkins and Richards's art to be more profound than that between Richards and Dylan Thomas: "Ceri's stylistic clarity was definitely more akin to Watkins's poetry . . . just like Watkins's vision, which is the ability to create out of abstraction an *object* which can be immediately understood".[51] Sanesi recalls an afternoon in the garden of "The Garth" when he and Vernon Watkins were deep in poetic/philosophical discourse. Ceri Richards arrived:

> He sat down on the grass with us and whilst he was listening to us he seemed to be elsewhere, but not apart from us: in fact he seemed to be absorbed, amazed. Then, almost unexpectedly, he quoted some lines of Henry Vaughan: I think they were from the poem "They are all gone into the world of light". Then pulling a pencil stub from his pocket he pretended to sketch some shapes in the air, quickly, as if that blue and untouchable transparency were a piece of paper. Then, with an identical movement, he sketched out the same shapes on the fly-leaf of a book that was lying on the ground. Calmly, he said these words, which I will never forget: "It's what is different which always makes us realise what is the same."[52]

The Henry Vaughan poem Richards quoted projects a life that continues beyond the physical:

> They are all gone into the world of light!
>   And I alone sit ling'ring here;
> Their very memory is fair and bright,
>   And my sad thoughts doth clear...
>
> He that hath found some fledg'd bird's nest, may know
>   At first sight, if the bird be flown;
> But what fair well of grove he sings in now,
>   That is to him unknown.[53]

Those are sentiments that would have been shared deeply by Vernon Watkins whose work, too, sought to draw the truth from that light into which we all go. Intellectually, temperamentally, and in spirit, the three men on the grass, together with the two dead poets, Vaughan and Thomas, were in accord and had a common purpose and confluent language: theirs was the self-appointed, self-defining task of translating the world's mysterious ways, through the forging of imagery, to the minds and hearts of men, "before becoming transformed / into the astounding white of the darkness".[54]

Through my research on Ceri Richards, I have been moved to look again, to consider more carefully the poetry of Vernon Watkins. I have kept honour in the memory of the man, but have neglected his poetry. In 1967 when I had tutorials with him in University College, Swansea it was not the voice that could instruct me as a young, developing poet. His poetry has not aged well; he strikes us as too sonorous, much of his work seems stilted even. Yet "The Feather", "Music of Colours", "The Mare", "The Heron" and "Ballad of the Mari Lwyd" are alive and may still have the power to move and instruct. If my own villanelle based on Richards's *La Cathédrale engloutie* achieves anything of lasting worth, then I would wish lines such as "and live by old rhythms, each fold of the sea" and "who are deaf to deep truths, can't see / light and music still plays beneath the waves" to evoke Watkins, and those qualities which Ceri Richards wished to celebrate in common with his friend from Pennard.[55] I believe that "we must learn to love / and live by old rhythms" and that is why Richards's Costers, and Sabines, the Pianists and Cathedrals and his multifarious bio-morphic forms, together with the word-music of Thomas and Watkins should be woven again into the contemporary life of Wales.

NOTES

An earlier version of this paper formed part of the 2003 Rhys Davies Lecture, given at University of Glamorgan. The author and editor are grateful to the Ceri Richards Estate for permission to reproduce the artist's work.

1. Other poets who have responded to the work of Ceri Richards include John Ormond and the present writer.
2. Speaking at the Ceri Richards Study Day, National Museum of Wales, Cardiff, 22 September 2002.
3. Mel Gooding, *Ceri Richards* (London: Cameron & Hollis, 2002).
4. Dean Powell, " A Lifelong Engagement", *Western Mail*, 29 March 2002.
5. Gooding, *Ceri Richards* 44.
6. Richard Burns, *Ceri Richards and Dylan Thomas—Keys to Transformation* (London: Enitharmon P., 1981).
7. W. Moelwyn Merchant, "Ceri Richard's 'Pagan Mystery'", *Fragment of a Life* (Llandysul: Gomer, 1990) 30-32.
8. In 1940 he was invited down to teach by Evan Charlton, but returned to London in 1944.

9. Alfred Janes, "Ceri Remembered", Catalogue to Ceri Richards Exhibition, University College, Swansea, 1984.
10. Alfred Janes, interview in Tony Curtis, *Welsh Artists Talking* (Bridgend: Seren, 2000) 21.
11. Richard Burns, *Ceri Richards—Drawings to Poems by Dylan Thomas* (London: Enitharmon P., 1980).
12. Burns, *Keys to Transformation* 61. Jung's letter is dated 21 May 1958.
13. Introduction to the 1973 Memorial Exhibition catalogue.
14. Gwen Watkins, *Portrait of a Friend* (Llandysul: Gomer, 1983) 153-54.
15. Quoted by Mel Gooding, *Ceri Richards* 178.
16. *Vernon Watkins 1906-1967*, ed. Leslie Norris (London: Faber, 1970) 95-96.
17. *Vernon Watkins 1906-1967* 95-96.
18. It was to Richards that Watkins showed the letter from John Berryman, describing Dylan Thomas's death in New York. This clearly had a deep effect on the painter. See *Portrait of a Friend* 150-51.
19. *Vernon Watkins 1906-1967* 95-96.
20. Preface to *David Jones: Letters to Vernon Watkins*, ed. Ruth Pryor (Cardiff: U. of Wales P., 1976) n.p.
21. Pryor 37.
22. Pryor 19.
23. 11 March 1963. Although Amis had moved from University College, Swansea to King's College, the show was staged in the next-door neighbour Clare College. Clare bought an Ernest Zobole painting for their collection.
24. For this and other references to Watkins's direct involvement with the artists, I am indebted to his widow, Gwen Watkins, with whom I spoke on 4 November 2002.
25. Gwen Watkins (in conversation 2002) quotes an occasion in the Kardomah when Alfred Janes, hearing Dylan and Vernon deep in a discussion about poetry, declared "Poems is muck!"
26. "Exuberance", *Viewpoint* 1.7 (1964): 12-16.
27. In conversation with the present writer, 4 November 2002.
28. Vernon Watkins, *Ballad of the Mari Lwyd* (London: Faber, 1941).
29. *Poetry Wales* 12.4 (1977). The editor was John Ward.
30. As related by Gwen Watkins in conversation, 4 November 2002. The book was, apparently, lost from their house while they were in the U.S.A., where Vernon Watkins died in 1967.
31. Related by Gwen Watkins in conversation with the present writer, 4 November 2002.
32. Vernon Watkins, *Cypress and Acacia* (London: Faber, 1959) 53.
33. In conversation with the present writer, 4 November 2002.
34. Vernon Watkins, *Fidelities* (London: Faber, 1968).
35. One wonders if Watkins had seen the huge Tintoretto crucifixion in the Scuola Grande di San Rocco in Venice at this time, in which the carpenter's trade is integral to the panoramic scene at Calvary.
36. Roberto Sanesi, *Viaggio Verso Il Nord / Journey Toward the North* (Milan: Cerastico Editore, 1971).
37. The poem was later included in *The Ballad of the Outer Dark and Other Poems*, ed. Ruth Pryor (London: Enitharmon, 1979). The lithographs were published, with the poem, in 1970 as *Elegiac Sonnet 1 & 2* in a limited edition of 149 by M'Arte Editizioni, Milan, in the *Immagini e Testi* series, ed. Luigi Majno and Roberto Sanesi.

38. Roberto Sanesi, *The Graphic Works of Ceri Richards*, trans. Richard Burns (Milan: Cerastico Editore, 1973) 111. Plates 63 and 64.
39. Vernon Watkins, *Selected Poems 1930-1960* (London: Faber) 43.
40. In his study of Neo-Romanticism in Britain, David Mellor points to its characteristics of "the body and sexuality; nostalgia and anxiety; myth making; organic fantasies; the threat of war and extinction"—many of which inform the work of the artists discussed in this paper. See David Mellor, *A Paradise Lost* (London: Lund Humphries, 1987).
41. *Vernon Watkins 1906-1967* 96.
42. Watkins's "Foal" was included in *Poesie, con testo a fronte*, ed. Roberto Sanesi (Parma: Guanda, 1968).
43. *The Collected Poems of Vernon Watkins* (Ipswich: Golgonooza P., 1986) 184.
44. *Collected Poems* 56.
45. *Collected Poems* 251.
46. Quoted in Roland Mathias, *Vernon Watkins*, Writers of Wales (Cardiff: U. of Wales P., 1974) 32.
47. Pryor 67.
48. Vernon Watkins, letter to Ceri Richards, January 1961, *Poetry Wales* 12.4 (Spring 1977): 61.
49. *Collected Poems* 185.
50. From "A Few Words for Ceri Richards", published on the occasion of the opening of the Inaugural Exhibition of the Ceri Richards Gallery, University College, Swansea, June 1984.
51. "A Few Words for Ceri Richards".
52. "A Few Words for Ceri Richards".
53. Henry Vaughan, *Poetry and Selected Prose*, ed. L. C. Martin (Oxford: O.U.P., 1963) 318-19.
54. Roberto Sanesi, "Elegy for Vernon Watkins", trans. William Alexander (London: Cape Goliard, 1970).
55. Tony Curtis, "Cathedrale Engloutie i.m. Ceri Richards", *Wading Through Deep Water* (Bridgend: Coychurch Press, 2001) 67.

Supercharging the Struggle: Models of Nationalist Victory in the Poetry of Harri Webb

Nicholas Jones

University of Wales, Swansea

I

In a 1954 editorial in the *Welsh Republican*, Harri Webb, poet, socialist and nationalist, discusses a speech given by Aneurin Bevan to the National Committee of the Chinese People's Consultative Conference. He agrees with Bevan's argument that different ideologies may be applicable to different nations, and that socialism can take different forms depending on historical circumstance. However, Webb then quotes Bevan telling his audience about the differences between their country and his:

> . . . the struggles which you have waged are at the same time a struggle for national independence against imperialism. This has the effect of supercharging the social struggle with the emotion derived from national self-consciousness and the yearning for liberation. You are therefore possessed of an emotional dynamic which is not present with us.[1]

Predictably enough, Webb disagrees; the idea that such a struggle for independence and liberation exists within Wales is perhaps the single most important theme throughout his writing, and the quotation leads Webb into one of his trademark polemical declarations:

> Mr. Bevan comes from the Tops of the Valleys. It is hard to believe that even in China he can have forgotten the difference between the exploitation of the English worker and the wholesale rape and ruin of that region where the epic desolation of Dowlais, the generation of despair that engulfed Blaina and Brynmawr, seal the utter damnation before God and man of the Gentlemen of England.[2]

Webb was never inclined to hold back from stating his views in the strongest way possible, and Bevan had of course not forgotten the Depression, but he blamed the Conservatives as a party, not the English as a nation, as seen in his infamous 1948 speech in which he described the

Tories as "lower than vermin" due to their policies during the 1930s.[3] Where Bevan sees the situation in terms of left and right, Webb thinks in terms of imperialism and nationalism. In Webb's view, Wales was clearly in a colonial situation:

> A colony, surely, is a country that, in the first place, has no Government of its own, or only an inferior Government with not much more power than, say, a County Council. And as a consequence of not having a proper Government, a Colony is an exploited country, that is to say, its economy is run for the benefit of the country that 'owns' the Colony, not for the welfare of the inhabitants themselves. Wales is a colony by both these tests.[4]

In 1971 Webb translated "The Burgos Trials", an article in which Jean-Paul Sartre describes the Basque people as being super-exploited[5]—once by capitalism as workers, but also colonially as Basques. Sartre also argues that:

> it is in colonies that the class struggle and the national struggle merge.[6]

Webb's own writings express similar ideas, and it is in this context that Webb sought to draw parallels between Wales and other nations, looking for inspiration, both literary and political, from other nationalist movements. Close to home, Webb looked to Ireland as a nation that had seceded from the British state and, informed by his own wartime experiences in North Africa and Palestine, he was drawn to both the Algerian fight for independence and the Zionist movement that led to the creation of Israel, writing poetry about all three nations.

However, these parallels are not without their difficulties. Webb said of "Homecoming", his 1971 verse play which depicts in a highly positive manner the life of Theodor Herzl, one of the founders of Zionism, that:

> It is finished exposition of a certain sort of nationalism, a certain idealistic, almost romantic mood. . . . All this, I believe, is relevant to our situation, despite differences in detail.[7]

That different examples of nationalism can, despite their differences, be applied to the Welsh situation is precisely the message of many of Webb's poems. However, in a letter to Gwynfor Evans in 1977, Webb was no longer able to access the kinds of feelings that had given rise to "Homecoming":

> I can't recapture the mood in which this poem was written, because that demands a quality of unflawed faith which I no longer possess. (*CP* 428)

This suggests some disillusionment on Webb's part towards the romantic nationalism that informed his previous writings. Such ambivalent feelings towards nationalist struggles can be traced throughout his writings, however, and Webb's descriptions of nations after independence are also often ambivalent. "August 1976", written after a trip to Dublin, is somewhat disappointed with the realities of postcolonial Ireland, while "Manuscript Found in a Bottle", written in 1967, the year of the Six Day War, is unable to take an entirely positive view of the Israeli state. Meanwhile "For Franz Fanon" (sic),[8] written in 1970 and dedicated to the Martinique-born intellectual who was heavily involved in the Algerian independence movement, offers no images of either postcolonial Algeria or violent revolt, and it seems that Webb was unwilling to address directly the violence and bloodshed of nationalist struggles, and the resulting complex moral issues. The intention of the present paper is initially to reconstruct some elements of Webb's nationalist thought as a basis for exploring the tensions and contradictions within a series of poems where Webb turns to Israel, Algeria and Ireland as enabling comparative examples of nationalist victory.

II

Harri Webb joined Plaid Cymru in 1948, but five years later joined the Labour Party, before eventually rejoining Plaid in 1960—oscillating between the twin poles of socialism and nationalism (like his hero Hugh MacDiarmid). In the same period, between 1949 and 1957, he was active in the Welsh Republican Movement, a radical left-wing nationalist group, editing its newspaper and engaging in various activities, including direct action such as burning Union flags and breaking into Cardiff Castle.[9] Such a history demonstrates an unease and disillusionment with mainstream politics, and in an article entitled "Remember Mafeking", Webb reports on a 1977 parliamentary debate on devolution, and directly attacks the Labour Party for betraying its radical past:

> The breathtaking effrontery of some of the phrases uttered in the Commons rather shocked some moderate and sober-minded people. . . . [T]he alleged successors of Keir Hardie and Lansbury and Henderson [are] invoking imperialist standards and values with a fervour worthy of Lord Kitchener or Rudyard Kipling.
> "Britain", they say, must be unitary, monolithic centralized, ruled paternalistically from Westminster and Whitehall, otherwise all is lost, all will be chaos and corruption. Rally around the flag chaps, Socialism hath need of you.[10]

Mainstream British socialism will not accept nationalist claims and is, according to Webb, espousing imperialist beliefs more suited to the right; it is this hostility to nationalism that caused Webb's irreparable breach with Labour. Elsewhere, Webb makes his rejection of British mainstream politics even clearer, arguing that:

> There is just one party, when it comes down to essentials, the English party. It calls itself by different names, Conservative, Labour, Liberal, but it stands for the same thing in the end.[11]

Interestingly, Frantz Fanon can be seen to have undergone a similar process of disillusionment. David Caute makes the point that Fanon lost all faith in Western radicalism following the actions of the French Communist Party in 1956:

> The Party hesitated, equivocated, called for "peace", but not for independence. In March 1956 the Communist parliamentary deputies voted in favour of special powers that enabled the government to do virtually as it liked in Algeria. Aimé Césaire was outraged [and] resigned from the Party. . . . Fanon's initial shock turned to fury—and contempt. Every reference he made to the PCF was a verbal molotov cocktail. But he did not stop there; his scorn embraced the whole French left-wing intelligentsia.[12]

Fanon therefore comes to represent a form of socialist thought removed from the mainstream left and based instead on anti-imperialism, something very similar to the project of the Welsh Republican Movement and other groupings. In Webb's view, the important division is not simply between progressives and reactionaries, but between nationalists and imperialists. A new type of politics opens up, rejecting the simple left-right divide, in opposition both to conservatism and imperial forms of socialism. Both Webb and Fanon rejected parties that they believed to fail in their radical intentions by being unwilling to denounce imperialism.

Fanon was also to offer uncompromising denunciations of bourgeois nationalism, and argued that merely legal or institutional independence was not in itself enough for freedom—it could mean simply exchanging one set of oppressors for another, with the colonized taking the place of the colonizers, keeping rather than transcending the colonial structures. In an essay on Fanon Neil Lazarus writes:

> In his essay on "The Pitfalls of National Consciousness" in *The Wretched of the Earth* he produced an excoriating critique of bourgeois anticolonial nationalism, an ideology aimed at (re)attainment of nationhood through means of the capture and subsequent "occupation" of the colonial state, and which on his reading represented only the interests of the elite indigenous classes.[13]

Rule by the colonial bourgeoisie will simply change foreign colonial rule for local capitalist exploitation, and Webb's critique of Plaid Cymru can be seen in similar terms. However, as Lazarus goes on to point out, this attack on one form of nationalism does not undermine all nationalisms:

> Some contemporary theorists of "postcoloniality" have attempted to build upon Fanon's denunciation of bourgeois nationalism. Yet Fanon's actual standpoint poses insuperable problems for them. One fundamental difficulty derives from the fact that far from representing an abstract repudiation of nationalism as such, Fanon's critique of bourgeois nationalist ideology is itself delivered from an *alternative nationalist standpoint*.[14]

Such a paradigm of bourgeois nationalism in opposition to a more radical nationalism could provide a framework for looking at such matters in Wales. Webb attacked what he called the "chapel-pacifist element in the Blaid",[15] and the W.R.M. represented a socialist alternative to the centralism of Plaid Cymru. In a 1951 *Welsh Republican* editorial, Webb describes dangers that the movement must avoid:

> We must never make the mistakes of approaching our task in a spirit of middle-class superiority and exclusiveness, of indulging in Welsh language snobbery, or of reproaching our fellow countrymen for their "lack of patriotism".[16]

This is clearly a thinly-veiled attack on what Webb saw as the failings of Plaid Cymru. Elsewhere, Webb argued that the appeal of the party was "to the right rather than to the left", prompting him to worry about the possibility that Welsh cultural heritage would become associated with political reaction.[17]

A sense of the diverse strands of nationalism within Wales may also be gained by looking at the views of Webb and Gwynfor Evans on the Easter Rising of 1916. Webb wrote several times about this and believed such a symbolic sacrifice might be needed within Wales:

> The Easter 1916 Rising failed, and as the leaders were being marched off by the soldiers, the Irish people of Dublin, whose lives had been disrupted by the battle, and who had been put in terror by the firing, spat on Pearse and Connolly and cursed them. But within a year that mood had passed, the true significance of events had sunk in, and the battle of Ireland was as good as won.[18]

Webb sees the rising as an important psychological turning point, and goes on to suggest something similar is required in Wales. By contrast, Evans argues that:

> Although I admire the sacrifice of those heroes, I think the Rising was a disastrous mistake, for it led to the Civil War from which the country took fifty years to recover.[19]

Evans, who can be seen to represent the pacifist, gradualist tendency within Plaid Cymru with which Webb disagreed, sees the cost of the Rising in the long term, where Webb chooses to see the more positive effects. Where Evans clearly had no wish to see Wales follow a similar path, Webb was no opponent of direct action and believed political violence could be justified. This point is reinforced by Webb's 1955 poem "The Disclaimers", one of his earliest satirical pieces, which contrasts the timidity of Plaid Cymru with the actions of other nationalist groups, for example the removal of the Stone of Scone from Westminster Abbey in 1950, an audacious symbolic act of which Webb certainly approved:

> When daring Scots reclaimed their Stone
> They had to do the job alone;
> The Blaid were asked if they had helped—
> "Not on your blessed life!", they yelped. (*CP* 39)

The second stanza then turns to an example from Ireland:

> When Irish bold pinched England's arms
> And filled the tyrant with alarms
> 'Mid all the panic that devolved
> The Blaid piped up, "We weren't involved!" (*CP* 39)

In Webb's view, Wales should learn from the actions of Irish nationalists, and once again Plaid Cymru is seen as timid and ineffectual. However, the poem does go on to praise some nationalists from Wales, and refers to the attempt, in 1950, to sabotage the Fron aqueduct, which carried water out of Wales and into England—another symbolic act of anti-imperialism from which Plaid Cymru was keen to distance itself:

> When valiant Welshmen had a try
> To blow the aqueduct sky-high,
> Through all the arrests, the search, the fuss,
> The Blaid was heard, "It wasn't us!" (*CP* 40)

In each stanza, different elements come to represent a radicalism missing from Plaid, the poem culminating in an example of violent direct action within Wales.

Such views are also seen in Webb's prose of the period; in the 1950s, he directly argued that violence might be necessary in order to free Wales:

The Welsh Republican Movement was formed largely by returned ex-servicemen whose knowledge of war is not academic. They do not want

> bloodshed between England and Wales, but if it comes, and with it national independence, then it will be a small price to pay to end the iniquitous tribute of subjection which has gone on too long.[20]

Webb believes here that bloodshed is preferable to acceptance of the colonial status quo. This, however, does not represent the most extreme point in Webb's political progression. Later, in 1963, Webb refers back to his earlier comments but rejects them as not going far enough, arguing that the Welsh people:

> have sunk so low, are so deeply stained with the guilt of servitude, that their condition may be likened (as Pearse likened it) to that original sin in which theologians say the human race is lost. The act of redemption can only come through the sacrifice, if necessary—and I believe it to be necessary—of the lives of the best. This I think goes beyond the old Republican doctrine. . . . The Republicans said they would not shrink from shedding blood if necessary. . . . I now say that such sacrifice is not only probably necessary, a predictable statistical likelihood, but absolutely necessary. Without it there will be no wholeness or health in any of the other actions that lead us forward.[21]

Webb sees sacrifice and violence as something that will have a spiritual effect, and similar ideas were also espoused in a different context by Fanon:

> At the level of individuals, violence is a cleansing force. It frees the native from the inferiority complex and from his despair and inaction; it makes him fearless and restores his self-respect.[22]

Given that Webb was attempting to justify the use of political violence, it is unsurprising he should look to Fanon and the 1916 Irish revolutionaries who also developed theories on such matters. Their ideas contrast explicitly with the pacifism of Gwynfor Evans and Plaid Cymru that Webb rejected. However, despite dealing with nationalist movements that used violence to achieve their ends, Webb's poems contain remarkably few direct images of violence. To some extent, this could be because a connection with such themes would damage the parallels intended with the Welsh situation. Equally, Webb sought a mass audience for his work, and may have felt that support for political violence would alienate potential readers. However, it is by no means clear that Webb's own attitudes were this straightforward. Webb did wish to see a more radicalized form of nationalism within Wales, but it seems that he was not willing to follow his own pronouncements to their logical conclusion—namely, that an independent Wales should be forged through violent rebellion. In this context, it is possible to see the poems as not simply straightforward pieces of propaganda, but as themselves containing the ambiguities and contradictions present within Webb's political thinking. In this sense, they act almost as a corrective to the more direct arguments put forth in Webb's more polemical prose.

III

"Israel", written in 1966, is Webb's first poetic encounter with Zionism, and strongly demands that Wales should learn from the Zionist example. In the chronologically-arranged *Collected Poems*, it immediately follows Webb's trio of diverse responses to Gwynfor Evans's by-election victory in Carmarthen.[23] "Israel" was therefore written at a time of nationalist success, and its message is essentially optimistic.

In contrast to "For Franz Fanon" in which Wales is only invoked in the closing lines, and even then indirectly, in "Israel" Webb directly addresses the Welsh people from the start, and demands to be heard. However, he does not in any way flatter the Welsh people—rather, he belittles them, his tone combative and angry:

> Listen, Wales. Here was a people
> Whom even you could afford to despise,
> Growing nothing, making nothing,
> Belonging nowhere. (*CP* 91)

Webb stresses the impoverishment and difficulties of the Jewish people before the creation of Israel, but sees the Welsh as being little better off. There is a sense of a people in decline, living by their wits and requiring salvation. This is seen as the state of the Jewish people before the creation of their state and, Webb insists, Wales is currently in a comparable predicament. However, Webb argues that renewal came to Judaism only after disaster:

> And because they were such a people
> They went like lambs to the slaughter. (*CP* 92)

This presumably refers to the Holocaust, and Webb seems to be suggesting that the state of Jewish culture contributed to this event, something that many would regard as historically inaccurate at best, and deeply offensive at worst, although given Webb's admiration for Israel it would be difficult to paint him as anti-Semitic. The Holocaust is, although not directly invoked, the central event of the poem, which is split into two sections, before and after the Shoah, and also before and after the creation of Israel, reinforcing the idea of change and a movement between two conceptions of the Jewish people. The physical blank space on the page between the two sections comes to represent this spiritual transformation and redemption that came after such horrific suffering. This very repression becomes the impetus for growth, and Wales has no excuses for failure. The creation of Israel is therefore seen as a catalyst for renewal and growth as well as an example to Wales:

> The mountains are red with their blood,
> The deserts are green with their seed.
> Listen, Wales. (*CP* 92)

These lines inevitably recall Webb's image of the green desert at the centre of Wales—"Israel" was included in *The Green Desert*,[24] Webb's 1969 collection, and is the only poem to use these words in conjunction. In this context "Israel" can therefore be seen as being important to Webb's poetry as a whole, affecting the interpretation of perhaps his best known image. In the poem, a literal and metaphorical desert is being cultivated and made fertile; by extension, Webb is offering an image of how the Welsh "desert" could be reclaimed; it is currently literally, but not metaphorically (politically or culturally) green; it should, and can, become both.

In addition to this new-found fertility, a cultural transformation is embodied in Webb's use of music in the poem. The Jews are described as a people:

> Who lived by playing the violin
> (A lot better, incidentally,
> Than you ever played the harp). (*CP* 92)

Later, Webb uses specific musical references to reflect the Jewish transformation:

> They have switched off Mendelssohn
> And tuned in to Maccabeus. (*CP* 92)

In his explanatory notes to the poem Meic Stephens indicates that these lines refer to:

> *Judas Maccabeus*, an oratorio (1747) by Handel (1685-1759); Judas Maccabeus was a Hebrew patriot who won victories over the Syrians in the 2nd century B.C.
> (*CP* 408)

It is therefore suggested that the movement is from Mendelssohn, a German whose family converted from Judaism to Christianity, to music concerning past Jewish victories, a change in musical style symbolic of a wider movement away from Europe and European culture towards the Jewish state in Palestine. Of course, Handel was also European, and it is not entirely clear that the poem refers to Handel's oratorio—only the single word "Maccabeus" appears, and a different reading could see this as a movement from art to action, from celebrating a composer to celebrating a patriot and rebel.

Despite its negative portrayal of Wales, "Israel" is essentially hopeful—redemption and regrowth are possible, though difficult. The message of the poem is comparable to the final lines of "A Whisper", the first of Webb's poems, written around the same time as "Israel", about the 1966 by-election:

> The draught is bitter we must drain
> Before the land is whole again. (*CP* 89)

Both poems accept that the task will be difficult, but the poet does not despair. In many ways the language of "Israel" is simplistic—reflecting Webb's desire to offer a clear, direct message—but it is not without its difficulties. A central problem raised by the poem is the extent to which the parallel with Israel can be taken. In an interview published in *Planet* with Judith Maro, who had written about Wales and Israel, Ned Thomas suggests that:

> perhaps the Israeli comparison is a dangerous delusory one for Welsh people. . . . I'm not quite sure where Harri Webb's powerful poem "Listen Wales"[25] leads us, if taken literally. "The valleys are green with their seed / The deserts are red with their blood" is one thing, if it arises under the pressure of necessity, but who would choose the situation of Israel, not only (I would argue) forced to fight, but forced in some ways to abandon her own original *raison-d'être*? In other words, can Israel be anything more in Wales than a metaphor for commitment and resolution which has to operate, thankfully, in a very different context?[26]

This highlights the difficulty of interpretation. The poem can be seen as essentially offering an inspiration, something to be admired but not directly emulated; alternatively, the parallel may be intended more precisely. It could be argued that, in this poem, Webb shies away from forcing the point he is making because the consequences are too problematic; just as in "For Franz Fanon" he does not directly say that violent revolution is the answer to the problems of Wales. Ned Thomas is uneasy about the parallel with Zionism, but he misquotes the poem, introducing the word "valleys", which gives the image a much closer connection to Wales. Green valleys would be a symbol of Welsh reconstruction and rebirth, perhaps, following their pollution by industry; the actual poem refers to Wales less directly.

The role of culture (the violin and Mendelssohn) in "Israel" is a theme that continues throughout Webb's writing, not least in "For Franz Fanon", where the link between culture and nationalist politics is explored in a different context. At the start of his book on Zionism, Michael Berkowitz says that:

The early Zionist movement sought to define and create a Jewish national culture in order to activate a sense of belonging to a Jewish nation among the Jews of Europe.[27]

The role of the nationalist artist becomes the assertion of culture in order to foster national identity, something that can be seen in the work of many writers from Wales. In *The Wretched of the Earth* culture is also an important theme. While nationalism is often seen as split between cultural and political manifestations, Fanon sees the two ideas as being linked:

> The colonised man who writes for his people ought to use the past with the intention of opening up the future, as an invitation to action and a basis for hope. But to ensure that hope and to give it form, he must take part in action and throw himself body and soul into the national struggle.[28]

This is very similar to Webb's highly-politicized conception of literature, and a good description of Webb's own poetic response to Fanon. Art becomes an explicitly political act, not only a way of supporting the struggle, but a part of the struggle itself, although not an alternative to political action. Fanon describes this as the "literature of combat", a phrase that can be applied to Webb's more polemical poetry. Importantly, Fanon also argues that Third World nations need to move beyond Western constructs:

> The Third World ought not to be content to define itself in the terms of values which have preceded it. On the contrary, the under-developed countries ought to do their utmost to find their own particular values and methods and a style which shall be peculiar to them.[29]

Culture becomes a way of expressing difference, and so asserting the right of a country to freedom. In Webb's case, asserting that Wales has more in common with Algeria or Israel than England is a way of distancing the nation from a British identity. The post-colonial critic Ania Loomba suggests that:

> Anti-colonial nationalism is a struggle to represent, create or recover a culture and a selfhood that has been systematically repressed and eroded during colonial rule.[30]

This is a situation familiar in Wales and very close to Webb's conception of the role of Welsh literature and politics, which he argues encompasses more than legal and social structures:

> Politics everywhere is a working out of social and economic pressures which affect everybody directly. And in Wales it has always been something more, an expression not only of immediate necessities but of wider ideas and ideals, embracing such fields of human activities as religion, language and culture.[31]

Such a widened conception of politics is seen in Webb's poem "For Franz Fanon" which highlights the relationship between cultural symbols and the practices of imperialism. The poem begins with a decontextualized image:

> Bronze hero against the sun
> Reined his horse to a prance,
> Bronzed and splendid
> (But what had he done?)
> An attitude of France. (*CP* 136)

A bronze statue of a horse and rider represents France; the poem begins with the oppressors, not the natives. A strong image is shown, and it is not immediately presented negatively, but as "balanced and splendid", words that, in the light of the rest of the poem, can be read ironically. However, the lines are perhaps not as simple as they seem. Webb is already questioning and undermining the image of power in asking "... what had he done?".

The action is then placed more specifically; by line 10, the setting is clearly Africa, and an opposing though linked image is presented:

> Bronze skins against carved stone
> Crouching in rags and sweat,
> Beating the ages away on a drum
> Africa sits, in wait. (*CP* 136)

The carved stone against which the natives crouch could be taken to be the statue, creating a highly striking visual image: the statue, high in the air against the sun, representing France, while beneath the natives crouch in rags. This itself becomes a metaphor for the structures of imperialism, while the full stop following "An attitude of France" suggests the idea of a division between the French and the natives—the Manichean divide which Fanon wished to overcome. Africa waits, although we do not yet know for what. Importantly, this first section of the poem was written during the 1940s, and it was only later that history provided Webb with the material to complete the piece. (Algeria gained independence in 1962 and the poem was completed in 1971, *CP* 422).

The next section of the poem places the location yet more precisely, revealing the city in question:

> The Opéra in the square,
> Has plaques on its facade,
> Florid phrases declare
> Cervantes and Régnier
> Were slaves and prisoners here.
> This was Algiers then. (*CP* 136)

Each of the first three sentences ends with the invocation of a place—first France, then the continent of Africa, then finally the country and city is revealed (although a knowledge of the life of Cervantes would reveal this slightly earlier). There is constant movement between different locations, which continues right up until the final line.

Miguel de Cervantes was captured by corsairs in 1575 while sailing from Naples to Barcelona. He was then taken to Algiers, where he spent five years in captivity before being ransomed and eventually freed.[32] Within the poem, this comes to represent an ironic reversal of colonization, with Europeans rather than Africans suffering subjugation. Cervantes can also be seen to represent western art, just as the opera is an alien, western cultural institution. "Florid phrases" shows an engagement with issues relating to language which carries on throughout the poem—the plaques are in French, and in a formal register, completely alien to the surroundings, humiliating Algerians by reminding them of their past—French culture becomes a symbol of oppression, and language is an especially important issue in the next three lines:

> Everywhere tricolours hang—
> *On s'en fout des indigènes*
> *Sales gen, ils sont bons pour rien.* (*CP* 136)[33]

Just as the tricolour is out of place in Algeria, so French is out of place in an English poem—an alien element. It is also the only point in the poem in which another voice other than that of the narrator's is directly heard. As so often in Webb's work, the political enemy is given a voice which is self-incriminating, and from those two lines French contempt and racism are made abundantly clear.

The movement of the poem then continues, leaving the capital for the *bled*, the rural interior of Algeria:

> Up in the hills, in the bled
> Poplar and white wall,
> And roofs of Roman red
> Extend Cézanne's Provence,
> No doubt about it at all
> This is clearly France. (*CP* 137)

While "bled" refers to the Algerian landscape, many readers are likely to be unfamiliar with this meaning of the word, and it is possible to construct other readings based on the English definition. For example, the word could be related to the discussion of colonialism within the poem; to be bled dry is a common metaphor, and so the line could be taken to refer to the metaphorical economic bleeding of Algeria by imperialism. The proximity of the colours "red" and "white" perhaps add weight to such an interpretation, and the economic exploitation of Africa was indeed one of Fanon's recurrent themes.

While such a reading is necessarily speculative, it does not, however, undermine the general significance of the landscape, something of which Fanon himself stresses the importance:

> Hostile nature, obstinate and fundamentally rebellious, is in fact represented in the colonies by the bush, by mosquitoes, natives and fever, and colonisation is a success when all this indocile nature has finally been tamed.[34]

An African landscape has been changed completely, both in terms of vegetation (poplar trees), and in terms of architecture. The red roofs recall Cézanne's Provence—not the actual place, but a dominant artistic representation of it. This is clearly France—or rather an image of France that has been fabricated. "This *was* Algiers"—has been replaced by "this *is* clearly France"; past nationhood has through time been lost. After this, the poem then ventures even further into the interior:

> Where the boulevard became
> The road to the empty sands
> Chiselled phrases proclaim
> *Mission civilisatrice.* (*CP* 137)

The French word "boulevard" once again suggests the colonization of language and landscape; even far away from the capital, colonialism still intrudes. The "chiselled phrases" recall the plaques on the façade of the opera house, and once again a French phrase is inserted into the poem. The poem has moved away from the political centre to the periphery of the country and it is here that Webb sees independence as happening. The idea of "*mission civilisatrice*", a divine mission to civilize Africa, is highly ironic, given the image of the end of imperialism that follows. It is then, after Webb has taken the reader to "the empty sands", that he returns to the colonizers:

> The colons of rich lands
> For whom life was sweet
> Privileged and serene
> Saw no end to the long peace
> Nor the coming of their dark. (*CP* 137)

Despite the fact the poem was completed after the struggle and the resulting independence of Algeria, Webb offers no images of postcoloniality or violent revolt; the only military image is that of the statue. If Algeria and Fanon are taken directly as a model, the message is that violent revolution is the way to independence. But in the poem the process of independence seems almost to be inevitable, a spontaneous historical imperative, rather than something that results from a political or military struggle. As well as evasiveness on Webb's part, the lack of violence in the poem can perhaps be linked to Fanon's argument that oppression *within* Western countries is maintained by non-violent structures of socialization:

> In the colonies it is the policeman and the soldier who are the official, instituted go-betweens, the spokesmen of the settler and his rule of oppression. . . . In the capitalist countries a multitude of moral teachers, counsellors and "bewilderers" separate the exploited from those in power. In the colonial countries, on the contrary, the policemen and the soldier, by their immediate presence and their frequent and direct action maintain contact with the native and advise him by means of rifle-butts and napalm not to budge.[35]

Webb is primarily interested in social, cultural and economic oppression, through institutions of government, education and so on, rather than direct military subjugation. In highlighting the cultural methods of upholding imperialism (tricolours, the opera, architecture) and ignoring more direct oppression and the military response to it, Webb is not simply expressing the history of Algeria, but, potentially, distorting aspects of it so as to better fit the parallel with Wales which Webb invokes at the end of the poem:

> I often think of the scene
> As I walk in St. Mary's Street
> As I walk in Cathays Park. (*CP* 137)

Webb does not make the connections between the two countries explicit; instead, the reader must work them out, re-reading and re-interpreting the poem in the light of these final lines. The poem itself becomes an exposition of Fanon's beliefs—a nationalist writer, committed to a political struggle, suggesting a model of successful decolonization that he implies his own people might follow. The poem recalls Fanon's description of storytellers in Algeria whose message changed as the struggle for independence grew more intense:

> The story-tellers who used to relate inert episodes now bring them alive and introduce into them modifications which are increasingly fundamental. There is a tendency to bring conflicts up to date and to modernise the kinds of struggle which the stories evoke, together with the names of heroes and the types of weapons. The method of allusion is more and more widely used. The formula

"This all happened long ago" is substituted by that of "What we are going to speak of happened somewhere else, but it might well have happened here today, and it might happen tomorrow".[36]

This is precisely the message of "For Franz Fanon"—showing a victory won in another country as an inspiration and model for Wales to follow. The moral is clearly that such things can happen, that freedom is not impossible. This is also the message of "Israel" and "Homecoming", but not all of Webb's output presents nationalist movements in such a positive manner. "Manuscript Found in a Bottle", which takes as its starting point Webb's wartime memories of Palestine, and "August 1976", about a visit to Dublin, are somewhat more ambiguous, and suggest a slightly different understanding of Webb's attitude to overseas nationalisms.

Indeed, Webb's poetry dedicated to Irish themes does not depict the nation simply as somewhere nationalism triumphed, although independence is indeed celebrated. Rather, Webb also sees deficiencies in its present state and looks back to the revolutionary past. In "August 1976", Webb looks to Easter 1916, which represents a national sacrifice the Welsh have still not been able to imitate; in the second half of the poem, Irish achievement is compared to Welsh failure:

> Sixty and more years into our future too
> Who have yet to make the first move.   (*CP* 270)

However, this achievement has been accompanied by a degradation of culture, and post-independence Ireland has regrettably lost touch with its past:

> Still, on Stephen's Green
> Father Hannan conducts a children's choir
> Sponsored by the Tourist Board, and a little girl
> Recites *Mise Eire*, the terrible words
> Accuse in vain, are politely applauded
> By people eating ice-cream.   (*CP* 270)

Patrick Pearse's poetry is read to uncomprehending tourists, and a serious piece of nationalist, revolutionary art becomes devalued in a context it was not created for—an appalling fate for the poem. "Mise Eire" has been translated from the original Gaelic as "I Am Ireland":

> Great my glory:
> I that bore Cuchulainn the valiant.

> Great my shame:
> My own children that sold their mother.[37]

Pearse describes two extremes of Irish history, glory and shame, and a present-day political position is refracted through mythological history to give it greater depth and import, a device used frequently by Webb. Indeed, in "August 1976" the 1916 Rising comes to occupy an analogous position as a glorious and mythologized event from the past:

> It has been sixty years
> Since the Proclamation, the agony.
> The spittle is still fresh on the face of James Connolly. (*CP* 270)

As in Webb's poetry about Welsh history, the past constantly permeates the present; in Dublin, the struggle for independence cannot be forgotten. Yet not everything has been devalued, and the city is still suffused with its history, even if many choose to ignore it. However, there are questions to be asked about its future:

> Two citizens argue in Slattery's as to whether
> Or not there are bogs in Kerry. There are men here
> Who will break stone, but for what roads? (*CP* 271)

These lines allude to W. B. Yeats's poem "Parnell", Webb thereby indirectly invoking the nationalist leader:

> Parnell came down the road, he said to a cheering man;
> "Ireland shall get her freedom and you still break stone."[38]

Following independence labourers will still break stone, and much will continue as before. To use Sartre's terms, the stonebreaker will be freed from super-exploitation, but not from the exploitation inherent in capitalism, while in Fanon's terms, he will not have found true liberation. Webb is aware that freedom from imperialism will not necessarily lead to socialism, and there is more to aspire to than simply independence, something not engaged with in the more polemical "Israel" or "For Franz Fanon".

However, this is not to suggest that Webb does not wish to emulate the Irish Republic, and the poem ends with a surprising image:

> The city is dressed for summer, smiling
> As only those may who have known sorrow.
> Tears, too, make the eyes sparkle. (*CP* 271)

Ireland has suffered for its freedom, and so has the right to be happy—Wales, however, has not yet begun on such a journey; and has not yet earned the right to smile. This links to the depiction of Jewish suffering in "Israel", where liberation is seen as coming out of tragedy. In his next poem about the Middle East, "Manuscript Found in a Bottle", Webb looks back to his time in Palestine during the war, and feels that:

> all my recollections of the Holy Land
> Should be, well, not exactly holy, but at least
> Respectable, part of a pattern, bearing some relation
> To the Good Book or Current Affairs. Deep down
> Perhaps some potent apocalypse is still brewing
> But somehow I hope not. It is better this way,
> With all my memories rather disreputable— (*CP* 95)

Webb goes on to remember his youthful actions, using appropriate vocabulary: for example, listening to a bishop while wanting to get "pissed":

> I avoided
> All shrines, tombs, temples, pilgrimages,
> Was resolutely profane, chose to take my liberty
> In Tel Aviv, on the beach and in the nightclubs . . . (*CP* 95)

Webb seems almost proud of his earlier actions and attitude, telling of his adventures with great enthusiasm. However, he is also somewhat uneasy—the "apocalypse" perhaps refers to the situation in 1967, when the poem was written, with the Middle East on the brink of conflict. If all-out war were to happen, Webb's irreverent memories would in some way be tarnished, offensive, and inappropriate. Webb's tales clash with the notion of "Current Affairs", the product of the media, which is almost equated with "the Good Book" itself—both officially-sanctioned discourses which do not, in the poet's opinion, entirely reflect real life. There are therefore two Webbs present in the poem, one a sailor in his early twenties, the other a writer in his mid-forties, the experiences of the former being mediated through the mind of the latter. In many respects, they are different people, particularly regarding the younger Webb's take on the inhabitants of the area:

> The dour drab Jews meant just as much to us
> And just as little, as the picturesque Arabs.
> Let the fuckers fight it out themselves, we said. (*CP* 95)

The poem could be seen as being about Webb's movement from his earlier, ignorant attitudes, to his current interest in and admiration for Zionism. However, such an argument can only be made with reference to Webb's other writings on the issue, since the poem itself ends on an ambivalent note, with Webb thinking:

> how irrelevant
> A place can be when you're there, if it isn't yours,
> It's only when you get back you see what matters
> And that the real truth begins and ends at home.   (*CP* 96)

When Webb was in Palestine it meant nothing to him; he merely wanted to leave. Only later, with his increasing knowledge of Zionism, did he realize its significance; and so the real truth can only be apprehended after returning home—in Webb's case, returning to Wales after demobilization. Yet the poem also denies that interpretation; if the truth begins and ends at home, Palestine can only play a very marginal part in Webb's Welsh truth. Webb needs this example, perhaps, to fully understand the significance of his own homeland; Palestine can only function as a place that has helped the poet to realize the "truth" of the situation in his own land.

IV

If a socialist struggle for justice can be "supercharged" by the addition of a nationalist emotional dynamic, so, Webb believed, the Welsh national struggle could also be intensified through the emulation of examples of successful anti-imperial movements from around the world. Unhappy with mainstream Welsh political parties, rejecting Labour for its opposition to nationalism and Plaid Cymru for its pacifism and timidity, Webb needed to look elsewhere for models—firstly to the W.R.M., then, after the movement's collapse, to overseas examples of nationalist victory. He thus sought countries where a radicalized form of leftwing nationalism had been successful, and that could offer encouraging models for Wales. His comparative poems, whilst depicting scenes in Ireland, Algeria and Israel, have at their heart a message to the Welsh people; these countries are models of nationalist victory. However, for all of Webb's undoubted polemical intentions, these poems do not operate as straightforward propaganda. While "Israel" does speak of regrowth and renewal following the creation of the Jewish state, Webb's poetry about postcolonial Ireland is deeply ambivalent and suggests that the principles of the revolution have since been betrayed. "Manuscript Found in a Bottle", meanwhile, questions the whole notion of drawing direct parallels between different nations, with Webb suggesting that Palestine was only important to him as it helped realize his own truth based on his own, individual, Welsh experience.

Fanon begins *The Wretched of the Earth* by declaring that decolonization is always a violent phenomenon; yet, despite dealing with three nations created, in part, through military struggle, there is—as we have seen—

remarkably little violence depicted within Webb's poems. To some extent this is in order to allow the parallels with Wales to operate more fully; however, Webb's attitude to political violence can be characterized as ambiguous. While he was happy to argue in the pages of the *Welsh Republican* that bloodshed was preferable to subjugation, a poem such as "For Franz Fanon" suppresses the violence of the Algerian struggle. To stress the violence would be to emphasize the difference between Algeria and Wales, whereas to emphasize images of cultural subjugation is to underline the similarity between two colonized nations. It appears that Webb would not allow an unpalatable history to compromise his message to the Welsh people. There is a direct political purpose to these poems, and, despite their ambivalences, they become examples of the type of art espoused by Fanon himself—directly politicized and, indeed, a very part of the struggle for national freedom itself; in this sense, they represent the application of highly radicalized ideas to the Welsh political debate, and an attempt to bring slightly closer the aim of an independent Wales.

NOTES

1. Harri Webb, "Against Imperialism", *No Half-Way House: Selected Political Journalism*, ed. Meic Stephens (Talybont: Y Lolfa, 1997) 98.
2. "Against Imperialism", *No Half-Way House* 98.
3. Michael Foot, *Aneurin Bevan* (London: Orion, 1999) 363.
4. "Letters to Mr. Jones", *No Half-Way House* 55.
5. Jean-Paul Sartre, "The Burgos Trials", trans. Harri Webb, *Planet* 9 (1971): 10.
6. "The Burgos Trials" 8.
7. Harri Webb, *Collected Poems*, ed. Meic Stephens (Llandysul: Gomer, 1995) 427-8. All subsequent references to Webb's poetry are to this edition and included in the text (*CP*).
8. "Frantz" is misspelled as "Franz" in all published forms of the poem.
9. For an account of the W.R.M. see Gweriniaethwr, *The Young Republicans: A Record of the Welsh Republican Movement* (Llanrwst: Gwasg Carreg Gwalch, 1996).
10. "Remember Mafeking", *No Half-Way House* 343-44.
11. "The Future of Wales is in Our Hands", *No Half-Way House* 346.
12. David Caute, *Fanon* (London: Fontana, 1975) 48-9.
13. "Disavowing decolonisation: Fanon, nationalism, and the question of representation in postcolonial theory", *Frantz Fanon: Critical Perspectives*, ed. Anthony C. Alessandrini (London: Routledge, 1999) 162.
14. *Frantz Fanon: Critical Perspectives* 162.
15. "Up the Republic!", *No Half-Way House* 46.
16. "We Believe in the Welsh People", *No Half-Way House* 65-6.
17. "Wales Defies the Tories", *No Half-Way House* 110-11.
18. "A Letter to Gwilym Prys Davies", *No Half-Way House* 234-35.
19. Gwynfor Evans, *For the Sake of Wales*, trans. Meic Stephens (Cardiff: Welsh Academic P., 2001) 66.

20. "No More Blood for England". *No Half-Way House* 92.
21. "A Letter to Gwilym Prys Davies", *No Half-Way House* 232. Cf Patrick Pearse, executed after the Easter Rising, who said that "Bloodshed is a cleansing and sanctifying thing, and the nation which regards it as the final horror has lost its manhood. There are many things worse than bloodshed, and slavery is one of them". See Raymond J. Porter, *P. H. Pearse* (New York: Twayne, 1973) 60.
22. Frantz Fanon, *The Wretched of the Earth* (New York: Grove P., 1963) 73.
23. "A Whisper", "When Gwynfor Got In For Carmarthen" and "Colli Iaith".
24. Harri Webb, *The Green Desert* (Llandysul: Gomer, 1969).
25. This was the original title for "Israel".
26. Ned Thomas and Judith Maro, "Israel / Wales", *Planet* 31 (1976): 19.
27. Michael Berkowitz, *Zionist Culture and West European Jewry Before the First World War* (Cambridge: C.U.P., 1993) 1.
28. *The Wretched of the Earth* 187.
29. *The Wretched of the Earth* 78.
30. Ania Loomba, *Colonialism / Postcolonialism* (London: Routledge, 1998) 217.
31. "The Political History of the Cynon Valley", *No Half-Way House* 315.
32. For more detail on the life of Cervantes see Donald P. McCrory, *No Ordinary Man: The Life and Times of Miguel de Cervantes* (London: Peter Owen, 2002).
33. Meic Stephens renders these lines as "We don't care about the natives / Dirty people, they are good for nothing", *CP* 423.
34. *The Wretched of the Earth* 204.
35. *The Wretched of the Earth* 31.
36. *The Wretched of the Earth* 193.
37. Raymond J. Porter, *P. H. Pearse* 128.
38. W. B. Yeats, *The Poems*, ed. Richard J. Finneran (London: Macmillan, 1983) 312.

Crossing the Border:
National and Linguistic Boundaries in
Twentieth-Century Welsh Writing

Geraint Evans

University of Sydney

I

The rise of interest in post-colonial literatures represents a continued interest in the idea of nation as a category of human identity. New literatures, or the recent developments of old literatures, are seen as what Gramsci and others have called "sites of struggle" in which the location and identity of nation might somehow be revealed.[1] One of the main sites of struggle in modern Wales has been the language of composition for writers, artists and academics. Should it be Welsh or should it be English or could it, perhaps, be both?

In Welsh-speaking Wales, for much of the twentieth century, the position was fairly clear: those who could write in Welsh generally did, and if they wrote in English as well, those works, particularly in the middle decades of the century, tended to be regarded by them as being of secondary importance, or were time-delayed translations of the Welsh original. At the end of the twentieth century, however, at a time of rapid political and linguistic change, a new position began to emerge, a position long established elsewhere—in Ireland, for example—though all but unknown in Wales. What this paper seeks to describe is the way in which the work of two writers, R. S. Thomas and Gwyneth Lewis, has crossed one of the most significant linguistic boundaries of modern Wales. And how it is in the relationship between the work of a writer such as Gwyneth Lewis and the work of R. S. Thomas that we can begin to chart the way in which such a change became possible at this point in Welsh history.

In many post-colonial literatures the battle lines are laid by linguistic rather than physical geographers, and in Wales in the twentieth century, this process was clearly visible. While many authors who wrote in English became increasingly supportive of the Welsh-language movement and of writing in Welsh, with a number learning Welsh and subsequently publishing in Welsh, very few writers who began by publishing in Welsh in the early and mid twentieth century went on to publish substantially in English. From at least 1962, with the birth of Cymdeithas yr Iaith Gymraeg, the Welsh Language Society, following Saunders Lewis's famous radio talk *Tynged yr Iaith* [The Fate of the Language], choosing to write in Welsh was for many a consciously political act, whose binary opposite was the treachery of writing in English.[2]

Writers in other communities during the twentieth century did not always take the same view. Many writers in Ireland wrote in both languages. Brian Ó Nualláin, who wrote in Irish as Miles nagCópaleen and in English as Flann O'Brien, is a famous example. Other writers, such as Vladimir Nabokov and Joseph Conrad, whose first language was not English, became famous as English writers, while Samuel Beckett, following a tradition of looking to Paris rather than London, began writing in English before publishing in French. But in Wales the linguistic boundaries were the boundaries of a struggle for nothing less than the survival of the language, and such cosmopolitanism was largely avoided. And the reasons, of course, relate to the survival status of Welsh in the twentieth century. Linguistic survival was not an issue when Polish or Russian or English were abandoned by a few individuals as the language of literary composition, and the decline of Irish had occurred sufficiently earlier than Welsh that its position in the early twentieth century was already quite different. What had been in Ireland since the 1890s a movement of language revival was, in Wales, a movement of linguistic maintenance, and the strategies of the two groups would by necessity be very different.

Linguists such as Bob Dixon, David Crystal, Nancy Dorian and others who are concerned with language survival talk about issues such as the discourses of institutional power as being key factors in determining survival, rather than critical mass alone. Dixon and Crystal both give extraordinary examples of language communities with a few thousand speakers which seem reasonably stable, in contrast with language communities of several million, which are not expected to last more than a few generations.[3] What they all describe, and what members of the language movement in Wales instinctively knew, is that survival is related not just to maintaining and increasing the number of speakers, but to the use and visibility of the language in institutional discourse. It is in education, publishing, broadcasting, public life and government that the lifeblood of linguistic survival flows, and it is in cultural production, in this case literary texts, that critics look for a reflection of those vital signs.

So in Wales, as part of a political programme of language maintenance, writers saw their determination to use Welsh as a medium for literary and scholarly publication as an important way of establishing the institutional significance of the Welsh language. And at a time when there was no

Assembly, and no Welsh Language Act, so no Welsh Language Board, and when the visibility of Welsh on official forms and in the business of government was so low, this was an important strategy. So the major literary figures of Welsh Wales generally avoided writing in English. One of the most influential, Saunders Lewis, had, of course, begun by publishing in English in the 1920s, when the hegemonic power of English was at its height. He published a play and a book of literary history in English before embarking on a remarkable career of scholarly and literary writing in Welsh.[4] And as late as 1969, he wrote to his friend, the writer David Jones, that:

> I've been pondering since I saw you whether I can write a little introductory volume on you in English as the Welsh Arts Council ask. It's mostly a matter of conscience—I don't mind an occasional review or article in English, but a book? I don't want to set a bad example for Welsh writers, and nobody was ever quite first rate in two languages. However, a little informative book on a very particular friend is, I have concluded, not a betrayal, and I'm writing to the Council to accept the commission.[5]

The book was for the Writers of Wales series and it is one of the lost critical gems of modern Wales, as Saunders Lewis was forced to relinquish the commission due to poor health.[6]

The point is that Saunders Lewis was repeating an orthodoxy which supported a post-colonial strategy of resistance to English hegemony. It was, as he says, "a matter of conscience" for Welsh writers to avoid the "betrayal" of publishing in English, as a way of forcing the non-Welsh world to notice the existence of the language and to engage with it at some level, rather than avoiding it entirely by reading the English translation as if that were in fact the text, or just reading a writer's English work as if that was the important part. So in Wales, in the middle decades of the twentieth century, there were very few writers who more than occasionally broke this taboo.[7]

So in the absence of self-determination, and in the face of an accelerating onslaught of Englishness, the use of Welsh as the language of artistic composition was an axiomatic instrument of nation building. And a number of well-known writers whose first language was English swelled the ranks of Welsh writing in what almost amounted to a form of literary apostasy. Writers like Waldo Williams and then, later, Bobi Jones championed the idea that choice alone could determine the language of composition for the "re-cambrianized" Welsh writer. This position rather uncomfortably contradicted the view that "nobody was ever quite first rate in two languages" though that contradiction was never problematized—never, that is, until R. S. Thomas strode onto the scene, clothed against the chill blast of appeasement by the mantle of steadfast integrity which he had inherited from Saunders Lewis himself. He appeared as the lone truthteller, railing against the iniquity of the modern world, and against the destructiveness of English life to the tender blooms of minority languages everywhere and of Welsh in particular.

R. S. Thomas became the conscience of a nation. He was the man who stood apart and told the difficult truths: industrialization was destroying the world around us, English imperialism was destroying the Welsh way of life and the indifference of the Welsh themselves was the English minotaur's main ally as it:

> . . . [elbows] our language
> Into the grave that we have dug for it.[8]

But the difference was that R. S. Thomas wrote poetry in English, and had always written poetry in English, and even when he became a key figure in the language movement and wrote politically-engaged Welsh prose, and refused to give interviews in English even though he was one of the most famous poets in the English-speaking world, he continued to write poetry in English. He did so because he felt he had no choice. English was his birth language and R. S. Thomas believed like Saunders Lewis that significant literature was something which could only be written in a genuine first language.[9] Welsh-speaking Wales took him on his own terms and he became, in a way that no writer in English before him had become, a truly national figure. And one includes in that observation Dylan Thomas, who probably had a higher international profile, but never enjoyed a status in Welsh literary circles equal to the great Welsh-language poets of the twentieth century, to Gwenallt and Waldo and Robert Williams Parry and Saunders Lewis.[10] It was to that elite that R. S. Thomas was admitted.

This extraordinary achievement for an English-language poet took place at a time when a number of institutional changes were taking place in Wales which would make the language more visible in public life and more of an active participant in the discourses of government. Through the accumulation of small legislative changes, and through the continuing desire of many Welsh people to foster the use of Welsh in public life, Welsh was beginning to develop codes for the major discourses of power. Official forms and signs, legal proceedings, education and above all broadcasting were beginning to give the language not just a legal status but a linguistic life in areas which were essential if survival was to be possible.

The significance of the language movement in Wales over the last fifty years cannot be assessed in term of whether or not the Welsh language has survived or will survive, something which at this stage is simply not knowable. The significance of the language movement is that it brought about the preconditions without which it could not ever hope to survive. The institutional changes which have been achieved over the last fifty years, limited though they are, have nevertheless created the conditions under which survival has now become one of the possible outcomes. And in that fight for survival strategies of language use, such as those employed by R. S. Thomas, can be crucial weapons. Language systems are so dynamic, however, and the conditions change so quickly, that no strategy is likely to be effective, or even felt to be possible, for more than a brief period. So R. S. Thomas, who was born before the outbreak of the Great War, came from a world in which his own linguistic dilemma, what he called the "scar" of his Englishness, arose from the educational and social conditions in which he had been raised.[11] But by the 1980s there was an entirely new generation of Welsh writers who had been raised with bilingual education and Welsh broadcasting and for whom the codes of language use were no longer defined in the old ways. For them, at a linguistic level, there was now a choice but it was a choice which required a political sanction or a literary model and, more than anything, that model came from the Welsh-speaking political campaigner with an international reputation for writing poetry in English. Part of the reason the model of R. S. Thomas made a difference lies in the way different parts of his output, in different languages, increasingly made a coherent whole, none of which was fully understandable without the other. In particular, from the early 1970s in prose works like *Y Llwybrau Gynt* and *Abercuawg*, he is writing to a bilingual audience, whose knowledge of his Welsh-language work informs a reading of his English poetry.[12] While he continues to write in English, it is as if he has cut off all but the Welsh-reading audience from aspects of his English-language work.[13] It is almost a version of choosing to write only in Welsh. But for the literary life of Wales it is a more far-reaching step than that. What he has begun to do is to construct a bilingual audience: to write a series of texts in two languages which are sufficiently interconnected that a knowledge of one becomes a precondition for understanding the other, so that it is only, in some ways, the readers of the Welsh texts whose readings of the English poems are fully informed. This situation—it need not be called a strategy, for it is the effect of the texts on his audience rather than Thomas's intent which matters here—was quickly recognized, even if it was not consciously debated. One proof of this is that many of his Welsh prose works were translated into English and eagerly read and quickly assimilated into the essential lists of sources for the study of his poetry. This brought an awareness of the Welsh language to an international audience, and foregrounded the significance of Welsh-language writing in the field of Welsh writing in English. It also drew attention, in the subject matter of works like *Abercuawg*, to the linguistic reality that no translation can do more than broadly indicate some of what might be signified by the original text itself. There are meanings in the lexis and the grammar of all languages which cannot be translated, a concept which will be central to the following discussion of Gwyneth Lewis.

So R. S. Thomas is not like his near contemporary Dylan Thomas, writing different kinds of text for different kinds of audience, and writing poetry which is part of the mainstream of international English writing. From the point at which he begins to publish prose works in Welsh, R. S. Thomas is increasingly writing a single, coherent body of work in two languages for a single audience.[14] And it is this radical and challenging body of work which forms the literary paradigm which helped to enable a generation of writers in late twentieth-century Wales to begin to cross the border from the neurosis of bilingual treachery to the code-switching fluency of a modern, self-determining multilingual nation which is a nation state in Europe rather than a colonial economy in the remnants of an empire. It is predictable within a post-colonial framework that a national literature which exhibits a period of defensive separateness, in which identity is defined in terms of difference from the imperial centre, will develop into one in which identity is self-referenced rather than externally referenced through opposition. But that process requires not only the historical changes of self determination, but appropriate literary paradigms. It is that paradigm which the work of R. S. Thomas, more than any other, supplied in late twentieth-century Wales.

II

One of the most interesting literary texts in recent Welsh writing is Gwyneth Lewis's poetic sequence, published in 1999 as *Y Llofrudd Iaith* [The Language Murderer].[15] The sequence is in the form of a murder mystery in which the body of an elderly woman, who is the Welsh language, is discovered knifed in the back, and whose death is investigated by detective Carma, who has studied Welsh at the University of Wales and Zen in Kyoto. In 2003, Gwyneth Lewis published *Keeping Mum*,[16] in which she recasts, in English, the plot, characters and location of the Welsh sequence. There are thirty seven poems in the sequence *Y Llofrudd Iaith* starting with "Cyffes y Bardd" [The Poet's Confession] and ending with "Dalen o Lyfr Coll Iaith" [A Page from the Lost Book of Language]. In *Keeping Mum*, however, there is something other than a straight English translation of the Welsh sequence. In the Preface, Gwyneth Lewis says that in *Y Llofrudd Iaith* she wanted "to explore how we could free ourselves of the idea of a 'mother tongue' with all its accompanying psychological baggage and its infantilising of native speakers".[17] But having been persuaded that "the fate of a language might be of interest to those concerned with the wider linguistic ecology" she found that the act of translation became a new act of composition. So the first section of *Keeping Mum*, "The Language Killer", contains just eleven poems, which represent as much of *Y Llofrudd Iaith* as Lewis was "able to translate in a fairly direct fashion" and "only a handful of the poems are literal versions".[18] Beyond those eleven poems there is a second sequence, itself called "Keeping Mum" which contains twenty poems which "radical[ly] recast" the themes of *Y Llofrudd Iaith* and are also "a meditation on mental illness and language". They are "entirely new poems in English . . . translations without an original text—perhaps a useful definition of poetry".[19]

Gwyneth Lewis is unusual in Welsh writing for having created an equally significant reputation for writing poetry in Welsh and in English,[20] for leading, in a way which does not mirror R. S. Thomas's career, what she calls "a double life".[21] Thomas's duality was that he wrote poetry only in English and, increasingly, wrote prose only in Welsh. Lewis's output is also different from other poets in Wales, such as Menna Elfyn, who has published Welsh poetry with facing-page English translations by herself and other writers, in a format well known in Ireland. But it is that ability, one might almost say that mandate, to write original work in two languages which connects her work with that of R. S. Thomas, and it is in *Y Llofrudd Iaith*, written in Welsh, that we see one of the most revealing examinations in modern Welsh writing of the many issues of language and identity which are central to the two literatures of Wales. Gwyneth Lewis has spoken of the code-switching imperatives which underlie her choice of language for poetic composition—that it is in no sense "a choice" but something which grows out of the act of composition.[22] This experience of multilingualism is so far from being uncommon that David Crystal has suggested multilingualism may be the natural state for humans, and yet in Welsh-speaking Wales, where daily life is clothed in the nuances of bilingualism, it is not an experience which has been much explored.[23]

Y Llofrudd Iaith begins, in classic police procedural style, with a confession, which may or may not be true: the character of the poet confesses to murder through lack of care:

> Fi lofruddiodd yr iaith Gymraeg . . .
> Mwrdrais fy mam.
>
> I did it. I killed my mother tongue.[24]

This establishes at the same time the common maternal metaphor for a birth language—*mamiaith* or mother tongue—which will later be developed in the linguistic pathology of family relationships.

In the wake of her death, as the investigation begins, some of the old woman's possessions, her books, are found to be missing from her house:

collections of idioms and rural sayings and a valuable, unpublished tenth-century manuscript which contained a rare tract about how to live in the moment without words. And in the course of a police interview, the poet, who had confessed to doing too little too late, describes how her seduction by another language had begun at school, where she acquired a taste for the nicotine-like habit of inhaling a second language:

> —a hoffais deimlo mwg
> ail iaith yng nghefn fy llwnc a brath
> chwerw ei gemeg.

> . . . the bite of another language's smoke
> at the back of my throat, its bitter chemicals.[25]

The odd word of English—"y tu ol i'r sied" [behind the shed]—becomes whole sentences and then whole books, some read illicitly, hidden inside the respectability of Welsh covers. But although this fails to trick an ever-watchful mother, it is, by then, too late. Moving on to French:

> . . . Rown i'n darllen mwy
> i gael yr un effaith nawr . . .
>   Un noswaith mi gefais lond bola o ofn.
> Ar ol darllen llawer gormod o Proust
> llewygais.

> . . . [I] Had to read much more
> for any effect. . .
>   One night I OD'd
> after reading far too much Proust.[26]

Travelling further and further from her old life, and adding new languages as the addiction grows, the "language fetishist" for whom "sex is part of the problem" yearns for a "multilingual man" whose many tongues can satisfy her linguistic cravings. It also becomes clear, as the sequence progresses, that the mother had two daughters, the poet and the archivist. The archivist daughter, who remained loyal, did everything for her mother, while the little, gallivanting poet of a daughter "carried on" with multilingual, married men. Nevertheless, it is the poet, who is confessing to the murder, who was the mother's favourite. Language delights more in the sometimes uncontrollable power of exploration and invention than in the well-meaning but conservative impulses of the conservator.

In one of the most successful poems in the sequence, which appears as "What's in a Name?" in *Keeping Mum*, we see the beginnings of the new world which is starting to emerge in the aftermath of the mother's death. In

"What's in a Name?" it is an indifferent, personified bird, who rejects the poet:

> Today the wagtail finally forgot
> That I once called it *sigl-di-gwt*.[27]

But in the original, darker poem "Dechrau'r Anghofio" there is a very different experience. The English couplet is a wonderfully inventive response to the problem of translation, but it lacks the sharp smack of recognition which comes with the opening lines of the Welsh poem:

> Heddiw, trodd y sigl-di-gwt
> yn *wagtail*
>
> [Today the sigl-di-gwt turned into
> a *wagtail*][28]

in which the italicized, alien lexis (later on there are also *swallows*) signals the phenomenon which is at the heart of the matter for supporters of linguistic plurality. When there is nobody left to call it "sigl-di-gwt", the bird does not acquire another name, it literally turns into something else. It is language, and the processes of classification and naming, which creates our sense of the reality of any environment. And often it is classification—the way we divide up the world—which, more than the way we name things, separates one language and culture from another language whose lexis does not share the same footprints of connotation. These are ideas which run through the literature and polemics of twentieth-century Welsh Wales, finding their most popular expression in that great poem of linguistic anthropology, "Cofio" [Remembering] by Waldo Williams, whose title and intertextual resonance echo through the title and argument of "Dechrau'r Anghofio":

> A geiriau bach hen ieithoedd diflanedig,
>   Hoyw yng ngenau dynion oeddynt hwy,
> A thlws i'r glust ym mharabl plant bychain
>   Ond tafod neb ni eilw arnynt mwy.
>
> Little words of old, fugitive languages
>   That were sprightly on the lips of men
> And pretty to the ear in the prattle of children—
>   But no one's tongue will call on them again.[29]

It is also interesting to note that Lewis herself hears the echo of another great Welsh poem of the twentieth century behind the whole sequence. In an interview prior to publication in 1999, she said that:

> Y gerdd fawr y tu ol i'r llyfr hwn yw "Hon" T.H. Parry-Williams. Hynny yw,
> mae'n anodd iawn imi feddwl sgwennu unrhyw beth ar y testun heb glwyed
> rhythmau'r gerdd honno . . . dw i'n edmygus iawn o waith T.H. Parry-Williams.

> The great poem behind this book is T.H. Parry-Williams's "Hon". That is, it's
> very difficult for me to think of writing anything on this subject without hearing
> the rhythms of that poem . . . I'm a great admirer of the work of T.H. Parry-
> Williams.[30]

But whatever literary cognates may be found for the form and ideas of
"Dechrau'r Anghofio" and "What's in a Name?", there are important semantic
and philosophical differences between them. Lewis's Welsh poem describes
what happens when the reality of the named environment begins to change as
the language which names it also changes. This argument is implicit in
"Dechrau'r Anghofio" where the literary and political discourses of language
loss provide a ready context for a Welsh audience, but it is explicity argued
through in "What's in a Name?":

> *Lleian wen* is not the same as 'smew'
> Because it's another point of view,
>
> Another bird.[31]

It is not just the obscure words which are lost. The things which they named
have also gone. With every language lost, another of the worlds we live in is
lost as well.

As the sequence gathers momentum, there is still speculation about the
identity of the murderer and even the cause of death. The pathologist's report
is ambiguous. There is evidence of trauma and also of poison. And others now
begin to confess: the farmer, the devoted archivist daughter, her secret lover,
the English-speaking doctor. It is clear that while the death has been certified,
the cause remains unknown. Meanwhile, the language is in its death throes,
haemorrhaging lexical items that are absorbed by the mortal enemy of
language, silence:

> Roedd y diwedd yn erchyll. Torrodd argae tu mewn
> ac roedd gwaed ym mhobman. Allan o'i cheg
> daeth rhaeadrau o eiriau *da yw dant*
> *i atal tafod* . . .
>
> The end was dreadful. Inside a dam burst
> and blood was everywhere. Out of her mouth
> came torrent of words, *da yw dant*
> *i atal tafod* . . .[32]

We read an eye-witness report of the death of the last speaker, a phenomenon well known in linguistics, where it is usually recorded in the ethnography of western observers, who often, as here, write in English. The final words as the person dies are spoken to a world where already there is nobody who can understand them. Although the Welsh phrases are translated in footnotes to "The Final Minutes", the poem would also work as a sociolinguistic text if they could not be understood by an English-speaking audience. The words drain out of the dying language like the last drops of blood out of a corpse, and "then she was gone".

<h2 style="text-align:center">III</h2>

In the wonderful extended metaphor of the narcosis of multilingualism which comprises "Cyfweliad â'r Bardd" and "Mother Tongue" the character of the poet suggests that it is her own linguistic promiscuity that has led to the death of Welsh. This is not a pathology which the literature of language survival supports, but the guilt expressed by the character of the poet is not necessarily the primary message of the book. Like the murderer's confession, it does not have to be true to be part of the story, and the primary argument of this poetic sequence, not least through its very existence and achievement, is that the results of travel and contact and plurality are in fact linguistic vigour and renewal. Despite the author's well-founded anxiety about language survival in the Preface, the achievement of the sequence implicitly argues, as the literature of language survival suggests, that it is not multilingualism that kills languages: what kills languages is the abandonment of one monolingual culture for another.

What can be seen in the different but related paradigms of composition which are apparent in the work of Gwyneth Lewis and R. S. Thomas is a growing linguistic self-confidence in which literary composition in Wales can be as plural as identity itself. The preconditions for this were established by the changing power structures in which Welsh began to establish itself in a number of important institutional discourses, but the literary paradigm which made the politics of choice a less than all-consuming neurosis for bilingual Welsh writers like Gwyneth Lewis in the 1980s and 1990s was the example of R. S. Thomas, the first truly national literary figure in post-industrial Wales, whose work crosses the border between Welsh and English.

NOTES

This is a revised version of a paper originally given at the 25th Annual California Celtic Studies Conference / Celtic Studies Association of North America Conference, University of California, Berkeley, April 2003.

1. See Antonio Gramsci, *Selections From the Prison Notebooks*, ed. and trans. Quintin Hoare and Geoffrey Nowell-Smith (London: Lawrence & Wishart, 1971).

2. Saunders Lewis, *Tynged yr Iaith* [The Fate of the Language] (London: BBC, 1962); trans. G. Aled Williams, *Presenting Saunders Lewis*, ed. Alun R. Jones and Gwyn Thomas (Cardiff U. of Wales P., 1973) 127-41.

3. See R. M. W. Dixon, *The Rise and Fall of Languages* (Cambridge: C.U.P., 1997); David Crystal, *Language Death* (Cambridge: C.U.P., 2000); Nancy C. Dorian, ed., *Investigating Obsolescence: Studies in Language Contraction and Death* (Cambridge: C.U.P., 1989). Crystal describes the survival of differently-sized communities, Dixon describes a new model of language survival called "punctuated equilibrium", and Dorian brings together contributions from many leading practitioners in fields relating to language survival.

4. *The Eve of Saint John* (Newtown: Welsh Outlook, 1921); *A School of Welsh Augustans* (Wrexham: Hughes, 1924). On *The Eve of Saint John* and Lewis's early plans for a literary career in English, see Bruce Griffiths, *"The Eve of Saint John* and the Significance of the Stranger in the Plays of Saunders Lewis", *Welsh Writing in English: A Yearbook of Critical Essays* 3 (1997): 63-77.

5. Unpublished letter from Saunders Lewis to David Jones, 13 December, 1969, NLW Casgliad David Jones [NLW David Jones Collection].

6. The book was eventually written by René Hague, Writers of Wales Series (Cardiff: U. of Wales P., 1975).

7. It is interesting to look at writers such as Emyr Humphreys who did publish in both languages but the argument here is about the primary significance of the absence of a general movement towards multilingual composition.

8. R. S. Thomas, "Reservoirs", *Collected Poems 1945-1990* (London: Dent, 1993) 194. For the image of the English minotaur see Gwenallt, "Rhydcymerau", *Eples* (Llandysul: Gomer, 1951) 20-21; trans. Tony Conran, *Welsh Verse* (Bridgend: Seren, 1992) 285-86.

9. On the position of the writer who has learned Welsh as a second language attempting to write creatively in that language, see R. S. Thomas, "The Creative Writer's Suicide", *R. S. Thomas: Selected Prose*, ed. Sandra Anstey (Bridgend: Poetry Wales P., 1983), 172-73. The essay was originally published as "Hunanladdiad y Llenor", *Taliesin* 35 (Rhagfyr 1977): 109-13.

10. For an early view from Saunders Lewis on the status of Dylan Thomas, see his pamphlet "Is There an Anglo-Welsh Literature?" (Cardiff: Guild of Graduates of the University of Wales, 1939).

11. R. S. Thomas uses the term "scar" in a documentary about his work, broadcast on I.T.V.'s *The South Bank Show*, Season 14, no. 20, episode 334, which was first broadcast on 14 February 1991.

12. For translations of *Y Llwybrau Gynt* [The Paths Gone By] (1972) and *Abercuawg* (1976), see *R. S. Thomas: Selected Prose.*

13. It is the Welsh-reading audience who will, for instance, pick up the wealth of R. S. Thomas's allusions in his poetry to Welsh-language literature and myth; see Jason Walford Davies, "'Thick Ambush of Shadows'": Allusions to Welsh Literature in the Work of R. S. Thomas", *Welsh Writing in English: A Yearbook of Critical Essays* 1 (1995): 75-127, and the same author's *Gororau'r Iaith: R. S. Thomas a'r Traddodiad Llenyddol Cymraeg* (Caerdydd: Gwasg Prifysgol Cymru, 2003).

14. Since R. S. Thomas's first essays in Welsh were published in 1945 and his first collection of poetry, *The Stones of the Field*, in 1946, this has effectively been true of his whole career.

15. Gwyneth Lewis, *Y Llofrudd Iaith* [*The Language Murderer*] (Felindre: Barddas, 1999).

16. Gwyneth Lewis, *Keeping Mum* (Tarset: Bloodaxe, 2003).

17. *Keeping Mum* 9.

18. *Keeping Mum* 10.

19. *Keeping Mum* 10.

20. Her other collections of poetry in Welsh are *Sonedau Redsa* (Llandysul: Gomer, 1990) and *Cyfrif Un ac Un yn Dri* (Felindre: Barddas, 1996) and in English *Parables & Faxes* (Tarset: Bloodaxe, 1995) and *Zero Gravity* (Tarset: Bloodaxe, 1998).

21. *Keeping Mum* 9.

22. See "Parable a Ffacs", *Taliesin* 91 (1995): 68-74.

23. See David Crystal, *Language Death*, Ch. 1.

24. "Cyffes y Bardd" [The Poet's Confession], *Y Llofrudd Iaith* 7; "A Poet's Confession", *Keeping Mum* 13. A more literal translation of the Welsh quotation, which is the first and last words of "Cyffes y Bardd" is "I murdered the Welsh language. . . . I murdered my mother".

25. "Cyfweliad â'r Bardd" [An Interview with the Poet], *Y Llofrudd Iaith* 14; "Mother Tongue", *Keeping Mum* 15.

26. "Cyfweliad â'r Bardd" [An Interview with the Poet], *Y Llofrudd Iaith* 14; "Mother Tongue", *Keeping Mum* 15.

27. "What's in a Name?" *Keeping Mum* 14.

28. "Dechrau'r Anghofio" [Beginning to Forget, literally, The Beginning of the Forgetting], *Y Llofrudd Iaith* 22; my translation.

29. For the full text of "Cofio" and an English translation see Tony Conran, *The Peacemakers: Poems by Waldo Williams* (Llandysul: Gomer, 1997) 62-63.

30. "Hon", *Ugain o Gerddi* [Twenty Poems] (Aberystwyth: Gwasg Aberystwyth, 1949); for the Welsh text and a translation see R. Gerallt Jones *Poetry of Wales: 1930-1970* (Llandysul: Gomer, 1974) 60-61. The excerpt from Gwyneth Lewis's interview with Jerry Hunter is taken from "Ar Drywydd y Llofrudd Iaith" [On the Trail of the Language Murderer], *Taliesin* 107 (1999): 19-31; my translation.

31. "What's in a Name?" *Keeping Mum* 14.

32. "Y Munudau Olaf" [The Final Minutes], *Y Llofrudd Iaith* 41; "Her End", *Keeping Mum* 21, where the Welsh proverb is translated in a footnote as "A tooth is a good barrier for the tongue".

COMMENTARY

Lost and Found: Reflections on Translation as a Threat and a Promise

Joseph P. Clancy

My title refers, of course, to the much-quoted dictum by my countryman Robert Frost that poetry is what gets lost in translation. That is a memorably succinct way of saying that what delights us in a successful poem is the co-inherence of expression and meaning, the absolute "rightness" of *these* words in *this* order, that the essential mark of a good poem is that it is untranslatable.

True, true, all too true. And yet, for those of us who persist nonetheless in practising this art of the impossible, it is not as simple as that. Literary translation takes place within a four-way tension: between, most obviously, the original poet's achieved expression of a particular experience in his own language and the translator's attempt in another language to express the experience of reading that poem, through what George Steiner affirmatively calls "counter-creation", "metamorphic reiteration"[1]—but also between the demands of a reader who knows the original language and poem, and the needs of a reader who doesn't. It is the former reader, who is usually the reviewer, who will understandably be keenly aware of what has been lost and may therefore see the translation as a threat, but it is the latter reader, all too seldom a reviewer, who is the translator's intended audience, for whom translation means the promise of literary pleasure in finding a new poem. Perhaps I should have said a five-way tension: it is well to remember that what gets lost or found may depend less on translators than on the tastes of editors and publishers, and on the financial constraints within which they play their role in what Steiner terms "the household of imagining".[2]

I want to explore not only what gets lost but what can be found by translating Welsh poetry into English. Poetry, because that is where I've concentrated my own efforts as a translator, and because that is where the losing and the finding are most immediately apparent—but my observations can also apply, though perhaps in a lesser degree, to translating from and into what Dryden appropriately called "the other harmony of prose", as I know very well from attempts at translating the stories of Kate Roberts and the plays of Saunders Lewis, John Gwilym Jones, and Gwenlyn Parry. I want to consider as well some of the consequences of translating Welsh literature into English, the possible responses of Welshless readers and the possible effects on bilingual Welsh writers, for whom, Dafydd Johnston has remarked, translation into the "majority language" may be "a welcome means of cultural dissemination" but "can also be seen as an act of betrayal".[3]

I

Let me begin, then, with two poems that have a great deal in common. Both were composed about a dozen years ago in the same place and on the same subject, though neither poet was aware of the other's poem at the time.

THE WILD GEESE AT GREGYNOG

To the pond, we say, giving to our walk
Not a destination but a terminus.

A mid-March afternoon, chill breeze,
Weak sunshine. Stark boughs and twigs
Seem dormant still, although in listless grass
Bright clumps of crocuses proclaim the spring.
A blackbird whistles his agreement. Files
Of daffodils stay huddled in their sheaths.

The pond is dull, its darkling surface
Unruffled by the reeds within the shallows
And ripples here and there where unseen fish
Catch bugs too small for sight. Dull, dull.
The only thing that could produce a stir
Is jumping in. Then suddenly

Two geese are gliding, side by side,
Out into the middle. Their easy progress
Leaves the pond untroubled,
But here is life in motion. No thrum of wings,
No soaring off as an epiphany:
Ignoring us, they linger at the centre,
Then circle back to what we now can see
Is a small island near the other side.

They vanish in the bushes, and we turn
Back to the road. The pond has been
A sort of destination after all.

GEESE AT GREGYNOG

The geese have gone. There's no scarcity
of commotion on the surface of the lake: the raucous
pontificating coot on busybody rounds,
its black fuss ruffling the cosy greyness;

the wild ducks, quaa, quaa, rising in terror
and circling, flailing the rushes, raising an uproar
in the tanglewood of the island; on tranquil wing
an old buzzard, chilling on a summer evening.

No lack. But the straight-backed fleet I've watched each night
again this year, rowing trim nautical
single file through the rushes at the sunset hour,
they fledged wings, they left. It's a sorry world!

Lacking their head-high dignity, bereaved
is a lake's civility. And the image imposed
on geese? How false! They were gentle creatures,
their progress soft and graceful across water's mirror.

At nightfall they'd walk, a cautious band,
from their browsing in the tall hay to their rightful stand
in the rushes and sword-grass, slipping so smoothly
into their element and claiming possession of a patch.

Six little ones, brown and flimsy, proud father in front
guiding, and one at the rear, every moment
keen her concern for the goslings—
a tidy organic family, a nucleus of nurture.

Over months of disturbance in a lake—crows' yakking,
jay's shriek of malice, man's two heavy feet,
they were the civilized element, the constant activity
of their care and their growth affirming continuity.

But tonight, at summer's end, winter is at hand,
its sudden forward cold a guarantee
that I will see, next year perhaps, a springtime when
the geese will not ever come back to the lake again.

As I said, the two poems, while seasonally and thematically different, have
much in common. Not only the subject and the setting, but the conversational
style and what Tony Conran has called "empirical" structure, the speaker's
movement from the particulars of an experience through an exploration of the
possible meaning of that experience, the structure common to most meditative

poems in English since Coleridge and Wordsworth.[4] What they also have in common is the precedent of W. B. Yeats's poem on the wild swans at Coole. And there is one more thing they have in common: although the poems are by different poets, both are in a sense mine—one of them is a translation. But which? That, I acknowledge, is a bit unfair—in our normal reading experience authors are identified and translations are so labelled from the start. I've done this as a way of making several points which become especially apparent through translation—that much contemporary poetry in Welsh shares common ground with much contemporary poetry in English, and that apart from the setting, an estate in Wales for whose place-name most non-Welsh readers would need a footnote, there is nothing particularly Welsh about either poem. Once I've noted that the second poem, "Geese at Gregynog", is a translation of a poem by the late R. Gerallt Jones, there is still another point. My own poem, "The Wild Geese at Gregynog", explicitly acknowledges Yeats's poem and contrasts the experience—that is its very basis. But though Gerallt Jones's poem surely could not have been written had not Yeats's existed first, there is no such acknowledgement—and in Welsh, no need for it. Might some readers find it as a poem in English a bit too derivative from Yeats? But what one experiences in reading Gerallt Jones's poem in its own language, on the contrary, is that an Irish poem in English has made a poem in Welsh, based on a similar experience, possible—one's sense of this is lost, or at least seriously diminished, when the poem is read in translation.

GWYDDAU YNG NGREGYNOG

Mae'r gwyddau wedi mynd. Does dim prinder
cynnwrf dros wyneb y llyn: y gotiar
groch ymhongar ar drywydd busneslyd,
ei ffws du'n annifyrru'r llwydni clyd;

yr hwyaid gwylltion mewn dychryn yn codi
a chylchu, cwaa, cwaa, chwipio'r brwyn, cadw
stŵr yn nryswig yr ynys; hen foda
ar adain lonydd, ias oer yn hwyr ha.

Nac oes. Ond y llynges gefnsyth a wyliais
feunos eleni eto'n rhwyfo'n un rhes
drefnus forwrol trwy'r brwyn awr machlud,
magodd adenydd, aeth. Diriaid yw'r byd!

Heb eu hurddas penuchel, amddifad
gwareiddiad llyn. A'r ddelwedd osodwyd
ar wyddau? Mor ffals! Llariaidd rai oeddynt,
mwyn a phrydferth dros drych dŵr oedd eu hynt.

Fin nos cerddent yn fintai ofalus
o'u pori yn y gwair tal i'w gwir wanas
yn y pabwyr a'r gellhesg, gan lithro
i'w helfen mor llyfn a meddiannu bro.

Chwe fechain yn frown a bregus, tad balch ar y blaen
yn arwain ac un o'r tu ôl yn fain
ei chonsárn bob eiliad dros y cywion—
teulu organig twt, meithringell gron.

Dros fisoedd o styrbans mewn llyn—clochdar brain,
malais sgrech y coed, trymder deutroed dyn,
hwy oedd yr elfen wâr, dycnwch gwastad
eu meithrin a'u twf yn hawlio parhad.

Ond heno, ddiwedd haf, mae'r gaea'n agos,
a'i oerni annhymig dirybudd yn ernes
y gwelaf, hwyrach y tro nesaf, ryw wanwyn
pryd na ddaw'r gwyddau fyth eto'n ôl i'r llyn.

What else is lost, and how much of the original Welsh poem has been found, I will try to demonstrate by reconstructing, insofar as I can recall it, this particular wild-goose chase, the choices (to use an actor's term) and the constraints in what Bobi Jones once called (in conversation) "diplomatic negotiations" between the two languages. I must first note that Gerallt Jones himself had translated this poem along with others for the Welsh issue of *Modern Poetry in Translation*. He also contributed to that issue a short comment in which he termed what he had done "'versions' rather than true translations" and questioned the wisdom of self-translation, because the poet is likely to be tempted "to use the original as a springboard for another poem". "Someone else," he wrote, "at least comes to the task with a degree of objectivity, and bases the work of translation on a text rather than on a text plus a remembered experience".[5]

In the case of this particular someone else, when I was asked to provide the translation for a memorial publication by Gregynog Press I carefully avoided looking at Gerallt's "version" of his poem until the very last stage of my own work. This is my regular practice when I'm aware of prior translations—I want first to translate my direct experience of the Welsh poem, after which I'm happy to have any help I can get that may provide corrections or suggest improvements. When I finally consulted Gerallt's version, it proved helpful in several instances which I'll note later, but I also found, not surprisingly in view of his comments, that he had taken more liberties with the poem than I thought I could allow myself.

Gerallt's poem opens with an apparently simple statement of fact, and I didn't think twice about rendering *Mae'r gwyddau wedi mynd* as "The geese have gone". There seemed to be no choice, and, allowing for the unavoidable differences in syntax and sound, no problem. But I remember that a Welsh-language reviewer of my twentieth-century anthology some years ago, while generally favourable, regretted that I had not conveyed more of the distinctive features of the Welsh language in my use of English. Some specialists in Translation Studies call this "foreignizing" the translation, an ugly if expressive neologism which itself, I suggest, cries out to be translated into a more naturalized English. I do, in fact, try to do this on occasion, when it appears possible within the stylistic context, but as a general rule it seems best, as here, to use plain English for plain Welsh. It may be worth considering what my reviewer's suggestion would mean in this case. An extremely literal "Is the geese after going" would be absurd. Should I translate the sentence as "The geese are after going"? That would surely suggest an Irish speaker—I've never heard a Welsh person talk this way—and most importantly it would be a stylistic distraction from the almost prosaic way in which the poem begins and from which it moves into a more elevated style. For that "simple statement of fact" is not, for the person in the poem, simple at all—how the "fact" affects him, its significance for him, is what he discovers, meditatively explores, through the remainder of the poem.

There seemed to be not much choice and no real problem either in translating *Does dim prinder / cynnwrf dros wyneb y llyn* as "there's no scarcity / of commotion on the surface of the lake". I was briefly tempted to render the whole first line as "The geese have gone. No scarcity", as a way of energizing this opening, but I reflected that the relaxed, seemingly casual style was exactly what was needed, and not least to counter in the second part of the line the relative terseness, the near abruptness, of the English in the first part, in contrast to the easier flow of the Welsh. I have frequently dithered in dealing with the Welsh genitive construction, e.g. whether it would be better in this instance to translate *wyneb y llyn* as "the surface of the lake" or "the lake's surface", but this time the former seemed a clearly better choice for keeping the conversational style, even though as always this meant being wordier and therefore somewhat slacker than the Welsh.

Choice, if not problems, really began with that coot, *y gotiar*, at the end of the second line. Not that I saw any choice about moving it down to the next line so that normal English syntax of adjectives preceding noun would match the normal Welsh syntax of noun preceding adjectives. But every word in line three except the preposition *ar*, "on", offered a variety of options. In literal prose translation, the poem says "the loud assertive coot on a meddlesome trail"—I turned this first into "the loud / outspoken coot on a busybody course", then "the loud / outspoken coot on busybody circuit", and finally "the raucous / pontificating coot on busybody rounds". This is, I think, a good example of what Gerallt Jones remarked in his essay, that "if some at least of [the verbal music] is to be conveyed in another language, then a compromise will almost certainly have to be arrived at in terms of the dictionary definitions of the actual words used".[6] In moving somewhat away from the prose sense of the lines, I was trying, paradoxically, to capture more of their poetry, above all to make my coot in English as noisy as she is in Welsh: *y gotiar / groch ymhongar ar drywydd busneslyd.*

It was sound, too, as much as sense that led me to translate *annifyrru*, "annoying / vexing", as "ruffling". It provided both an assonantal and an alliterative echo of "fuss", and an element of onomatopoeia expressive of the physical disturbance created by the bird. I am not fond of using abstractions in the way *llwydni*, "greyness", is used here, but that is what the Welsh means, and translating quite literally as "the cosy greyness" provided a good contrast in rhythm and music to the first half of the line. I should note at this point that while it felt natural to employ the same metre as the original—what Robert Frost once called "loose iambics"—I didn't think it necessary, or rather, frankly, I didn't think it possible, at least for me, to create a reasonably close poetic translation while retaining Gerallt Jones's unusual and attractive rhyme-scheme, with its partial rhyme for the first couplet of each stanza followed by rhyming an unstressed with a stressed syllable for the second couplet. I have usually found that giving priority to the rhyme pattern would result in losing the poetry, or at least in substituting too much of one's own poetry for the original. I did in places achieve more end-rhyme and internal rhyme in this translation than I had expected, but this was a serendipitous consequence of searching for the most expressive words in the most effective order, rather than of any conscious effort.

What I do attempt as a translator is to stay as close as the considerable syntactic differences between the languages permit to the sequence, the movement, of thought and feeling in the original poem. But there are times when the English language, the rhetorical effect, and the rhythm seem to require a difference. That is why those ducks in stanza two quack much earlier in English than they do in Welsh, and why the uproar they raise, *stŵr*, ends the second line in English whereas it begins the third line in Welsh, and why the old buzzard, *hen foda*, at the end of line three in Welsh is delayed until the start of line four in English. There is probably no need to discuss the choices of "terror" for *dychryn* and "flailing" for *chwipio*, or of turning *ias oer*, "a cold shiver", into "chilling", but the rendering of *dryswig* as "tanglewood" calls for some comment. It is a quite literal translation of the compound *dyrys*, "tangled", plus *gwig*, "wood, forest", and in noting this I remembered that Nathaniel Hawthorne had called a collection of his stories *Tanglewood Tales*. That *dryswig* doesn't appear in the Welsh-English section of "The Complete

Welsh-English English-Welsh Dictionary", *Y Geiriadur Mawr*, or in the much larger University of Wales dictionary, *Geiriadur Prifysgol Cymru*, didn't disturb me—I've grown accustomed to Welsh poets coining compounds, especially in my translating of Bobi Jones. But when I came to look at Gerallt Jones's English version of his poem, I found that he had rendered *yn nryswig yr ynys* as "in the island jungle". I then turned to "jungle" in the English-Welsh section of *Y Geiriadur Mawr*, and there it was, *dryswig*, though the first Welsh word listed was *jyngl*. After all that, I decided that I much preferred "tanglewood", and it stayed.

The third stanza in Welsh begins with the standard form for a negative response, *Nac oes*, providing a transition to the heart of the poem by confirming the *Does dim* of its opening line. Simply translating this as "No" was an obvious possibility, but that wasn't sufficiently emphatic; too much had been going on in the preceding sentence for it to have full force, and the rhythm of the line required something more than a monosyllable. I tried "No indeed", but when I consulted Gerallt's version, I saw that he had translated *prinder* as "lack" rather than "scarcity" and then repeated this with "No lack" for *Nac oes*. I was not tempted to change "scarcity" to "lack", but "No lack" would make, I thought, the strongest way to begin this third stanza, and so I blatantly and gratefully borrowed it.

Most of the work on the third stanza was otherwise a matter of finding by trial and error not only the best single words but the most satisfactory equivalent for the complexity of the Welsh sentence, and it was the final line that gave me the most trouble. That Welsh could dispense with pronouns in *magodd adenydd, aeth* didn't help. I eventually concluded that using "they" to refer back to *llynges*, "fleet", was more effective than "it", however much grammarians might frown, and that however striking it might be to follow the Welsh by translating monosyllabic *aeth* as monosyllabic "went", "they left" worked much better in the total context. Rhythm played its part here too, since there was no choice but to turn trisyllabic *adenydd* into monosyllabic "wings". (No one, I presume, would wish to suggest "pinions".) Whether it is quite ornithologically or semantically correct to say "they fledged wings" I don't know, but since *magu plu* means "to grow feathers, to fledge", this struck me as preferable for both sound and sense to something like "they developed wings".

It was the exclamation at the close of stanza three, however, that presented the greatest problem. *Diriaid yw'r byd!* translates literally as "Ill-fated / Evil / Wretched is the world!" I don't presume to know exactly how this proverbial-sounding phrase strikes a contemporary Welsh reader, with its archaism, its echo of the *contemptus mundi* theme, of Llywarch Hen, Siôn Cent, Pantycelyn. Literally translated it is likely to seem an excessive response, and as if a contemporary poem in English suddenly quoted Chaucer's "Swich fin hath false worldes brotelnesse". Here, I believe, is a case of something Gerallt Jones touched on in his essay, when he wrote that

> . . . in addition to problems which are specifically linguistic, the translator also faces difficulties which might be more properly thought of as sociological . . . it seems still possible and valid to make the kind of direct, explicit statement in a Welsh poem that would no longer be regarded as valid in a conventional English poem. . . . [I]t may sometimes seem necessary, when translating, not only to change the words of the poem but to change its stance as well.[7]

I have experienced the truth of this fairly often in reading modern Welsh poetry. The self-conscious self-questioning ironic stance, distrustful of simple strong emotions, has so permeated poetry in English that it would seem virtually impossible to translate certain Welsh poems, just as it is perhaps impossible to find a poetically satisfying way of translating this phrase. My worksheets show an almost ludicrous effort to arrive at an expression that could carry what is, essentially, a cry of the heart that is the heart of the poem, in such a way that English-language readers would respond appropriately. I tried "How wretched is the world!"; "How grim is the world!"; "So goes the world!"; "So it is with the world!"; "It's the way of the world!"; "It's a wearisome world!"; "Heartless is the world!"; "It's a heartless world!"; "It's a miserable world!"; until at last I hit upon "It's a sorry world!" as perhaps just barely adequate, a change of words and a modification of stance that would not be a complete betrayal of the original.

I was curious to learn how the author himself had dealt with this, and I was amused and a bit envious to discover that he had avoided the problem altogether by changing the exclamation to a statement and substituting the meaning of *amddifad*, from the first line of the next stanza, for *diriaid*, ending this third stanza with "The world's bereft". As, of course, he had every right to do, since it was his poem, but I didn't feel free to follow his lead.

I kept "bereaved" where I thought it belonged, at the end of the first line in the fourth stanza, and I thought it appropriate to reflect the heightened style into which the original poem had moved by inverting the sentence structure: "bereaved / is a lake's civility". Initially I even tried to keep the Welsh nominal sentence form, something I have occasionally found it possible to do in dealing with other poems, by translating *amddifad / gwareiddiad llyn* literally as "bereaved / a lake's civilization". This struck me, though, as unduly awkward, and I accepted the necessity of adding "is". And while "civilization" is the usual meaning of *gwareiddiad,* that not only made for a metrically clumsy line but did not seem quite the right word to convey what the Welsh actually meant. "Civility", in one of its older meanings, offered a better choice, and it contributed an internal rhyme with "dignity" as well. I was pleased to feel that decision was confirmed when I saw that the author had chosen to translate *gwareiddiad* not as "civilization" but as "gentility".

I am usually hesitant to use inverted sentence structure (too hesitant perhaps at times), since contemporary English speech ordinarily achieves emphasis by tone of voice rather than the inversion that is normal in Welsh. *Llariaidd rai oeddynt* in the third line of this stanza, for example, would sound very stilted if translated as "Gentle creatures they were". But with the last line of the stanza, *mwyn a phrydferth dros drych dŵr oedd eu hynt*, while it couldn't be comfortably rendered as "mild and beautiful across the mirror of the water was their course", I did find a way to keep the style appropriately heightened in English: "their progress soft and graceful across water's mirror".

Rather than treat the second half of the poem in as much detail as I have the first, I want to single out a few words and phrases that illuminate still further what happens in the process of poetic translation. The final word in stanza five, for exemple, *bro*, posed a special problem. It always does whenever it is used to mean something more than "region" or "vale"—I have never found a wholly satisfactory way to capture the connotations of the word, its full resonance, in English. The University dictionary does not help much when it lists "neighbourhood" and "native haunt" among its definitions. The best translation I have been able to come up with is "home patch"—and after I had toyed with "taking possession of a homestead" (which was not only metrically awkward but smacked too much, I thought, of American pioneering in the mid and far West), I settled on "claiming possession of a patch" as carrying, I hoped, at least something of the meaning in *meddiannu bro*.

I was able, at one point in stanza six, to reproduce a Welsh syntactic pattern fairly comfortably in English with "keen her concern" for *yn fain ei chonsárn*. In the last line of that stanza Gerallt Jones coined a compound to praise this "tidy organic family" as *meithringell gron*, "a complete nurturing-cell". I couldn't manage to invent an equivalent English compound, but I worked my way, after consulting *Chambers'* definitions of "cell" and then "nucleus", from "a total cell of nurture" through "a nurturing nucleus" to "a nucleus of nurture", and felt, I confess, rather smugly satisfied to have come up with this as the best way to convey the expressiveness of the Welsh compound.

I was less sure about translating *clochdar brain* in the next stanza as "crows' yakking"—was this perhaps too American (I do not feel obliged always to translate modern Welsh into British English, and if Americanisms are more expressive, I am happy to use them, but I try to avoid jarring usage), and too slangy? *Chambers* does not note the word as American, though it does

146 • REFLECTIONS ON TRANSLATION

indicate that "yak" is slang. What finally matters for poetry, though, is expressiveness, and "yakking" seemed to me a good deal more expressive here than "chattering" or "cackling", closer indeed to what the Welsh is expressing in the sound as well as the sense of *clochdar.*

Another noisy bird sounds off in the following line, but I didn't realize this until I looked at Gerallt Jones's version. In blissful ignorance I had translated *malais sgrech y coed* as "the wood's shriek of malice" —I had never come upon *sgrech y coed* before, and it didn't cross my mind that this could be, very expressively indeed, the name of a bird, the Welsh for "jay". Having been put right by the poet, I couldn't resist keeping that racket in by translating the phrase as "jay's shriek of malice".

Translating *trymder deutroed dyn* ("the heaviness of man's two feet") as "man's two heavy feet" was, on the other hand, the result of an immediate and perhaps rather arbitrary decision to avoid the abstraction in this context: Welsh poetry is apparently more comfortable with this than is English. It would have been wrong, however, not to translate the dance of abstract nouns *as* abstract in the last two lines of this stanza, *dycnwch gwastad / eu meithrin a'u twf yn hawlio parhad*, "the constant activity / of their care and their growth affirming continuity": the abstract nouns here have the dignity, the force, the paradoxical concreteness of Chaucer investing his Knight in "Trouthe and honour, freedom and curteisye".

The poem ends with a return to the present and to the plain style of the opening lines. Literally and prosaically, the last two lines say "that I will see, perhaps the next time, a spring / when the geese will never come again back to the lake". I first rendered this as "that I will see, next time perhaps, a spring / when the geese never return again to the lake", thinking it important to end with "lake" as the Welsh poem did with "llyn". But this was not so much plain as flat, was rhythmically wrong, and certainly failed to capture adequately the quiet poignancy of this closing moment, with the speaker's implicit awareness not just of mutability but of his own mortality. So I brought the final line closer to the Welsh by replacing "return" with "come back" and "never" with "not ever", in both instances thereby slowing down and intensifying the line with two successive stressed syllables, and I made "again", with its alliterative echo of "geese", the emphatically last word. As a result, however, the final line was too long—and so, with a change for metre's sake of "spring" to "springtime" and then of "time" to "year" to avoid repetition, I shifted "when" from the beginning of the fourth line to the end of the third, and discovered that this not only improved the rhythm of both lines but produced, quite unexpectedly, a rhyming couplet that now seemed the right, the only, way to close this poem as translation, this translation as poem:

> that I will see, next year perhaps, a springtime when
> the geese will not ever come back to the lake again.

When a friend of the American writer Elmore Leonard remarked that it was a shame how a film version had ruined one of his novels, Leonard pointed to a copy in his bookcase and answered, "They haven't ruined it. It's still there." So it is too with a translation, of this or any other work. As the American poet, critic, and translator Stanley Burnshaw has said, "the words of the original poem remain there, wholly unaffected, looking in several directions at once, giving and receiving echoes, suggestions, and the other qualifications that create the uniqueness of their life".[8] And awaiting, since no translation is ever definitive, the next wild-goose chase.

II

Enabling a reader to compare original with translation in this way and thereby illuminate both is one advantage of parallel texts in bilingual editions, though it is only a small minority of readers who can (or may wish to) enjoy the exercise, and such enjoyment is a by-product rather than the purpose of literary translation. Bilingual editions have, however, become for some publishers the preferred format for translations from Welsh: I've heard both commercial and cultural arguments in favour of this, and not only have recent selections of Euros Bowen's and Waldo Williams's poems, Menna Elfyn's latest collections, and an anthology by Robert Minhinnick been published with facing texts but a new translation of Caradog Prichard's 1961 novel *Un Nos Ola Leuad* was brought out by Penguin in a bilingual edition,[9] while Gwasg Gomer, with its Trosiadau/Translations series that includes both poetry and fiction, intends to publish translations only in this format for the foreseeable future.

I believe, though, that there are reasons for questioning whether such editions are the best way to serve Welsh authors and their translators. And I am concerned less with the commercial aspect than with the aesthetic, with the ways in which bilingual publication may, if not exactly threaten the original work, then create problems in securing for it the widest possible audience, whether this is through literal or literary translation.

Two recent examples of literal translation are bilingual editions of Dafydd ap Gwilym and Iolo Goch—the latter by Dafydd Johnston for Gomer's Welsh Classics series, the former by Rachel Bromwich, also for the Welsh Classics series but subsequently revised for publication by Penguin Books.[10] Both are extremely useful volumes, and I am indebted to both in working on translations for a new anthology of medieval Welsh poetry. Dafydd Johnston's purpose as a translator is stated clearly and modestly: "The translations have no pretension to literary merit in their own right. They are intended merely as an aid to the understanding of the Welsh text, and aim above all at a literal rendering: the sense of the Welsh, as far as that is consonant with good English, has been retained as far as possible".[11] The publishers go further, however, in recommending the book to "the general reader", and Professor Johnston himself expresses the hope that his introduction "will encourage the reader to keep one eye on the Welsh text in order to appreciate some at least of the rich music which is entirely lost in prose translation"[12]—the reader he has in mind is clearly different from those being assisted in reading the fourteenth-century Welsh poems.

The Penguin edition of Dafydd ap Gwilym is even more obviously aimed at both Welsh-speaking and Welshless readers. Rachel Bromwich declares that her purpose "has been two-fold: firstly, to aid the interested student, who may have 'little Welsh' or none, to understand and appreciate the originals, and secondly, hopefully, to introduce some English readers . . . to a distinguished European poet . . . whose achievement fully deserves their sympathetic interest and attention".[13] Dr. Bromwich goes a good deal further than Johnston when she defends "adopting straight prose for my translation, since this is the only means of conveying an approximation to the meaning of the original. . . . I believe that straight prose has been the most successful medium employed by translators of Celtic poetry, both Welsh and Irish, in the present century".[14]

In both cases, the translators have succeeded in providing what Dr. Bromwich calls "serviceable" translations that can assist readers with some command of Welsh "towards the interpretation and appreciation of the originals".[15] But for others? Welshless readers may be intrigued rather than bewildered by the facing pages and willing, on the basis of the scholarly introductions, to accept the status of Dafydd ap Gwilym and Iolo Goch as major poets, but I am very doubtful that in either case the translations themselves, lacking as they do what the Scottish poet and translator Edwin Morgan refers to as "the rhythms and exhilarations necessary for the creation of even translated poetry",[16] will give much pleasure or convince those readers of the quality of the original work.

When the original text is paralleled by a literary translation, it is, of course, a different matter. But here too I question the wisdom of trying to satisfy the needs and interests of two classes of readers. An editor informed me lately that Welsh learners have a great desire for bilingual editions, and perhaps this is true, though I think they would learn more by tackling the Welsh text with dictionary and grammar at their elbows. Fully bilingual readers are likely to find the parallel texts a distraction—when the eye is constantly drawn from one language to the other, one does justice to neither the original nor the translation, and in my experience it requires some effort to concentrate on either text. For completely Welshless readers, a bilingual edition is likely to be a distraction in a different way—it may be good for them to realize, as one author said to me, that Welsh is not simply a dialect of English and that what they are reading is in fact a translation, but the presence of the Welsh text is like having a stranger constantly looking over one's shoulder. In my view literary translation serves not only the intended readers but the original authors best when it is permitted to stand alone, to be, as John Dryden said of his own distinguished translations, "a passable beauty when the original muse is absent."

Translators can be grateful that, ironically, the situation of English as "the majority language" has created a market for translations in Wales itself. I suggest, though, that it would be good for Welsh publishers and others to look outwards as well as inwards more than they appear to do at present, to be more aware that there is now a world market for translations into English. Within the last few decades it is English that has become not only the target language for translation from any other language but also the source language for translations *into* other languages: recent translations of Welsh poetry and prose into Catalan, Italian, German, Czech, Dutch, and Japanese have been based on prior English literary translations. As George Steiner has observed,

> for the nuclear physicist, the banker, the engineer, the diplomat, the statesman, English is the indispensable window on the world. It is fast becoming so for the writer. [For the writer in a 'small language', small in respect of the number of speakers, of the area in which it is spoken,] to go untranslated, and specifically, untranslated into English and/or American English is to run the risk of oblivion. Novelists, playwrights, but even poets—those elect custodians of the irreducibly autonomous—feel this achingly. They *must* be translated if their works . . . are to have a fair chance of coming into the light.[17]

For the "small language" that is Welsh, whose writers are themselves bilingual in a country where 80% of the population cannot use the language, the global status of English may indeed pose a threat as well as offer a promise. That Welsh-language reviewer of my translations some years ago anxiously advised his readers that they would do much better to read the poems in Welsh. He was right, to be sure, but I think translations are no threat in this way to the language—they are more likely to lead a Welsh-language reader back to the original and to tempt a Welshless reader to learn Welsh. It is the necessity of translation in social and political situations for communities where only a minority are truly bilingual that directly threatens the language. Literary translation does not, but it may threaten it indirectly, by threatening the literature.

It might seem that one threat is that the attraction of a much larger readership can lead fluently bilingual writers to practice their craft or sullen art in English rather than in Welsh, but this is a complex matter, as Glyn Jones in English and Alun Llywelyn-Williams in Welsh, Bobi Jones in Welsh and R. S. Thomas in English, have testified. For them as for others, it has not been a question of them choosing a language but of the language choosing them. I wonder though whether there are not potentially gifted youngsters now being bilingually educated for whom English with its global status will seem their natural medium. We are unlikely to have many who become, like Gwyneth Lewis, highly original poets in both languages.

Gwyneth Lewis has said that "self-translation seems to me a very barren activity",[18] and she has usually preferred to have her Welsh-language poems translated by Richard Poole. Self-translation has been increasing lately in Wales, and I've given elsewhere reasons for regarding this as dangerous.[19] Here I will simply cite the strongest argument against self-translation, as remarked to me by my son Thomas, Reader in Celtic at the University of Glasgow: in reading another's translation, one views it and responds to it *as* a translation, but with a self-translation, this essential distinction is lost, so that the reader sees it and responds to it as if it were the original work. When self-translation fails to do justice to the original, as has been in my experience all too often the case, the result is unfortunate. An English reviewer of Menna Elfyn's latest collection rather naively wished that she had translated her own poems: Menna Elfyn is wise enough to know better. The promise offered by translation is most likely to be fulfilled, I suggest, when someone else does the translating.

George Steiner, in his essay on translation from which I've been quoting, noted that

> many writers in such countries as Norway, Denmark, Sweden, in Holland, in Israel, compose their books in the native tongue *and* in 'world-English'. They act either as their own translators or collaborate from the outset of the relevant project with an English-language interpreter. More obliquely . . . writers have, more or less knowingly, angled their work towards an English-speaking market, thus making the hoped-for translation more important, more expectant of echo than is the original. Sensibility bends towards an Anglo-American resonance.[20]

I am doubtful that this has yet become the case with Welsh writers, but it is plainly a possibility, even perhaps a probability, if Welsh-language authors and publishers feel compelled to seek a global market. For the present I find it heartening that such younger poets in Welsh as Iwan Llwyd, Twm Morys, Ifor ap Glyn, Myrddin ap Dafydd, and Geraint Lovgreen, in a collective volume entitled *Syched am Sycharth*,[21] show no signs of having one eye on being translated.

Quite the contrary, in fact. *Syched am Sycharth* has been for me a healthy reminder of the limits of translating, not only because of the poets' frequent use of the translation-resistant traditional Welsh verse-forms of *englyn* and *cywydd*, with their employment of the intricate sound-patterning known as *cynghanedd*, but because even if the poems can be adequately translated, the non-Welsh reader will still encounter what C. S. Lewis once labelled "unshared backgrounds". Take the title—translating it as "Thirst for Sycharth" of course loses the Welsh music, but most importantly, what meaning can the reference to Sycharth have outside Wales? It was the magnificent manor of Owain Glyndŵr, celebrated by Iolo Goch and other poets, destroyed by the English during Glyndŵr's rebellion, and this collection of poems was composed as a celebration and a reminder six centuries later of that rebellion within the context of present-day Wales. And what is true of this volume applies as well to much in contemporary as in earlier Welsh-language poetry: however many footnotes we supply, we cannot expect allusions to Catraeth or Taliesin, Blodeuwedd or Cilmeri, to have the resonance that only comes from a fairly long and deep acquaintance with Welsh literature and history.

I am not, however, arguing against translating a work because of the loss of such resonance. I believe the attempt must be made, footnotes and all, if Welsh poetry is to be fairly presented to non-Welsh readers. And in other ways too I am less concerned with sensibility bending "towards an Anglo-American resonance" in the poets themselves than in translators', editors', and publishers' selection of what is translated. For a good deal of modern Welsh poetry is, to coin a phrase, seriously unfashionable. Consider, for example, in contrast to the ready acceptability for an English-language reader of Gerallt's "Geese at Gregynog", this poem by Alan Llwyd:

CLOCH LLANGYFELACH AR FORE O FAWRTH

Yn gyfeiliant i gloch Llangyfelach,
bregliach y brain
ar fore o Fawrth:
brain du, a'r bore'n dywyll,
yn crawcian uwch tincial uchel y clychau,
brain du yn cecru'n y coed,
a chawod ysgafn o eira'n disgyn
ar y canghennau.

Y gloch brudd a bregliach brain
yn ymrwyfo ar y gwynt, yn ymrafael
a'i gilydd ar y awel rewfain,
fel ewyn gwyn yn taro'n erbyn y nos:
tincial y gloch yn chwalu
uwch y bregliach briglwyd

fel eira'n bwrw
cawod wen dros geinciau du:
nodau crynedig y gloch
yn oerfel y bore'n ymffurfio'n gaenen gynnil
ar y canghennau.

Yn fawl dros Langyfelach,
uchel yw clychau'r eglwys sŵn y bregliach
cyn cilio, pendilio'n dawelach,
cilio wrth ildio i'r baldordd,
cilio ymhell, ond y tincial mud
yn aros,
aros, wrth i'r eira feiriol,
yn nhincial y ceinciau.

LLANGYFELACH'S BELL ON A MARCH MORNING

As accompaniment to the bell of Llangyfelach,
the crows' yakking
on a morning in March:
black crows on a dark morning
squawking above the bells' loud chiming,
black crows squabbling in the trees,
a light shower of snow
descending on the branches.

The solemn bell and the crows' yakking
tumbling on the wind, contending
with each other on the freezing breeze,
like white foam flailing against the night:
the chiming of the bell dissolving
above the hoary-headed yakking,
like snow shedding
a white shower upon black branches:
the quivering notes of the bell
taking form in the morning cold, a delicate film
upon the boughs.

Praise over Llangyfelach,
the church bells loud above the yakking's racket,
before fading, tolling more slowly,
fading in giving way to the gabble,
fading far off, but the silent chiming
remaining,
remaining, with the snow thawing,
in the branches' chiming.

A fine poem, but I cannot think of any contemporary poems in English that behave in quite the same way. W. H. Auden, in his usual binary fashion, employed characters from Shakespeare's *The Tempest* to deal with the relationship in poetry between beauty (Ariel) and truth (Prospero), declaring that "though every poem involves *some* degree of collaboration between Ariel and Prospero, the role of each varies in importance from one poem to another: it is usually possible to say of a poem and, sometimes, of the whole output of a poet, that it is Ariel-dominated or Prospero-dominated".[22] Alan Llwyd's poem is clearly by Auden's definition "Ariel-dominated", in that "if one tries to explain why one likes . . . any poem of this kind, one finds oneself talking about language, the handling of the rhythm, the pattern of vowels and consonants, the placing of caesuras . . . etc".[23] And this would be especially true for discussing the original Welsh poem, with its adaptation to free verse of the strict and complex harmonies of *cynghanedd*, which translation into English can only attempt to suggest. There is more to the poem than its music, to be sure, but the significance of counterpointing the snow's whiteness with the birds' blackness, the church bells' chiming with the crows' gabble—it is in essence a religious poem—is conveyed chiefly *through*, so to speak, the interplay of consonantal patternings and rhymes.

Welsh poetry from its beginnings has tended to be "Ariel-dominated" in this way, something a non-Welsh reader can usually readily accept for the medieval poems. A considerable body of modern Welsh-language poetry, however, continues this tradition, and frequently the pleasure it offers comes from melodic expressiveness rather than freshness of thought and feeling or even, at times, of imaginative language. It should not be thought that such poems, delighting as they do in aural virtuosity, are necessarily superficial, but the problems they pose for a translator are apparent. It is hardly surprising that not many of the best of these poems find their way into English.

There are plenty of modern poems in *cynghanedd* as well as in less demanding forms, including a number by Alan Llwyd, that are, in Auden's terms, "Prospero-dominated", in which "the beautiful verbal element . . . is subordinate in importance to the truth of what is said".[24] They often share, though, some basic characteristics of the "Ariel-dominated" poems. The poets see no need to emphasize individuality—the speaker is sometimes, as in Alan Llwyd's poem, implicit rather than explicit, and in any case is likely to be an everyman rather than an ego. The appeal is in expressing what most of us would think and feel on such an occasion, through, to use Tony Conran's term again, "non-empirical" structure: the speaker assumes shared beliefs and values, and proceeds without uncertainty to celebrate these as incarnate within a particular experience. Such poems are at the opposite pole from Frost's view that a poem should end in "a momentary stay against confusion". They are grounded in a different aesthetic, likely to be foreign to a non-Welsh reader, and something even less easily "translated" than the poem as a verbal artifact.

In an overview of Welsh-language contemporary writing, a major poet whose work however idiosyncratic in style is nonetheless thoroughly in this tradition, Bobi Jones (wearing his critical hat as Professor R. M. Jones), has explained why such poems are still part of the mainstream:

> The thrust of the Welsh poetic tradition of praise has left its mark on contemporaries. The praise posture is still so pervasive that, despite regular tendencies to conform to the English—and even the European—post-imperial norm of irony and defensive scepticism, there seems to be a uniqueness about the Welsh stance that even with the younger generation maintains itself despite inevitable pressures. It is to be detected particularly in three fields: in the bias towards praise of people, in the 'green' nationalist function (which has not only opened up themes of universal significance but given bite to expression), and in the continuity of Christian affirmation (a bias that has maintained seriousness and defended much verse from superficiality). All three would be quite odd from the English perspective.[25]

"Welsh praise," Professor Jones added in that essay, "can be uncomfortably positive and direct".[26] So, I will add in turn, can the other side of the coin, Welsh satire. Uncomfortable or not, it is essential that Welsh praise poetry and its counterpart, satirical poetry, not be lost in selecting poems for translation, however great the temptation by translators and publishers to accommodate to "an Anglo-American resonance". How the non-Welsh reader may respond to poetry that is so blatantly out of sync with the current post-modernist climate is another matter. It may well find a cool reception, a lack of comprehension and appreciation; it is likely to be scornfully described as "pre-modernist". And so, from one perspective, it is, though I prefer like Bobi Jones to see it rather as "post-post-modernist"—better still, to resist such categorizing and hope those readers find in it a realization of poetry's traditional and essential function, to "praise all it can," as Auden said, "for being and for happening".[27]

I have tended, like others before me, to pay more attention to what must and what may be lost in translation, to actual or potential threats rather than to what translation promises. That was probably inevitable, since what can be found, what is promised, access to a rich store of insight and pleasure, to beneficial communication between differing cultures, is obvious. Without translations I would never have discovered Homer and Greek tragedy, Icelandic saga, Goliardic songs, *The Divine Comedy*, Tolstoy, Ibsen, Chekhov, Lorca, Chinese and Japanese, Arabic and Hebrew poetry. Most importantly, without coming upon Gwyn Williams's translations in my college library in

Manhattan some forty-five years ago, I would not have found the poems of Dafydd ap Gwilym and decided I had to learn Welsh, and my life and literary career would have been unimaginably different.

So, to borrow from E. M. Forster's qualified praise for democracy, two cheers for translation—with the full three reserved for those who are keeping literature in Welsh alive, who entertain and enlighten through imaginative use of its language, and who will continue, with or without translation, to follow their demanding and rewarding vocation.

NOTES

An earlier version of this essay was delivered at the Cardiff University Centre for Lifelong Learning conference on "Translations: Wales and Ireland", 3 November 2001. It includes material from an unpublished talk entitled "Gerallt's Geese", given at the conference of the Association for Welsh Writing in English on "Acts of Translation", Plas Gregynog, 17-19 March 2000.

1. George Steiner, "An Exact Art", *No Passion Spent: Essays 1978-1996* (London: Faber, 1996) 202.
2. Steiner 199.
3. Dafydd Johnston, "Introduction", *Modern Poetry in Translation* 7 (Spring 1995): 15.
4. Tony Conran, "Waldo Williams's Three English Poets and England", *New Welsh Review* 11 (Winter 1990-91): 4-9.
5. R. Gerallt Jones, "The Problems of Translation", *Modern Poetry in Translation*: 74.
6. Jones 73.
7. Jones 73.
8. Stanley Burnshaw, *The Seamless Web* (Harmondsworth: Penguin, 1970) 208-9.
9. Euros Bowen, *Priest-Poet / Bardd-Offeiriad*, ed. Cynthia and Saunders Davies (Penarth: Church in Wales Publications, 1993); Waldo Williams, *The Peacemakers: Selected Poems*, trans. Tony Conran (Llandysul: Gomer, 1997); Menna Elfyn, *Cell Angel* (Newcastle upon Tyne: Bloodaxe, 1996) and *Cusan Dyn Dall / Blind Man's Kiss* (Tarset, Northumberland: Bloodaxe, 2001); Robert Minhinnick, *The Adulterer's Tongue* (Manchester: Carcanet, 2003); Caradog Prichard, *One Moonlit Night / Un Nos Ola Leuad*, trans. Philip Mitchell (Harmondsworth: Penguin, 1999).
10. Dafydd Johnston, ed., *Iolo Goch: Poems* (Llandysul: Gomer, 1993); Rachel Bromwich, ed., *Selected Poems of Dafydd ap Gwilym* (Harmondsworth: Penguin, 1985).
11. *Iolo Goch* xxii.
12. *Iolo Goch* xxiii.
13. Bromwich xxvi.
14. Bromwich xxvii.
15. Bromwich xxvii.
16. Edwin Morgan, *Collected Translations* (Manchester: Carcanet, 1996) 185.
17. Steiner 197.
18. *Modern Poetry in Translation* 81.

19. Joseph P. Clancy, "The Value of Translation", *Other Words: Essays on Poetry and Translation* (Cardiff: U. of Wales P., 1999) 120-2.

20. Steiner 197-8.

21. *Syched am Sycharth* (Llanrwst: Gwasg Carreg Gwalch, 2001). One of these poets, Twm Morys, winner of the chair at the National Eisteddfod in 2003, refused permission to include translations of his work in *The Bloodaxe Book of Modern Welsh Poetry*, ed. Menna Elfyn and John Rowland (Tarset, Northumberland: Bloodaxe, 2003), because "he is content to address his Welsh language audience, and regards translation as an aberration", Introduction 23.

22. W. H. Auden, *The Dyer's Hand* (New York: Random House, 1962) 338.

23. Auden 339.

24. Auden 340.

25. R. M. Jones, "The Present Situation", *Guide to Welsh Literature c.1900-c.1996*, ed. Dafydd Johnston (Cardiff: U. of Wales P., 1998) 289.

26. R. M. Jones 290.

27. Auden, "Making, Knowing and Judging", *The Dyer's Hand* 60.

NOTES

T. J. Llewelyn Prichard:
A Manuscript Found

Sam Adams

Thomas Jeffery Llewelyn Prichard, writer and actor, was baptized plain "Thomas Prichard" at the parish church of St. Mary's, Builth, on 29 October 1790. The parish register tells us he was the son of a lawyer, also Thomas Prichard, and his wife, Anne. The same source suggests that the family moved from Builth, or at least severed its connection with the church, after 1791. Place-names mentioned in a poem Prichard included in his most successful book, *Twm Shon Catti*, point to a boyhood spent in the parish of Trallong, near Brecon.[1] Apart from this nothing is known of his upbringing. He turns up next in London, appearing under an assumed name, "Jeffery Llewelyn", as one of the contributors to the *Cambro-Briton*.[2] In 1822 and 1823 he brought out pamphlets of poems as "Thomas Jeffery Llewelyn Prichard".[3] Subsequently, on the title pages of books, on documents and letters, he used versions of this combined name, settling finally on "T. J. Llewelyn Prichard".

There is a good deal of evidence, though none of it conclusive, that he acted at the Theatre Royal, Covent Garden under another name, "Mr Jefferies".[4] He left London with the ambition of making his name and fortune as a writer by returning to Wales to sell his first substantial book of poems, *Welsh Minstrelsy*,[5] but with indifferent success. A scheme to publish, in parts, a guide to the spas of Wales foundered on the apathy and poverty of his chosen audience.[6] Selling from door to door, he made barely enough to cover his expenses. Nevertheless, he married Naomi James in 1826 and, in 1828, while residing at Aberystwyth, published *Twm Shon Catti*. He settled once more in Builth and, over the next decade or so, three of the couple's four children were baptized at St. Mary's, as he had been. He seems to have left the family home after the publication of a second edition of *Twm Shon Catti* in 1839. Correspondents to the "Bye-Gones" column of the *Oswestry Advertiser*[7] in the 1880s bear witness to his having acted on stages at Brecon and Aberystwyth about 1841, and to have been in the employ of Lady Llanover,[8] by which time he had a wax nose, having lost the original, allegedly, in a sword fight.[9] For a long time he was engaged in historical research, in which he was aided by Rev. William Jenkins Rees, the Rector of Cascob, a long-suffering supporter of his ventures, who had a fine library.[10] The outcome was his last hope, *Heroines of Welsh History*.[11] When this ample volume failed to bring him the financial security he sought, he was done for.

The meagreness of the biographical outline offered above serves to confirm that we know very little of Prichard's life—apart from events surrounding his death. He died on 11 January 1862, from (to quote the death certificate) "Burns on the body caused by his clothes accidentally taking fire in his bedroom" two days previously, at a hovel known as "Major Roteley's Cottage, World's End, Swansea". The story will bear repetition.

Some seven weeks earlier, while out walking, "Mr W. Yorath", landlord, we presume, of the "Bird-in-Hand, High-street, Swansea", the address he gave, and good-hearted citizen of the town, came upon a scene that distressed him. He witnessed "a number of ruffians, boys and girls . . . most ruthlessly molesting" a cottage that gave the meanest of shelter to "an aged and infirm old gentleman". He wrote to his local newspaper, *The Cambrian*, describing the scene.[12] The children were "throwing stones in showers at his door and windows, and when he came out and bade them desist, they mercilessly insulted him". Yorath's Samaritan instincts aroused, he must have chased the children off, for he had spoken to the victim and discovered that he was a writer, "author of the 'Heroines of Welsh Poetry' [sic] and other works of considerable note". He urged neighbours, who had probably seen this baiting of the helpless old man before, to call the police if the hooligans returned. Yorath's purpose in writing to *The Cambrian* was to bring Prichard's predicament to the attention of Mr. Dunn, Superintendent of the police, who was a relative newcomer to the town and, if the pattern of the Metropolitan force held good in Wales, may well have been an ex-soldier.

Dunn reported to the magistrates that he had subsequently visited "the late Major Roteley's Cottage" and

a more pitiable and distressing scene he had never witnessed. The unfortunate man was lying on his bed apparently seriously ill, and so far as could be discovered completely destitute; the single room on the ground floor which he inhabited, was as cheerless and as wretched as any Grub-street garret in the last century could possibly have been—a chaos of dirty and dusty books, pamphlets and MSS. in prose and poetry, and scarcely a vestige of furniture, and without provisions of any kind. Among the heap of papers with which the chamber was crammed, were copies of various of Mr. Prichard's published works, and a manuscript volume entitled "Medallions of the Memorable, in a series of historic essays and sonnets". The works in question, both published and unpublished, seem to display considerable literary merit as well as great historical research.[13]

Part of Dunn's mission was to bring Prichard into the workhouse, where (quite widespread evidence suggests) he could have received the medical treatment he needed. The workhouse regime was far less humane in other respects. In 1861, the year before the events described in Swansea, Dickens published *The Uncommercial Traveller*, with its harrowing description of Wapping workhouse. Swansea Union Workhouse, situated near the junction of Mount Pleasant and Terrace Road,[14] may have been less rigid than was common in its interpretation of the Poor Law Amendment Act of 1834, the tacit purpose of which was to create institutions so inexorably harsh that paupers would prefer any hardship outside them to the usually brief existence within.[15] In any event, Prichard would have none of it. *The Cambrian* reported that he "positively refuses an asylum in the Union, declaring that he will starve rather than being an indoor pauper".[16] Whether, as a writer of some note, he was considered a special case it is now impossible to say, but the Board of Guardians agreed to allow him five shillings weekly "outdoor relief" and "Mr Essery, surgeon of the Board" was deputed to oversee the thorough cleaning of the cottage and the provision of a new iron bed, bedding and decent clothes.[17]

The newspaper's editor, Samuel C. Gamwell, a man of some culture, was not satisfied with this improvement in Prichard's circumstances. He sought to raise money for him more widely by inviting contributions from readers, some of whom would surely remember the man or his work. Characteristically, a committee was formed. It had its first meeting, *The Cambrian* tells us, on 27 November 1861, at the home of William Morris, who ran the Stamp Office in the High Street.[18] Gamwell and Morris were certainly acquaintances, perhaps friends, and there were other good reasons for the choice of venue: Morris had a local reputation as a literary gent and already knew Prichard, as the title page of *Heroines of Welsh History* (which names him as one of the publishers) clearly reveals. He would become the key figure in the preservation of some scraps of manuscript among the dirty "chaos" of papers Yorath and Superintendent Dunn had seen at Major Roteley's cottage, and merits a little attention on his own account.

Morris was an aspiring writer. A report of the "Llangollen Grand National Eisteddfod" occupying two full pages of *The Cambrian*, deals in some detail with the Gorsedd ceremony, presided over by the Rev. J. Williams (Ap Ithel), held on Tuesday, 21 September 1858, at which William Morris was admitted as an ovate. He took as his bardic name "Gwilym Tawe" and, "amid much applause", read lines he had composed for the occasion:

> Let each, in submission, express his regards
> To him who presides o'er this "Gorsedd of Bards",

> By the people's free choice, who in Powys's chair
> Has been called NOW the rod of the umpire to bear.
> May "God and his peace" o'er this Eisteddfod reign,
> And justice be done, so that none may complain.[19]

It is easy to see how a versifier of such quality could be an admirer of Prichard's art. Morris was then a keen eisteddfodwr,[20] and also an occasional contributor of poems to *The Cambrian* and lecturer at the Royal Institution of South Wales (which later became Swansea Museum).[21] Furthermore, in his official capacity at the Stamp Office, he was prominent in the business community.

The Stamp Acts required that certain goods, notably newspapers and pamphlets, be stamped, the fee for the stamp going to the government. The law gave government oversight of the products thus regulated and, by increasing prices, restricted their popular appeal: in 1815 the fee was a staggering four pence per copy. In 1836 it was reduced to one penny and in 1855 it was abolished, but by this time, Morris had become involved in commercial and property interests.[22] His duties at the Stamp Office also gave Morris connections with printing and publishing that he was not slow to exploit. He published an *1861 Swansea Almanack*, a guide to the town and its businesses, and in 1862 successfully tendered for the printing work of Swansea Corporation, beating the proprietors of *The Cambrian*.[23]

It is impossible to tell now precisely what Morris did as one of the listed "publishers" of *Heroines of Welsh History*, along with W. and F. G. Cash of London and C. T. Jefferies of Bristol. They may well have been jointly responsible for financing the printing of the book—at almost six hundred pages no mere trifle. Marketing it remained the writer's responsibility and, while he was in good health, Prichard sold it, as had long been his custom, by knocking on doors. Each copy cost him three shillings and it was priced at seven shillings and sixpence to the customer, when he could find one. This we gather from a letter to an unknown correspondent, dated 24 November 1857, included in Charles Wilkins's account of meeting Prichard.[24] He would request parcels of the book to be sent to the Post Office at the next destination on his list and, with a dozen or so copies in his pack, set out on his selling, but with scant success.

Morris also knew Major Roteley, Prichard's landlord, who had served on the *Victory* at Trafalgar and was a well-known Swansea character.[25] Both were members of the Swansea Association for the Prosecution of Felons.[26] Prichard might have become acquainted with Roteley because of a shared enthusiasm for the theatre: the major is reputed to have performed Shakespearian roles on the stage at Swansea. The suspicion remains that he was living in "Major Roteley's cottage"[27] as a result of his connection with Morris—who should therefore have been aware of his plight and may have chosen to ignore it. It would be consistent with what we know of the writer's soured relationship with Lady Llanover[28] that whatever arrangement he and Morris came to over the publication of *Heroines of Welsh History* had in the end gone wrong and left Prichard sick, friendless and alone.

Nevertheless, Morris had an important part in the brief remission from despair granted to Prichard at the turn of 1861. As a member (perhaps chairman) of the committee set up to organize aid for Prichard, Morris would have visited the newly-cleaned cottage and examined what had been salvaged from the litter of books, pamphlets and manuscripts. Ap Thomas, an otherwise unknown *Bye-Gones* correspondent,[29] refers to Prichard's "literary executor . . . a gentleman residing at Page Street, Swansea" and we can now link that address to Morris because the one item named in Mr. Dunn's report to the magistrates, "Medallions of the Memorable", has come to light.

Suspicion that some trace of Prichard still lay in Swansea, and that the connection with Morris might be significant, hardened to confidence during the time I was engaged upon the Writers of Wales monograph on the writer. Several months after its publication, I reopened the quest at Swansea Library, where the Cambrian Indexing Project, an inestimable boon to researchers, disclosed Morris's literary and business interests. Soon afterwards I approached the West Glamorgan Archive Service and, at their suggestion, Swansea Museum. The archive holds nothing on either Prichard or Morris but, rather to their surprise, librarians at the museum turned up a slim volume, eight inches by five, bound in dark blue buckram, the upper board detached. The paper is thick and glossy and the first page, framed in blue rules, bears the title "Medallions / of the / Memorable / in a series of / Historic Sonnets / By T. J. Llewelyn Prichard" followed by a four-line epigraph from Horace Walpole.[30] The early history of the manuscript is revealed by a cancelled line immediately beneath the main title, "A Pen-Pictured Annual for 1842". The text throughout is neatly written, though cramped here and there, sonnets on the right hand page and accompanying explanatory essays on the left. The pages are not numbered but, like the title page, each is bordered on all sides by blue rules. The manuscript may be a fair copy prepared for publication, or perhaps a curious mixture of doubt (that it would ever be published) and vanity prompted Prichard to give so much time to its making.

Inside the detached cover is a bookplate printed for formal presentation of the manuscript to Swansea Museum: "From the library of the late Mr. Samuel C. Gamwell, late Editor of the Cambrian Newspaper (presented by his wife Feb. 1897)". However, the flyleaf bears the faint inscription: "W. Morris, 17 Page Street, Swansea". This serves to confirm that the manuscript had previously been in the possession of William Morris, and that Morris's home was in Page Street.[31] There can be little doubt either that it had been acquired directly from Prichard in the last weeks of 1861 or early in 1862, when Morris was a member of the committee set up to rescue the writer from penury, for that fits the statement by Ap Thomas in *Bye-Gones*.

Furthermore, it now seems incontrovertible that the "literary and patriotic gentleman of independent means then living in Glamorganshire" (mentioned in the note added by the publisher, John Pryse of Llanidloes, to the posthumous third edition of *Twm Shon Catty*[32]) to whom Prichard "previous to his death made over, by a properly constructed deed of sale, all his MSS and Copyrights" is also Morris. In the same note, Pryse spares himself the task of writing a few details about Prichard's life by saying that the same "benevolent gentleman" who had long been "one of Mr. Prichard's kindest and best friends" planned to write "a biographical account of the author's life". This may have been the intention, but nothing came of it.

The purchase of Prichard's copyrights turned out to be more an act of renewed friendship than a shrewd investment. As we have seen, "Medallions" remained unpublished and Morris waited eleven years or so before putting *Twm Shon Catty* into the hands of a printer. If he made any money out of the latter venture, he did not live long to enjoy it. On the last day of 1875, *The Cambrian* reported the death on 26 December "at Page Street, Swansea, of William Morris (late of the Stamp Office) aged 60 years".[33]

"Medallions of the Memorable" contains forty-four sonnets, all evidently written before 1842, when Prichard completed the manuscript and added that description "A Pen-Pictured Annual for 1842" to the title. The phrase and, indeed, the appearance of the manuscript, indicate completion so far as the writer was concerned and perhaps optimism that it could bring him a little profit from the 1842 Christmas book market.[34] But it was not published and a glance at the contents may explain why. There are no topical poems about memorable contemporaries that might have aroused interest, and few opportunities for the writer to exploit his strength as a satirist. Humour is entirely absent. Rather, the collection confirms Prichard as an avid reader of poetry and histories. He was afflicted with a reverence for history that, in the end, did him no good. In the letter quoted by Wilkins, Prichard laments the commercial failure of *Heroines of Welsh History* "which, I regret to say, is far from meeting with similar popularity to that accorded to Twm Shon Catty— although it deserves it far more, being Historical".[35] His sonnets take themes from Rome, from medieval France and Spain and, oddly one might think, from Russia, which seems to have been a special interest.[36] His Welsh subjects are "Arthur Johnes's Translation of the Welsh Bard Davydd ab Gwilym" [sic], the Tudors, "Henry VIII", "Mary Tudor" and "Elizabeth",

"Tydvil" [sic] and "Gwenllian". The number of women in this small group is some indication of the gender balance overall: no fewer than sixteen of the titles bear the names of women.[37]

Twelve sonnets are concerned with poetry; individual poets are named in the titles of ten. The essay that accompanies the sonnet on "The Portable Poets" (that is, those whose works may be conveniently carried in a pocket to provide companionship on a walk) is a robust sally on behalf of the cultivated mind, though the civilizing influence of poetry does not extend to the ruder element in society:

> To speak of Poets and Poetry to those ignoble nobles, and ungentle gentlemen, who in spite of their stamp of caste, betray their native plebianism by their daily haunts and habits, were as ridiculous and out of place as to discourse with the red Indian on the beauty of civilization and the triumph of the fine arts. What is poetry or the Poet's fate to them? Their kindness is towards the kennel; their delight in the dog-fight, or the bull-bait; their raptures in the race-course and the prize-ring; where the slang of the blaguard [sic] and the cant of the felon has been rendered fashionable by their adoption. No, black-legs and black-letter are not more opposed to each other than the wrenchers of door-knockers and assaulters of Police, to the humanizing sons of song. . . .
>
> After all, to particularize the Poets by name, ought to be unnecessary; as, in the present cheapness of literature, a complete edition of Poets and Essayists, from the days of Chaucer to our own, should be found in the possession of everyone who aspires to the honors [sic] of a cultivated mind. Such an acquisition, for use more than ornament; for the table more than the dusty shelves of a library; with passages of the quotable beauties marked with the pen, according to the recommendation of Watts, would effect more towards regenerating the manners, and re-invigorating the decaying taste of our times, than any Satires that could be written on such interesting subjects.

Dante and Petrarch feature together in one sonnet, and Petrarch is honoured again in celebration of his part in the recovery of Latin literature. Among the English poets individually honoured are Falconer, now rarely heard of, others hardly better known, such as Prior, Savage and Churchill, and some, such as Chatterton, Goldsmith and Dryden, whose names are still familiar, though they may be now little read.[38]

A few examples will be sufficient to provide a flavour of the whole. Prichard is no prose stylist and the essays would not be read for their intrinsic charm. What merit they have chiefly resides in what they tell us about Prichard's reading, the subjects that attracted him and the pains he took as a researcher. His writing becomes interesting when he is most personally engaged. Anger, especially at the exploitation of the poor and vulnerable by the rich, and at the incomprehensible neglect of deserving relatives in the wills of richer family members, stirred him to a fluent vehemence that has the power to animate readers. Richard Savage, for example, aroused his sympathy, and the strength of his emotion is evident in the essay and the poem:

"Fact is strange—more strange than fiction;" and we may add, the life of the poet Savage is one of the most wonderful of narratives amongst facts and fictions. As Dr. Johnson's life of this unhappy poet is so easily attained, we need not mar that splendid piece of biography further than to give something like a table of its contents. The misfortunes of Savage may be said to have commenced even before his birth. In the year 1697 his mother, the Countess of Macclesfield, in order to get divorced from her husband whom she hated, made a public confession of adultery, naming Earl Rivers as the father of her unborn child. That noble man owned him accordingly, stood for his godfather, and gave him his own family name of Richard Savage. The worthless wife became the most unnatural of mothers; she sent her infant to be nursed by a poor woman who was charged to rear him as her own, in ignorance and obscurity, nor ever to inform him of his birth. Through the kindness of Lady Mason—his maternal grandmother, he was educated at a grammar school near St Albans where he was known only by his nurse's name. Earl Rivers on his deathbed desirous of making a provision for him, would have bequeathed £6,000, but was informed by his mother that he was dead. "This was," says Dr. Johnson, "the first instance of a lie invented by a mother to ruin her son without enriching herself." To rid herself from the danger of being at any future time made known to him, an attempt was made, at her initiative, to get him kidnapped and sent off to convict slavery in the American plantations. This scheme failing, she determined on burying him in poverty and obscurity; to which end she placed him with a shoemaker in Holborn, where he worked at the trade as his apprentice. His nurse, whom he considered his mother, died soon after; and on taking possession of her humble property he discovered by certain letters, the secret of his birth, and the reason of its concealment. His application to another soon followed; but as every art to soften her heart or open her hand proved in vain, being reduced to the utmost extremity of want, and having no profession, by necessity he became an author. The great misfortune of his life happened on the 21st Novemr. 1727. In a quarrel that took place at a tavern between a party opposed to him and his friends it was his unhappy lot to wound his opponent with his sword, of which he died. For this he was tried and condemned to death. When a pardon was solicited for him from the queen, he had to learn to his horror that his mother had been doing her best to get him hanged by declaring him a dangerous character—and that he had one night entered her house secretly with the intent to murder her. It was at this perilous crisis of his life that the Countess of Hereford, who had learned the whole particulars of his life, placed the unhappy affair in its true light before the queen, who not only caused him to be pardoned, but allowed him a small pension during his life. By his spirited poem the Bastard his mother from Society. [sic] By his severe satire called London and Bristol delineated he drew on himself the hostility of the Bristolians. A merchant of that ancient city was found, base and cruel enough to buy up the poor poet's debts, on which he cast him into prison; where soon after, in extreme poverty but unsubdued spirit, he died; and this eminent poet and man of eventful life was buried like the meanest pauper in the common prison ground.

The Poet Savage

Wild truths that cast care's fictions into shade
Thy life—the very martyrdom of song,
Stern poverty was thine;—thy struggles strong
Rose thee a hero, by the Muse's aid:
And thou didst greatly grapple with thy fate,
And master'd Murder, and a mother's hate;
But wander'd o'er the earth a homeless wretch:—
Yet Pity wept for thee—and lent her lyre—
And thou didst touch it with a master's fire,
While Admiration did the strains beseech
Till Rapture shouted plaudits. Though lowly laid
Within a prison's tainted ground, thy wrongs
And matchless sufferings that to faults betray'd
Could not obscure thy name—for genius nerv'd thy songs.

Prichard was clearly ambitious to be a sonneteer: a sonnet about manliness and talent blighted by poverty stands as a bitter and personal epigraph to the long sequence "The Noble of Nature" in *Welsh Minstrelsy*. He practised the form more assiduously for this project but, as that quoted above clearly shows, is not comfortable in it: his metrical skill was limited.

Unexpectedly, in one respect he approaches our own contemporary concerns. As might be guessed from the opening paragraph of the essay on "The Portable Poets" above, he was an early environmentalist, opposed to the pleasures of the chase. If he were still with us, he would be found in the anti-hunting lobby. A brief essay and the sonnet "Lewchew"[39] (one of his better efforts) confirm his affectionate regard for God's creatures and conservationist credentials:

From McLeod's "Voyage of the Alceste" we learn that among the many virtues which distinguish the amiable Islanders of Lewchew, their tenderness towards the dumb creation is not the least to be admired. "When they observed the effect of our fowling pieces in the hands of some of our gentlemen, they begged they might not kill the birds, which they were always glad to see flying about their houses; and if we required to eat, they would send in their stead an additional quantity of fowls every day. An order was immediately issued to desist from this sort of sporting."

Lewchew

"Kill not our birds good strangers; if ye need
Flesh for food, we'll send ye goodly fare;
Refrain in kindness, and in pity spare,
Nor let the innocent in anguish bleed;
We love the tuneful tenants of the air,

And muse to see them on the wing of speed;
Kill not our birds, good strangers—'twere a deed
Our children could not love ye for—for they
Compassionately weep whene'er they heed
The meek birds stricken by the beak of prey."
Such were the words the men of Lewchew used,
When Englishmen, for sport forsooth! destroy'd
The harmless creatures that the air enjoy'd
And thus, to foreign hearts great England's name abused.

As a whole, the collection hardly merits publication. That may have been the conclusion Prichard, too, reached—though it would imply unusual freedom from self-delusion. As we have seen, the manuscript tells us about (or, rather, confirms) certain characteristic Prichard attitudes and interests and little more. Yet, it is also a rare (probably unique) thing: a surviving fragment, in his own hand, of the creative endeavour of one of the earliest Welsh writers in English to have a conscious awareness of his linguistic medium and his audience. The preface and several footnotes in *Heroines* debate the relative value and status of Welsh and English, invariably favouring the latter at the expense of the former. The notes on pp. 374-75 are particularly relevant. For example: "Happily the English writers of Wales, however opposed by the sticklers for the supremacy of the Welsh language, have met with due encouragement these many years past, and goodly fruit they have borne . . . " Much earlier he described the contents of one of his pamphlets as "English-Welsh blossoms . . . hastily formed into a bouquet".[40]

One cannot help wondering how he survived from day to day. About the time he was completing "Medallions of the Memorable", he might have been on a selling tour with the second edition of *Twm Shon Catty* (1839). But then again he might not, since there is more than a hint that he had sold the copyright to a certain "E. Pool[e]".[41] Prichard was not resident with his family in Builth for the 1841 census nor when the birth of his last child, Llewelyn Felix, was registered in March of that year by Naomi Prichard. Thereafter we are reliant on the memories of the correspondents to *Bye-Gones*, and Charles Wilkins's recollection of meeting Prichard in the later 1850s, struggling with his wax nose and his burden of unsaleable books. Prichard's labour on *Heroines of Welsh History* shows that he long harboured a hope of gaining a fortune by his pen, but it was forlorn and ultimately dashed by a combination of the poverty and lack of interest in history of his readership, the rural and industrial working class of south Wales. And so, at last, he declined to the abject state in which Mr Yorath and *The Cambrian* found him, at that most desolate spot, "World's End", Swansea.

NOTES

1. *The Adventures and Vagaries of Twm Shon Catti; descriptive of life in Wales: interspersed with poems*, 1828. In his preface to the second edition (Cowbridge: J. T. Jones, 1839) Prichard thanks, among others, Archdeacon Beynon of Llandeilo, who, in the Town Hall at Carmarthen, "warmly eulogised the Author's attempt at the production of the first Welsh novel". On this claim, see Andrew Davies, "From Fictional Nation to National Fiction? Reconsidering T. J. Llewelyn Prichard's *The Adventures and Vagaries of Twm Shon Catti*", *Welsh Writing in English: A Yearbook of Critical Essays* 8 (2003): 1-28.
2. A short-lived journal (1820-23) edited by John Humffreys Parry, dedicated to the language, history and culture of Wales.
3. *My Lowly Love and other petite poems, chiefly on Welsh Subjects* (Worthing: William Phillips, 1822) and *Mariette Mouline, the Death of Glendower, and other poems, partly on Welsh Subjects* (London: W. Hersee, 1823).
4. In the Writers of Wales monograph *Thomas Jeffery Llewelyn Prichard* (Cardiff: U. of Wales P., 2000) 61-3, I bring together such evidence as is available and suggest, for example, that the publication of the pamphlet *My Lowly Love* in Worthing coincides with the six weeks in 1822 that "Mr Jefferies" was absent from his usual roles at the Theatre Royal, Covent Garden.
5. *Welsh Minstrelsy: containing The Land Beneath the Sea; or, Cantref y Gwaelod, a poem in three cantos; with various other poems* (London: John and H. L. Hunt, 1824; printed by John Cox, Aberystwyth).
6. *The Cambrian Balnea: or guide to the watering places of Wales, marine and inland* (London: John and H. L. Hunt, 1825), actually printed in Wales, probably in Aberystwyth by Cox. The title pages of copies held at Cardiff City Library differ; one gives the printer as "E Nicholas, Printer, Newport", another "Price, Printer, Hay".
7. *The Oswestry and Border Counties Advertiser* is a weekly, launched in 1849 by the brothers, William and John Roberts. It continues to be published and is currently also available on-line. In the nineteenth century, its "Bye-Gones" column was reprinted in quarterly parts and often bound, with an index, in annual volumes. The column continued with some interruptions to 1931.
8. *Bye-Gones relating to Wales and the Border Counties*: the relevant references to Prichard occur in the volumes for 1880-81 and 1882-83. Responding to an earlier query, "F.S.A." (Vol.V, 2 Nov. 1881: 350) testifies that he had seen Prichard on stage at the Brecon theatre in 1841; "Ceredig Cyfeiliog", another correspondent, (Vol.VI, 22 March 1882: 34) tells of meeting Prichard, who was already wearing a false nose, at Llanover, where he was employed by the then Lady Hall to draw up a catalogue of the printed books in her library, and also mentions "well-remembered" stage performances by Prichard at the Assembly Rooms in Aberystwyth.
9. Charles Wilkins, "Men Whom I Have Known", *Cymru Fu* II, Pt.V (July-Dec 1889): 80.
10. Rees was an antiquary (elected F.S.A. in 1840) and on the editorial board of the Welsh MSS Society. His library included the MS of the Genealogies of Thomas Jones J.P. of Tregaron, the historical Twm Shon Catti, now held in Cardiff Central Library (MS 2.136 Cardiff 59), where it is part of the extensive Tonn collection. In a letter dated 4 April 1826 Prichard thanks Rees profusely for access to his "rare and valuable books" (W. J. Rees Correspondence Tonn MS 3.104).

11. *The Heroines of Welsh History: Comprising Memoirs and Biographical Notices of the Celebrated Women of Wales etc.* (London: W. and F. G. Cash; Bristol: C. T. Jefferies; Swansea: William Morris, 1854).

12. *The Cambrian* 22 November 1861: 5, under the heading "A Case of Real Distress". The newspaper came out weekly, on Fridays. Its circulation extended far beyond the town of Swansea.

13. *The Cambrian* 22 November 1861: 5. Dunn's report appears in the same column as Yorath's letter:

14. Later in the nineteenth century it became Mount Pleasant Hospital. In 1997, after lying derelict for a time, the accommodation was refurbished and transformed into apartments.

15. The extent and depth of poverty were such that the horrors of the workhouse regime did not serve to decrease numbers of inmates. In 1838, the 443 Unions in England and Wales held 78,536 paupers; in 1843 there were 197,179. See E.P. Thompson, *The Making of the English Working Class* (Harmondsworth: Penguin, 1968) 296.

16. *The Cambrian* 22 November 1861: 5: the conclusion of Dunn's report.

17. *The Cambrian* 29 November 1861: 5, under the heading "Mr. Llewelyn Prichard".

18. The column identified in the preceding note also tells us that the meeting was held "Wednesday evening last", that is 27 November.

19. *The Cambrian* 8 October 1858: 6-7.

20. *The Cambrian* reveals that he gave addresses at the Aberavon eisteddfod (24 June 1853: 5) and the Aberdare National (23 August 1861: 5-6); won prizes in literary competitions at eisteddfodau in London (27 July 1855: 6) and Ystalyfera (29 June 1860: 8); attended a National Eisteddfod Council meeting in Shrewsbury (24 April 1863: 6), and bought the old wooden eisteddfod pavilion (26 February 1864: 5)!

21. The Royal Institution of South Wales was founded in 1835 as the Swansea Philosophical and Literary Society. Its founding members included three Fellows of the Royal Society: Lewis Weston Dillwyn, John Gwyn Jeffreys and William Grove. The building, now the museum, which became its base was opened in 1841. See Glanmor Williams, ed., *Swansea—an illustrated history* (Swansea: Christopher Davies, 1990) 161.

22. From 1852 he was trustee or director of a clutch of building societies (*The Cambrian* 25 June 1852: 2; 29 October 1852: 2; 5 July 1867: 1) and agent for an insurance company (*The Cambrian* 2 January 1852: 2). In 1861 he was nominated as one of the new income tax commissioners (*The Cambrian,* 1 November 1861: 5).

23. *The Cambrian* 15 August 1862: 2.

24. Charles Wilkins, "Men Whom I Have Known", *Cymru Fu* II, Pt. V (July-Dec. 1889): 80-81.

25. Information, or gossip, about Major Roteley is contained in an anonymous and unpublished account of nineteenth-century Swansea in the possession of Michael Gibbs of Swansea Museum.

26. *The Cambrian* 1 February 1861: 8.

27. The cottage, at the junction of Thomas Street and Edward Street, was destroyed by bombing during the Second World War or bulldozed subsequently. Its former location is somewhere under the car park to the south of the Quadrant shopping centre.

28. "Ceredig Cyfeiliog" informs us that Prichard was employed at Llanover (see note 8 above). The evidence that he quarrelled with Lady Llanover is to be found in

Charles Wilkins's account of his meeting with the writer (*Cymru Fu* II, Part V (July-Dec 1889): 80), and in the dedication and preface to *Heroines of Welsh History*. In both cases it is coded. Wilkins has Prichard "declaiming against the narrow-souled inheritor of riches who wouldn't help him" and refers to "his patron", who at first encouraged him but then began to find fault with "the great historic work" on which he was engaged: "He had to choose between historic accuracy or the entire withdrawal of his patron's support. He was not required to make false statements, but to slur over facts. And this he would not do". Prichard dedicated *Heroines* to "The Virtuous Votaries of True Womanhood ... As Contra-Distinguished From The Fantastic Fooleries And Artificial Characteristics Of Fine Ladyism In the Middle Walks Of Life", and begins his preface with an attack on "Certain parties in our principality, who may be designated The Fanatics of Welsh Nationality". See also the Writers of Wales essay on Prichard, 90-92.

29. *Bye-Gones* Vol. V (14 Dec. 1881): 347.
30. The manuscript bears the catalogue number RISW 34-28.
31. The house, which is inconspicuous, still stands.
32. "*The Adventures & Vagaries Of Twm Shon Catty, Alias Thomas Jones, Esq., Of Tregaron, A Wild Wag Of Wales* by J. T. [sic] Llewelyn Prichard, Third Edition With Additions . . . Now First Printed From MSS Left By The Author . . . Llanidloes: Printed And Published By John Pryse, 1873". The spelling "Catty" rather than "Catti" was introduced at the second edition (1839).
33. *The Cambrian*, 31 December 1875: 12
34. The "annual" was already a regular feature of the book market. Thomas Hood's *Comic Annual*, for example, came out about Christmas and kept him and his family, though in no great style, for the rest of the year.
35. Charles Wilkins, "Men Whom I have Known', *Cymru Fu* II, Part V (July-Dec. 1889): 81.
36. In the same letter of 24 November 1857, quoted in Charles Wilkins's article, Prichard mentions the work he has done "towards future publications—especially one which will bear the title of / Raps At The Russians". If this was written, it seems not to have survived.
37. This is consistent with his later decision to concentrate upon the "heroines" of Welsh history.
38. William Falconer (1732-69); Matthew Prior (1664-1721); Richard Savage (c. 1697-1743); Charles Churchill (1732-64); Thomas Chatterton (1752-70); Oliver Goldsmith (?1730-74); John Dryden (1631-1700). Poets of the nineteenth century are strangely absent.
39. John MacLeod, *Narrative of a Voyage, in his Majesty's late ship Alceste, to the Yellow Sea, along the coast of Corea ... to the island of Lewchew etc.* (London, John Murray, 1817). The "island of Lew Chew" had long been of interest to Prichard; a poem so entitled appears in *Welsh Minstrelsy*, 195-98, together with an accompanying note, 304-5.
40. See the preface to *Aberystwyth in Miniature in Various Poems*; Carmarthen: printed by Jonathan Harris, 1824.
41. Although the agreement with the printer, J. T. Jones of Cowbridge, was signed by Prichard, the book was printed "For E. Pool", probably the "Edward Poole", then or later ordained in the Anglican priesthood, who lodged with Prichard's wife, Naomi, at the time of the 1841 census and lived next door to Prichard's family in Builth at the time of the 1851 census.

"The lesser of the least": Elizabeth Davies (c.1769-1857), an Anglo-Welsh *bardd gwlad*

Sally Roberts Jones

University of Wales, Swansea

O ne of the advantages of the change in terminology from "Anglo-Welsh literature" to "Welsh writing in English" has been that it allows for the growth of interest in English-language writers in Wales before 1915; the Gothic novelists of the eighteenth and early nineteenth centuries have been studied by Moira Dearnley, Jane Aaron and others, and there have been studies too of what might, in contrast, be called their "realist" successors: Anne Beale, Amy Dillwyn and Allen Raine.[1] Very often these writers are of interest for their socio-political significance as much as for their purely literary achievements, but this is not unusual in the literatures of smaller countries. English literature, like Italian art, is an exception to the rules in that it is so rich in both quality and quantity that critical study has no need to look beyond the aesthetic dimension.

The prime essential for almost all writers is an audience, and one reason why the beginnings of Anglo-Welsh literature have sometimes been placed so late was the assumption that until the early twentieth century there was no sufficient English-using community to act as an audience—or if there was one, it was confined to the gentry and clerisy. There is a certain truth in this; the educational pressure for ordinary men and women—the *gwerin*—to learn English did not really come into being until after the infamous Blue Books episode of 1848, and the circulating schools which had earlier helped to create a literate public were basically Welsh-language institutions. On the other hand there were areas such as the Vale of Neath which were industrialized from a very early date; at first the English-speaking element resulting from this came largely from the upper and professional classes, but by the later eighteenth century a new English-language audience had begun to arrive, in the shape of navvies and other workmen brought in to build and man the canals and ironworks now mushrooming from Resolven to Pyle. Some moved on when their job was finished, but many stayed, married local girls and started families. These were the audience—"the working class of people"—for whom Elizabeth Davies of Neath wrote and who inspired what was probably her first appearance in print.[2]

She was born Elizabeth Jenkins in about 1769, the daughter of Richard Jenkins of the Paper Mill, Llangyfelach; in a letter to George Tennant of Cadoxton she described her father as a "gentleman", but he was most probably a farmer with a coal level on his land and entrepreneurial ambitions.[3] While Elizabeth was still young, her father went into business as a colliery owner and canal builder, but with no great success, and when he died, on 14 August 1788, of a chill caught by walking on boggy ground, her mother was left destitute, with six children. Elizabeth was about nineteen years old at the time and what happened to her next is unknown, but at some point between 1788 and 1824 she married a Mr. Davies and went into business as the proprietor of a sweetshop in Wind Street, Neath. She had also begun to write poems and ballads on local subjects. Very little is known so far about her later life, but she was a widow by the 1851 census, when she is listed as a pauper, and was living in the Almshouse in Water Street, Neath; she died in the Union Workhouse on 27 April 1857, aged eighty-eight.[4] (She was probably moved to the Workhouse because she became ill; there would have been no medical facilities in the Almshouse.) She had still been busy writing as late as 1850, and apparently travelling to Swansea, since her ballad on the opening of the South Wales Railway in 1850 suggests personal knowledge of the great occasion.

At the moment there appear to be some twenty of Davies's poems extant. The earliest dated example is her ballad on the Neath and Red Jacket Canal, written on 1 March 1824, but it is possible that her poem to the memory of Peter Price, the Quaker ironmaster of Neath Abbey, was written earlier; Price himself died in 1821, and though his widow, Anna, did not die until 1845, stanzas V and VI suggest that her bereavement was fairly recent:

> In harmony and peace and frugal fare,
> For many years, lived this happy pair;
> 'Till he was summon'd from this vale of woe,
> He left his faithful partner here below.
>
> Tho' she has parted with her earthly prop,
> She does not mourn like those who have no hope;
> Tho' earth is closed around the mortal frame.
> The spirit's gone to God from whence it came.

After the Neath Canal ballad there is a gap until 1845, in which year Davies produced "Lines on the Passing of the South Wales Railway Bill in the House of Lords"; the poem was dedicated to I.K. Brunel, Esq, and went into at least two editions. Although Davies appreciates the economic and social results of the passing of the bill—employment, cheap foreign food, the rush for shares in the railway—she also celebrates the lighter moments:

> Now to and fro we'll jaunting go
> With mirth and joy abound,
> Like lightning fly o'er the railway
> To see the country round:
> And telling tales through all South Wales
> What we have heard and seen.
> The bill hath pass'd the lords at last
> Signed by the British Queen.

Next we have a cluster of ballads and lyrics dating from 1849-50. Ten of the twenty surviving poems are, or can be, dated; these are mostly celebrations of public events or elegies for the departed. Thirteen poem sheets were printed by Whittington of Neath, the two earliest were by printers in Swansea, and one of the two Welsh-language poems was published by Francis of Neath (the other merely says "Printed for the Author"). Her more lyrical poems are mostly undated, or dated only by being included with a dated poem. Since it is highly unlikely that she wrote nothing between 1824 and 1845, it is evident that what has survived is only part of her total output, and the fact that most of the surviving sheets were printed by Whittington suggests that this was a factor in that survival. Certainly D. Rhys Phillips, whose exhaustive *History of the Vale of Neath* provides most of our information about Davies, was given his own set of ten of her poems in about 1894 by Walter Whittington.

Though the Neath Canal ballad is certainly not Davies's best work, it may well be the reason why her work came to be printed. The ballad had evidently been circulating in manuscript and, on 1 February 1825, Davies wrote to George Tennant of Cadoxton Lodge, the man behind the new canal, to ask for permission to have the verses printed. The canal had opened to traffic the previous May, and Davies had been inspired to compose a poem about it while she was walking along the newly-constructed towpath shortly before the opening. In her letter to Tennant she comments modestly that she "did not think they [her verses] would be noticed", but the "working class" had been much pleased with them, and had asked her to have them printed. It would seem that the gender of the poet was no barrier to success with what was, presumably, a largely male audience.

It has to be conceded that the verses are not great literature—as the poet herself freely admitted: "there is nothing in them but plain simple truth that suits [the workers'] taste and understanding better than the fine language of the great authors". On the other hand, to read them on the page does them less than justice; what seems awkward written down, flows relatively smoothly when read aloud. The complete ballad is nineteen stanzas in length, but these four give an idea of the style and content:

1. O! Could I make verses with humour and wit,
   George Tennant, Esquire's great genius to fit;
   From morn until even, I would sit down and tell,
   And sing in the praise of Neath Junction Canal.

2. To his noble genius, great merit is due,
   The increase of traffic he'll daily pursue;
   Employ to poor Labourers, it is known full well,
   He gave them by making Neath Junction Canal. . . .

5. Where two crystal rivers in union do meet,
   The skill of the builder must be very great;
   All for to contend with the torrents that swell,
   By building the arches of Neath Junction Canal. . . .

8. All you that are lovers of gazing around
   On the grand work of nature where 'tis to be found,
   Rich woods, pleasant valleys, groves, rocks, hill and dell,
   You can view as you walk by Neath Junction Canal.

It is the repetition in the last line of each stanza that gives the ballad what one assumes to be its unconsciously comic effect, but it does also suggest that Davies's reading may have included Ann of Swansea's ode, "Swansea Bay", which uses a similar device, and would have been available to the Neath poet.[5] Was this an example of the "fine language of the great authors" that was too grand for Davies's audience of workmen? If one compares Davies's Canal poem with Ann of Swansea's ode,

> In vain by various grief opprest
> I vagrant roam devoid of rest
> With aching heart, still ling'ring stray
> Around the shores of Swansea Bay. . . .
>
> Then Kilvey Hill, a long adieu
> I drag my sorrows hence from you:
> Misfortune, with imperious sway,
> Impels me far from Swansea Bay.

then "Swansea Bay" is smoother, more elegant, but not totally beyond the skill of Davies in the lyrical mode of "Reflections on the Grave of a Young Officer who destroyed himself in a fit of despair at Neath, and was interred in Neath Churchyard, With all respect due to a British Soldier":

> Where the long grass obscures yon lonely grave,
> And deadly weeds of poisonous odours wave,
> A gallant soldier with the silent dead,
> Unnoticed, unlamented, rests his head.

No weeping friends was [sic] seen to deck his bier,
No mourning kindred shed a tender tear,
But buried in the grave, sad mouldering heap,
His sorrows and his fate in silent sleep. . . .

Fond love and passion turn'd to a furious rage
Brought him thus low e'r in the bloom of age,
When all most dear to him was lost but death,
In moody madness he resign'd his breath.

Some idea of the public nature of Davies's poetic role can be seen from the note beneath the title of the "Reflections", which explains that "Though an entire stranger to the place, a Subscription was made for a respectable funeral, and the most respectable Tradesmen of the town followed him to the grave in a solemn procession". Even when being lyrical, she does not indulge in personal emotions—with the possible exception of the Christian faith which was clearly an integral part of her existence.

Though the workmen appreciated her Neath Canal ballad, it seems to have attracted mainly derision from the local literati. When Walter Whittington presented his set of ten of Davies's poems to D. Rhys Phillips, he described them as "Mother Davies's doggerel",[6] while a later historian, Elis Jenkins, presenting his own set of the poems to Neath Borough Library in 1965, comments of the Canal ballad: ". . . these verses must surely rank with the worst ever written; even as pure doggerel they have never been excelled'"[7]— which suggests that he had only a limited knowledge of the possibilities of folk verse! D. Rhys Phillips himself is more generous: "Jerome says that the singer of the hedgerows, if his note ring true, deserves a hearing; and such was Elizabeth Davies. Her sincerity and loyalty is her best commemoration".

Bearing these responses in mind, one might ask whether Elizabeth Davies merits any serious attention, but in fact her life and work open up several intriguing avenues. Firstly, we have an ordinary shopkeeper producing and publishing, by popular demand, a body of verse in English at a time when many would suggest that English was still a foreign language in the area. Secondly, the shopkeeper is a woman, at a time when we are often given to understand that women were confined to the drawing room and the kitchen; there is no hint in Davies's work that she felt herself in any way marginalized (and her printer, at least in later years, was also a woman, Mary Whittington. Possibly this was a legal ownership, following Mary's husband's death, not an active role, but her son Walter would have been still young in c.1850, and more recent generations of Whittington women have certainly taken part in the business).

Lastly, though most of what survives is in English, Elizabeth Davies was a first-language Welsh speaker and writer. This is plain from her letter to

George Tennant, which is fluent enough, but has a number of constructions which are clearly from the Welsh, while her spelling is often phonetic, the creation of someone writing by sound, not the dictionary: "It gave great satisfaction to hear the leas was sind . . . the gentleman that had the manigment of the workes did not understand to manig it well. . . ." In the poems, too, she often uses the third person singular with a plural subject, as Welsh does (third person plural is used only with "they"):

> The nation's arms and kings of yore
> Was richly laid down on the floor.

Interestingly, either she took more pains with her verses than with her letter, or someone—her printer?—-copy-edited them for spelling errors, but the Welsh grammatical constructions remain.

Among Davies's poems is "Verses to the Ivorites for their Great Love of the Welsh Language"; the Ivorites were a native Welsh benefit society, named after the medieval prince Ifor Hael (Ivor the Generous), and many Welsh towns have, or had, an Ivorites Hotel where the local branch of the society held its meetings. The preface to the poem begins: "The Welsh people are more attached to their native language than any others; it is a more perfect and impressing [sic], and fuller of meaning than any other language". Interestingly, she makes a firm connection between the Welsh language and the Scriptures; if Bishop Morgan's translation of the Bible saved the language from deteriorating into a patois, it was the missionary zeal of the eighteenth-century Revivalists in seeking to make that Bible accessible to all that created a literate Wales, and Davies is clearly a child of that zeal:

> In Welsh brave Welshmen do delight
> To talk both night and day,
> In Welsh they love to read about
> The cross on Calvary.
>
> They have got the holy scriptures
> In their native tongue . . .

The last stanza, offering the poet's good wishes for the Ivorites, sums it up neatly (with perhaps a judicious sting in the last line—the society was "men only"):

> I hope that God will prosper them,
> Both succour and defend,
> To keep their native language
> Quite perfect to the end.

And whilst they sojourn here on earth,
What pleasure more'll they need,
Than Welsh to sing to Christ our King,
The woman's conquering seed.

Happily, we do not simply have to speculate as to Davies's own competence in the Welsh language, since two of her Welsh poems (or, more appropriately, hymns) have survived, with her own parallel English translations. Whatever one's critical judgement of her English verses, the Welsh hymns have a claim to be at least on the fringes of poetry proper:

Y Cristion yn yr Eira

Pan o'wn ar forau gaua', yn gadarn oedd y rhew,
Yn teithio ar y mynydd, tra syrthiai'r eira'n dew;
Heb gennyf sac na swcwr i'm cynnal ar fy nhaith,
Fy ngwisg oedd dlawd oddeutu'm cnawd, a'm siwrnai oedd yn faith.

Fy yspryd oedd yn isel a'm calon oedd yn wan,
Yn barod i ddiffygio a syrthio lawr bob cam;
Ymdrechu wnawn i fyn'd ymlaen trwy nerth fy Mhrynwr mawr,
Dan roi fy mhwn ar ysgwydd hwn, cynhaliodd fi bob awr.

Myn'd yn gryfach yr oeddwn i bob cam,
Gan sugno nerth oddiwrtho fel llaeth o fronnau mam;
Mor dawel a mor dirion cymmerodd fi'n ei gôl,
Ei gariad mwyn a ddarfu ddwyn fy nghalon ar ei ôl.

Fy nghalon ddilyn Iesu tra byddwyf yn y byd,
Trwy ffydd i dramwy'r llwybrau sy'n myn'd i'r ddinas glyd;
A phan gyrhaeddwyf ben fy nhaith, mi gaf orphwysfa wiw,
A gwel'd y gair fu ar fronnau Mair, uniganedig Duw.

Os tewaf i a moli e gân y cerrig mud,
Hosanna iechydwriaeth i Brynwr mawr y byd;
Am adael gorseddfaingc ei Dad a marw yn ein lle,
A thalu'r iawn i'r ddeddf yn llawn, ag agor pyrth y ne.

The Christian in the Snow

'Twas on a winter's morning I travel'd thro' the snow,
My way was rough and rugged to climb the mountain's brow,
My food was very scanty, my garments very light,
The day was short, my journey long, I was fearful of the night. . . .

I felt my strength renewing, as if refreshed with wine,
My soul within me panting to call the Saviour mine;

He kindly took me by the hand, as gentle as a dove,
And led me onward on my way, my heart was filled with love. . . .

If I'll be still and silent, the stones will shout and sing,
Hosanna and salvation to Christ, my God and King,
Who freely left his Father's throne, and died upon the tree,
The atonement made, the ransom paid, that sinners may be free.

The second poem, "composed on a journey from Neath to Swansea, between four and seven o'clock on a fine May morning", is entitled "Ar Harddwch y Greadigaeth" ("On the Beauty of the Creation"). It begins as a celebration of nature, but in the last two stanzas becomes a hymn of thanks to the Creator. Interestingly, the last of the five Welsh stanzas comments on the writer's wish for "doniau'r bardd", the poet's gifts, something that is not quite expressed in the equivalent English-language stanza. Instead there is an extra note:

The Muse was early on the watch,
To see what Poet she could catch;
So early, no one did she see,
That was the way she arrested me:
Before my eyes she did display,
Creation dress'd in rich array;
And nature's beauty did invite,
The lesser of the least to write.

These two poems, together with the odd verses found attached to one or two of the English poems, are most unlikely to have been the only examples of Davies's Welsh-language writing, but whether she was basically a Welsh-language poet who also, when required, wrote in English, or whether the bulk of her output was in English, is something that cannot finally be determined from the material we have at present. In either case, Davies's English-language role was clearly the very Welsh office of *bardd gwlad*, the journeyman poet who celebrates local events and personalities, writing for the widest possible audience; what she represents is the carrying over of a particularly Welsh strand of poetic practice into Anglo-Welsh literature.

Elizabeth Davies was not to be unique in this, except insofar as she was a woman (and we cannot be sure whether this particular uniqueness was the result of survival or existence), but most of her successors still lurk in the darker corners of local history, not sophisticated enough in literary terms to have made any impact on critical studies of Welsh writing in English. This is especially the case because there is no real equivalent in the literature of England to the *bardd gwlad*. Hence, no doubt, the perplexity of a reviewer commenting, in the *Independent* newspaper, on the recent *Bloodaxe Book of Modern Welsh Poetry*, that "Too many of the poems read as if they do not merit inclusion. There is too much lame doggerel".[8] The poem that inspired this comment seems to have been Cynan's Eisteddfod-winning "Mab y Bwthyn", and I have to admit, as its translator, that regardless of the quality of the translation, I did wonder how an English audience would respond to it.

It is not a question that is easy to answer. Does one select only those poems and approaches to writing that when translated will appear to be authentically English literature? Or does one accept the work of a writer like Elizabeth Davies as a serious contribution to the literature of Wales and attempt to provide some idea, however imperfect, of the range and styles of a literature for which, to quote that more recent *bardd gwlad,* Harri Webb, "English standards do not apply"? If one chooses the first alternative, then Elizabeth Davies remains just a writer of doggerel—and more importantly, the largely unrecognized common ground between the two halves of the literature of Wales remains unexplored, a liability, not a source of strength.

NOTES

1. Moira Dearnley, *Distant Fields: Eighteenth-Century Fictions of Wales* (Cardiff: U. of Wales P., 2001); Jane Aaron, "The Hoydens of Wild Wales: Representations of Welsh Women in Victorian and Edwardian Fiction", *Welsh Writing in English* 1 (1995): 23-39; David Painting, *Amy Dillwyn* (Cardiff: U. of Wales P.,, 1987); Sally Roberts Jones, *Allen Raine* (Cardiff: U. of Wales P., 1979).
2. The main source of biographical information on Elizabeth Davies is D. Rhys Phillips's *History of the Vale of Neath*, first published by the author in Swansea in 1925, reprinted in facsimile by West Glamorgan County Archive Service and Neath Borough Council in 1994. This includes a transcript of Davies's letter to George Tennant, brief quotations from her verses, and reminiscences of her as a shopkeeper.
   The main source for the present paper is a collection of fifteen leaflets bound in boards, with a marbled paper design on the outside of the cover (similar to a small account book); this was probably put together in the late nineteenth century, and is now in the possession of Mr. J.V. Hughes, who bought the book some years ago from an antiquarian book dealer in Cardiff. The poems are printed on sheets of paper eight by eight and a half inches, each folded in half to make a four-page leaflet.
   The British Library has copies of sixteen of the leaflets, most in duplicate; the relevant shelf marks are 11647.aaa.62. and 11652.aaa.53. Neath Public Library has copies of some of the poems, probably from the set presented to it by Elis Jenkins in 1965. No titles are listed in the main database of the National Library of Wales for the Elizabeth Davies discussed in this paper; there is a listing for *Dwy Gan . . . Golwg ar Sefyllfa Cristionogrwydd,* a twelve-page pamphlet published in Aberystwyth in 1813, but it seems unlikely that this is the same author. The late Walter Haydn Davies included the full text of "Lines on the Neath and Red Jacket

Canal" in his manuscript collection of ballads, but gave no source for any of the ballads.
3. D. Rhys Phillips, *The History of the Vale of Neath* (Swansea: privately published by the author, 1925) 705-6, gives the letter in full, with the original spelling.
4. *History of the Vale of Neath* 568.
5. "Ann of Swansea" [Julia Ann Hatton, 1764-1838], *Poetic Trifles*, 1811.
6. *History of the Vale of Neath* 568.
7. Letter from Elis Jenkins to the Librarian, Neath Borough Libraries, 27 July 1965. Photocopy supplied to the author by Mr. J.V. Hughes, formerly Local Studies Librarian, West Glamorgan County Library Service, whose assistance in tracking down Elizabeth Davies's poems is gratefully acknowledged.
8. Michael Glover, "A fine lyricism bedevilled by brooding", *Independent* 13 November 2003.

"Heartsickness": An Early Short Story by Pennar Davies

With an introduction
by D. Densil Morgan
University of Wales, Bangor

T he rather bland "poet, novelist and scholar" which describes Pennar Davies (1911-96) in *The New Companion to the Literature of Wales* does scant justice to a very significant if somewhat neglected contributor to twentieth-century Welsh literature.[1] William Thomas Davies (as he then was) was born into a mining family in Mountain Ash in the Cynon Valley and experienced the adversity of the time at first hand. Educated at the Mountain Ash primary and grammar schools, he commenced what would be an extraordinarily successful academic career in the University College of South Wales and Monmouthshire at Cardiff in 1929 where he gained a first in Latin in 1932 and, along with W. Moelwyn Merchant, a first in English a year later. After winning his teaching diploma, he proceeded to Balliol College, Oxford, where he wrote an exceptionally powerful B.Litt. thesis on the Protestant polemicist and dramatist John Bale, and then, on the strength of a Commonwealth Fund Fellowship, he transferred to the Yale Graduate School in Connecticut to begin doctoral work on the comedies of another Elizabethan man of letters, George Chapman, the translator of Homer. His two years in America were to prove vital for his personal development. It was there, three thousand miles from home, that he committed himself to Wales and decided that his calling, above all else, was as a writer. A University of Wales Fellowship followed, which he spent in Cardiff in 1939, and then, totally unexpectedly and not without some panache, he switched from what seemed an inevitable career in English Literature to theology and the work of the ministry. "The war", he wrote, "which brought me to a definite and unpopular political commitment also led me to give myself to Welsh rather than English writing and, somewhat to my amazement and to the consternation of friends on both sides of the language fence, to the quaint life of a 'Respected' among the unspeakable chapel people".[2] This took him back to Oxford, to Mansfield College this time, before being ordained in 1943 into the Congregational ministry in Minster Road Church in Cardiff. For a pacifist to minister at the height of the war was challenge enough; it was exacerbated by the fact that while at Oxford he had married a German refugee. His scholastic and pastoral apprenticeship now complete (and despite being nearly enticed back by Professor Gwyn Jones in 1946 to teach literature in the English Department in Aberystwyth), he spent the rest of his career on the staff of theological colleges in Bangor, Brecon and latterly Swansea. He died, aged 85, in 1996.

This short account of the externals of Davies's life hides as much as it reveals. Although scholarship came effortlessly to him, he was first and foremost a creative writer. His initial literary links were with Keidrych Rhys and the writers of the magazine *Wales*, indeed he did much to call for a cease-fire in what John Harris has called "the war of the tongues" and, along with Rhys, he instigated "the New Wales Society", a forum for young Welsh writers in both languages intent on "substituting energy and responsibility for the dilettantism and provincialism of Welsh life and literature".[3] Both the outbreak of the Second World War and Davies's religious conversion and subsequent commitment to the Christian ministry put an end to the scheme, though some half-dozen of his poems published under the *nom-de-plume* "Davies Aberpennar" appeared alongside verse by Idris Davies, Glyn Jones, Alun Lewis, Dylan Thomas, R. S. Thomas and Vernon Watkins in the Faber anthology *Modern Welsh Poetry* (1944) edited by Keidrych Rhys.

Despite being brought up in an English-speaking home and being trained academically in English literature, it was as a Welsh-language writer that Davies's reputation would be made. He had learned Welsh at school and had been much influenced by the poetry of Robert Williams Parry—Gwenallt and Saunders Lewis were also producing work of the highest quality at the time—while the company of such contemporaries as the poet Alun Llywelyn-Williams at Cardiff, Aneirin Talfan Davies and, especially, J. Gwyn Griffiths (with whom he would establish the avant-garde Cadwgan Circle of Welsh language writers during the war) had drawn him more and more towards creative work in Welsh. Conversely, he found the attitudes of his Anglo-Welsh contemporaries, Dylan Thomas and Vernon Watkins especially, lacking in moral seriousness and social commitment. Scholarly works aside—he published a significant amount of theology, church history and at least one interesting monograph on what we would now call "Celtic spirituality"—between 1946 and 1991 he published five volumes of verse, four novels, an exceedingly valuable confessional journal and two volumes of short stories. Thematically he ranged far and wide: he was, after all, a sophisticated cosmopolitan intellectual whose erudition tended to intimidate his contemporaries. Yet he would return again and again to the matter of flesh and spirit or how the religious impulse manifested itself within human contingencies; the idea of hope and messianism (given wry and witty treatment in his novel *Meibion Darogan*, "The Sons of Prophecy", 1968), and questions of faith and identity in the context of contemporary anxieties. "Dr.

Pennar Davies finds a function for Welsh Nonconformity in the darkening years of possibly the last of the centuries" was how Saunders Lewis reviewed his Cold War novel *Anadl o'r Uchelder*, "A Breath from on High" in 1961.[4]

Critics are divided as to whether Davies excelled most as a poet, a novelist or a short story writer. J. Gwyn Griffiths—his oldest friend and most unswerving advocate—rates his poetry highly[5] while M. Wynn Thomas is impressed particularly by his novels: *Meibion Darogan*, which was based loosely on the activities of the "Cadwgan Circle" of artists in the Rhondda during the war years, and further "his intellectually adventurous trilogy of novels", *Anadl o'r Uchelder* (1958), *Mabinogi Mwys*, "An Ambiguous Youth" (1979) and *Gwas y Gwaredwr*, "The Saviour's Servant" (1991).[6] Yet both Gareth Alban Davies and John Rowlands feel that he was at his most accomplished in his short stories.[7] There is much to be said for all three opinions, though certainly his two volumes of short stories, *Caregl Nwyf* ("A Sensuous Chalice", 1966) and *Llais y Durtur* ("The Voice of the Turtle-Dove", 1985), contain some exquisite examples of the craft.

"Heartsickness"—he was not sure whether it should be called "Heartsickness" or "The Sick Heart"—was written by Pennar Davies while a graduate student at Yale in early 1938 and was found among his MSS. A vignette of the despair of ordinary folk in the south Wales valleys during the Depression, it seems never to have been published. During his time at Yale he kept a diary which alludes to the hardship which his family experienced, especially after his coalmining father had been injured and wretchedly compensated following an accident underground. Although not directly autobiographical, there is no doubt that the story—its description of a miner's life and thwarted dreams, the tensions between husband and wife caused by abject economic hardships—draws on personal experience. It was only rarely that Davies drew on his family background in composing literary works. One of his most memorable short stories was located in Renaissance Spain and had to do with the spirituality and love interests of female mystics and Catholic courtiers.[8] To that extent he never was a typical "valleys writer" or indeed a typical Welsh writer at all. Yet this early work shows an alert mind, a powerful imagination, an ear for dialogue and colourful local phraseology and a feeling for the complexities of human emotion and motivation. It augured well for Pennar Davies's future as a creative writer of ability and renown.[9]

NOTES

1. *The New Companion to the Literature of Wales*, ed. Meic Stephens (Cardiff: U. of Wales P., 1998) 165.
2. "Pennar Davies", *Artists in Wales*, ed. Meic Stephens (Llandysul: Gomer, 1971) 125.

3. John Harris, "The war of the tongues: early Anglo-Welsh responses to Welsh literary culture", *'Let's Do Our Best for the Ancient Tongue': The Welsh Language in the Twentieth Century*, ed. G. H. Jenkins and Mari Williams (Cardiff: U. of Wales P., 2000) 439-61; cf. Meic Stephens, "Yr Academi Gymreig and Cymdeithas Cymru Newydd", *Poetry Wales* 4 (1968): 7-12.
4. "Welsh Writers of Today", broadcast on BBC Welsh Home Service, April 1961; see Gwyn Thomas and Alun R. Jones, ed., *Presenting Saunders Lewis* (Cardiff: U. of Wales P., 1973) 170.
5. See, for instance, "Pennar Davies: More than a *Poeta Doctus*", *Triskel Two: Essays on Welsh and Anglo Welsh Literature*, ed. Sam Adams and Gwilym Rees Hughes (Llandybïe: Christopher Davies) 111-27.
6. M. Wynn Thomas, *Corresponding Cultures: The Two Literatures of Wales* (Cardiff: U. of Wales P., 1999) 94-100.
7. Gareth Alban Davies in D. Ben Rees, ed., *Dyrnaid o Awduron Cyfoes* (Pontypridd a Lerpwl: Cyhoeddiadau Modern Cymreig, 1975) 48-62; John Rowlands, *Ysgrifau ar y Nofel* (Caerdydd: Gwasg Prifysgol Cymru, 1992) 219-40.
8. "Y Tri yn Un" in W. Pennar Davies, *Caregl Nwyf* (Llandybïe: Christopher Davies, 1966) 11-27.
9. See Densil Morgan, *Pennar Davies*, Cyfres Dawn Dweud (Caerdydd: Gwasg Prifysgol Cymru, 2003).

Heartsickness

The little kettle bubbled over. The man lowered his feet from the mantel-shelf ungracefully and leaned forward sullenly to take the kettle off the fire and put it on top of the oven.

"Reg'lar little spitfire, this kettle," he said peevishly. "Gives you no notice nor nothin'."

The wife looked at him quickly, drawing in her brows. Suddenly she saw that the blue alarm-clock said ten past six.

"You're forgettin' about the News, an't you?" she said. "For a wonder, too, on a Saturday night."

His only answer was a discontented mumble.

"Oh, o' course," she said. "You an't got nothin' on the Football this week."

Another discontented mumble.

"Well, you can't say that *I* stopped you from giving him the sixpence."

No answer.

"Can you, now?" she asked insistently. "*I* do say as it's worth sixpence a week to 'ave a 'appy man about the 'ouse. It do give you somethin' to look forward to."

He grunted.

"Don't it, now?" she said. "Even if you never win it do give you somethin' to look forward to."

He had been unemployed for three years. "There en't nothin' else to look forward to, that's sure," he said. "With Les on the dole, too." It was hard cheese, he thought, to have a married son living near London and not to have enough of the ready to go up there for the day. Pretty hard lines. Neither he nor Glad had even seen their daughter-in-law. She was a Welsh girl, from Llanelli. She had been in service in London long before Les had gone up there. A nice girl, by all accounts. But they'd never even clapped eyes on her. It was hard lines on a man.

"Well *possible* we can manage to spare sixpence a week," said Glad.

"It's no good. Sixpence a week en't enough. Not to win. I been trying now for the best part of a season. You don't stand much of a chance with sixpence a week."

"Well, it do give you a *chance*. That's better than nothin'. An' it's a shilling a week with Charley's sixpence too. An' Charley said you'd been knocking at the door for a long time!"

Glad sure knew the lingo. He made a noise that was something between a laugh and a moan.

"Ay, a 'ell of a long time," he said.

"I s'pose Charley 'ad his usual sixpen'orth this week again, by 'imself."

"Ay. The more fool 'im. I bet 'e's just switched off his set this minute an 'e's sayin' 'Another bee tanner gone west'!"

"Ay," she said. "P'r'aps you were both mugs to *start* the game. But I do say, now you've started, you might as well keep on till you've got somethin' out of it. Use your bit of common, mun. If you stop now, it's as good as chuckin' all you've spent already down the sink. En't it, now? 'S as good as chuckin' it all down the sink."

"That's what Charley said last Saturday."

"An' 'e's right too. 'E likes his drop, I know, but we've all got our faults. 'E en't no fool, any'ow. Fair dooze. 'E en't no fool."

"Well, it's different with 'im." He turned round to scowl at her. "'E's workin'. It's just a side-line with 'im. 'E can go up to Luton to see 'Aydn an' Wyndham whenever 'e wants to. A tanner a week is just a drop in the bucket with 'im."

He turned round and glowered at his feet.

"Good lor', you talk about Charley like as if money was no object with 'im at all. Chware teg. 'E's not been working long himself. You don't want to say anything against Charley. 'E's been a good pal to you. If it 'adn't been for 'im droppin' in to play a game of draughts with you twice or three times a week you might 'ave—you might 'ave gone off your rocker."

"Go an' shove a sock in it!" he said savagely.

He spat into the fire and glared at it as if he hated it. He knew what Glad had intended to say before she changed her mind. She had been going to say "You might 'ave chucked yourself into the reservoir". He thought of the early days of his unemployment before he had become friendly with Charley, when he had fallen into the habit of relieving his misery by talking about suicide. He had never meant it, of course. Not really. But it had relieved him. And there had been some pleasure in tormenting his wife. "Duw, duw," she would say, "don't talk like that, mun! You en't got nothin' when you're dead!" And then, when he had almost frightened her out of her wits, she would scream, "Don't leave me, Bryn! For God's sake, don't leave me!" Somehow there had been some comfort in that. And then she would add, with her voice shaking, "This is better than nothing, Bryn."

Glad was also thinking of those days. She began to wash the tea things. She thought that the best bit of luck they had had was Bryn's picking up with Charley. Charley was always running in for a game of draughts. His talk did much to take Bryn's mind off his troubles. And early last winter he and Bryn had begun to spend a shilling between them every week on football pools. Bryn had become a different man. She had not "believed in betting". But a peaceful household at the cost of sixpence a week was a splendid bargain. What if they didn't win? There was always another week. But now Bryn was getting fed up with it. He wasn't going to chuck any more tanners away! He had missed a week for the first time since he had started. And he had been sulky during the last few days, and he was getting nasty again!

"You don't want to talk to me like that!" she said at last with a kind of hesitating boldness.

"Leave me alone then."

Neither of them spoke for a while. Then he spat into the fire and said, "I'm gettin' danted, I am."

She looked at him with dread. This was how his bad moods had always begun. He would be talking about doing away with himself soon.

"Don't talk like that. You must keep on 'oping."

"It's all right for Charley. 'E's workin', an' his kids are workin'."

"Well, do somethin' with the Football next week. You never know— "

"Charley can afford a tanner a week better than I can."

She did not know way to say. Miserably she hung the cups on the dresser.

"It's come to something," she said at last.

"What did you say?"

"Come to something if we can't manage sixpence a week for a bit o' pleasure. Possible!"

"What's the use of it?"

"It gives you somethin' to 'ope for. That's better than nothin'."

"'Better than nothin'!" He mimicked her as he had often before. "When you die I'll get that put on your gravestone."

He got up and put a dirty muffler round his neck, standing before a cracked looking-glass. Looking in the mirror he saw the old terror lurking in his wife's eyes.

"Where are you goin'?" she asked.

"Out", he said, threatening.

"Where?"

He answered with a heavy and ugly irony. "I'm going round to dear old Charley's to see if 'e's copped."

"There's no need to." She pretended, for the moment, to believe him. "You can venter 'e'll be round 'imself in 'alf a sec." She wished to God he would.

"Well, p'r'aps I don't want to see 'im after all. P'r'aps I don't want to see nobody any more."

"Don't talk soft, for God's sake. Sit down by there till 'e comes." She pointed to the armchair. "Duw annwyl, I got no patience with talk like that."

"Well, what's the use of goin' on?"

"What's the use of stoppin'?" She pushed him towards the chair. "Jowk, mun, there's always life while there's 'ope. Isn' there, now? I mean there's always 'ope while there's life. Isn' there, now?"

He pushed against her, making for the door. Then he stopped, hearing steps in the passage.

"Charley!" she said quietly. You could hear the relief in her voice.

"Ay, you can venter," he granted, and suddenly felt very foolish.

And Charley it was, a brisk, expansive little man, with a fleshy chin that was blue with stubble, a chattering little man who was the same everywhere and at all times, in his house and with his friends: very different from Bryn, who changed all the time with his company. Bryn was changing now, beginning to grin rather sheepishly.

At first Charley said nothing, which was very unusual for him. He just stood there, looking from one to the other, with a queer grin on his face, and with his hands in his pockets.

"I was just thinkin' of goin' round to your 'ouse," said Bryn.

"You was, was you?"

"Ay, ay. To see 'ow you done. Did you catch?"

For answer Charley pulled an elaborately miserable face, took his hands out of his pockets and pushed his thumbs down in a despair that was too abject to be real.

"What let you down? Your bankers let you down? I 'aven't 'eard the results."

Charley could contain himself no longer. He grasped Bryn by the shoulders and shook him in laughing ecstasy.

"God God, mun," he almost screeched. "I've copped! I've *copped*! What did I tell you? With a bit o' luck I'm made! If the prices are 'alf as 'igh as they was last week! Cissie, she's landed. Don't know 'ow we can wait to 'ear from them! Christ a'mighty! If them people don't pay up 'andsome I'll go up there an' knock 'em into the middle of next week! Sup me God, I will. An' if them there prices are anything like they was last week, I won't do another stroke o' bloomin' work for the rest o' my bloomin' natural!"

Bryn sat heavily in a kitchen chair, smiling mechanically, with a sick feeling in his throat.

"Well, I'm jiggered," he murmured. "That's a piece of blinging luck for you! 'S bloomin' great," he said, remembering himself. "Them prices, though, they're up an' down, you know. Up an' down."

"Penny pool, I s'pose?" said Glad.

"Ay, penny pool." Charley turned to Bryn. "Don't I flamin' well know it! But they'd better be up this week. Ay, by jingo, they better!"

"I 'ope so, for your sake," Glad said.

"Ay, I 'ope so," echoed Bryn.

Charley fizzed like a newly opened mineral drink. "You oughter seen me copyin' down them results, an' checkin' 'em. You just oughter seen me. I could 'ardly believe my eyes. 'Ardly believe my eyes. Not first goin' off, like, see. I just sat there gapin'. I felt almost too weak to carry clecks. Honest to God, I did. An' Cissie said, ''Ow've you done?' she said. An' I said, '*Done?*' I said. 'If I'm not blinkin' loopy, I been an' done the best thing that ever I done in all my natural?' An' so I 'ave, if on'y them prices—! An' I'd never 'ave thought I'd 'ave won with them forecasts as did win, like, see. I can thank my stars my bankers come up. But the rest of 'em, you'd never 'ave dreamt it! I just put in twos an' exes an' ones all 'ap'azard. An' they all came up, every man jack o' them! An' I've 'eard people say there isn' no God! They better not say that to me. 'E's been a real butty to me!"

"What you goin' to do if there's a good price?" asked Bryn, feeling his head.

"Do, my 'andsome! It's me for Luton, an' my old girl with me, for good. An' 'eck, won't our 'Aydn an' Wyndham be glad to 'ave us! Old Phillips the manager can put his job where 'is old 'oman puts 'er corn beef tins."

"I wouldn' mind if 'e give it to Bryn," said Glad. She loathed Charley for the first time since she had known him.

"Ay, I thought of poor old Bryn as soon as I could see I'd 'ad a bit o' luck." Charley tried to look as sympathetic as he could. "It's 'ard lines on you, in a way o' speaking. But I told you to stick with me, didn' I? If you'd come in with me this week you' be 'avin' your 'alf of the proceeds. An' now I've won on my own. Can't 'elp it, can I? You should 'ave come in with me, as per usual. I can't 'elp winnin', can I now?"

"P'r'aps Bryn was bringin' you bad luck all the time," said Glad with a hard note in her voice. "You never now, like."

"Well, you don't want to 'ave your 'air off about it. 'Ware teg, now. It's 'is fault. I told 'im last week to stick to it, told 'im till I was black in the face. I only 'ope '*e*'ll 'ave luck when '*e* tries by 'imself."

Glad looked at Bryn, wondering what he was thinking. The smile had left his face. He was looking almost stupid.

"'E ought to 'ave tried by 'imself all along, I'm thinkin'," she said. "There wouldn' 'a' been no ill-feelin' then."

"Well, good God!" said Charley, with righteous indignation. "Who's got any bloomin' ill feelin', I should like to know! I'm blinkin' sure I 'aven't. I'm as 'appy as a flea in a whist drive, I am! 'E could 'ave gone on 'is own if he'd wanted to. I s'pose 'e would 'ave if 'e 'adn' been afraid the dole people would 'ave made trouble if 'e'd won a little bit o' dough in 'is own name. I was doin' 'im a favour, I was, by lettin' 'im come in with me. Wasn' I, Bryn?"

"Ay, ay. 'Course you was. She don't mean anything."

"No. honest I didn't," said Glad. She felt tired and rather sorry for everybody. "You been a good pal to us. I only 'ope you'll get a good price up." But she began to cry softly, thinking of Bryn.

"Well, I go!" said Charley. "I go to sea! I'm surprised at you." He was, genuinely. "We've been pals together, 'aven't we? You don't want to treat me like as if I'd poisoned your bloomin' cat, or something. Fair's fair. If I've been a pal to you you ought to show a bit o' pleasure when I get a bit o' luck. 'Stead o' that, you go an' 'ave a good weep!" He began to show some good humour, and his tone became more persuasive and more teasing. "A sensible woman like you, too! An' I been 'oldin' you up as a model to Cissie!"

Bryn badly wanted him to go.

"Well, I won't ask you to play a game of draughts tonight," he said, "being as you're so excited, like." He attempted a joke. "I'd win too easy!"

"Ay, don't think I could tell black from white tonight. But I wasn' goin' to stay, any'ow. Thought I'd just come over an' spread the glad news, like. Couldn' rest if I didn't tell you. But look 'ere, Bryn, I'd like to make you a present of five quid out of my winnings. You won't mind takin' a little present off of me?"

"Five quid! Get on with you, mun. You don't 'ave to gimme anything. It's good of you, mind, but forget it."

"Jowkawopsticks!" said Charley with humorous, overbearing generosity. "It would only be the thing, like, see. 'Ave a 'eart, Bryn bach."

"'Course 'e'll accept five pounds off of you," Glad said quickly. "God knows we could do with it. It's very good of you to offer it, indeed it is."

"That's the 'ammer!" said Charley with enthusiasm. "Now we're all talking sense, like, see! But I'm off. Don't keep me. Goin' with the missus to see my in-laws. 'Ope the old man won't die of 'eart failure! The Lord's been threatening to smile on 'im for donkey's years. So long!"

And he was gone. They heard the front door bang and slowly turned to look at each other. For a while neither of them spoke. Bryn felt curiously helpless. Glad could think of nothing to say.

"Well, cryin' out loud!" said Bryn softly at last. "The very blingin' week as I didn' go in with 'im. For this to 'appen!"

He stared at the fire without moving. He felt that he was a fool and a victim and, though he could not said so, that the whole system of things had been created to outrage him, and him alone. His whole life seemed to be an unavailing struggle against all things that were about him, and all things seemed to be controlled by something vast and pervasive which was moving to defeat him. He looked about him, from wall to wall. The room seemed to have contracted. He was conscious of hostile immensities outside. For a moment he felt that there might be ugly presences inside too. The air seemed warm with their breath. Then he laughed bitterly at the idea.

Glad also stared at the fire. Under the heavy silence she almost lost awareness of the time and the occasion. Who are those two poor mugs? she almost asked herself. Those poor mugs sitting around like people in a doctor's waiting-room. They don't seem to know what the sun and the earth are for. Why don't they come and spend a month at our farm near Llanwonno? Then they'd find out what the sun and the earth are for. They are strangers, awkward and miserable strangers. God knows how they live since they have wandered so far from the things which give all men life. Hey, you, why don't you come and stay on our farm? Glad cried softly. The farm had been lost, and the farmer's daughter, too.

"Five quid, 'e said, did 'e?" asked Bryn in an ugly voice.

Glad lifted her head and nodded.

"Well, why don't you say it?" he shouted, getting up violently and knocking his chair over. He now felt irresistibly strong and wanted to break something, to tear something, to destroy something.

"Say what?" she asked.

"Say five quid's better than nothin'."

He went to her and clutched her hair with his hands.

She gave a little scream and sobbed. "We can go up an' see our Les on it," she said, crying and pulling his sleeves. "For a couple of days. Can't we now?" Her voice was twisted.

"Ay," he said dully, and let her go.

Dylan Thomas and John Donne: The Magpie's Magpie

Nathalie Wourm

Birkbeck College, University of London

I

John Donne's influence on Dylan Thomas is well documented. But what is less clearly understood is how alike Thomas is to Donne even in the very process of borrowing from him. T. S. Eliot famously described Donne as "a magpie", attracted to "broken fragments of systems", which he stuck "about here and there in his verse".[1] In Thomas's early poetry Donne's presence is felt principally in Thomas's use of ideas drawn from the Paracelsian system. But while none of the poems represents an exposition of Paracelsian philosophy, there are repeated images garnered from Paracelsus's concepts of cosmogony and alchemy.

II

In a passage about obscurity in modern poetry, Thomas claimed that his own obscurity was unfashionably based "on a preconceived symbolism derived . . . from the cosmic significance of the human anatomy".[2] Originating most clearly in Neoplatonist cosmology and having made its way into the Kabbalah, the idea of an analogy between the body of man and the cosmos was certainly more common in the Renaissance than in the twentieth century.[3] The first major exponent of the doctrine, sixteenth-century Swiss physician and alchemist Paracelsus, described man as a little world or *microcosm*, a replica of the whole creation or *macrocosm*:

> From the silt, the creator of the world created the small world, the microcosm, that is, humankind. Man is this little world which contains all the qualities of the great world. This is why he is called a microcosm. Man is the quintessence of the elements and of the stars or the firmament, of the sky and of the globe.[4]

The analogy was essential to Paracelsus's medical theory. He claimed that an understanding of corresponding components of the natural world, could help the physician understand the nature of a diseased body part:

[L]et cosmography be an anatomy . . . if you understand it thoroughly, you will understand the microcosm in its essence. Look at anatomia terrae, find in what order its hands and feet are distributed in it and consider what its fingers, its principal members are . . . the anatomy of water, find out what is its body and how the minerals constitute its limbs.[5]

John Donne, who was interested in the Kabbalah as well as in Paracelsus, referred to the concept of the microcosm repeatedly in the poems and *Sermons*, and the idea was central to the *Devotions*.[6] In Donne's use as in Paracelsus's, the microcosm is the last of God's creations, and is God's special work. In man, the secrets of nature are revealed, and to understand man, in return, the entire world has to be studied. Thus, nature is seen as corresponding to the spiritual, but it is the body of man which—itself corresponding to nature—provides the key to the spiritual.[7]

In the "Fourth Meditation" of the *Devotions*, Donne rebels against the idea of man as microcosm; he envisages an inversion in which man—because of his complexity—is the macrocosm: his veins are rivers, his sinews are the veins of mines, his muscles are hills, and his bones are stones. He considers that if this was the case, there would not be enough space in the universe for "this Orbe of Man to move in".[8] The analogy used by Donne here is highly reminiscent of Paracelsus's *anatomia terrae*. Again, in the Eleventh Meditation, Donne writes about man that:

Hee thinkes he treads upon the *Earth*, that all is under his feete, and the *Braine* that thinkes so, is but *Earth*; his highest Region, the flesh that covers that, is but *Earth*; and even the toppe of that, that, wherein so many *Absolons* take so much pride, is but a bush growing upon that *Turfe of Earth*.[9]

It is usually thought that Donne was a prime influence in Thomas's use of the idea of man as little world. Indeed, Thomas referred in one of his letters to what is probably Donne's Eleventh Meditation in the *Devotions*, as containing the "greatest description" of man's "earthiness" that he knew:

[Donne] describes man as earth of the earth, his body earth, his hair a wild shrub growing out of the land. . . . Every idea, intuitive or intellectual, can be imaged and translated in terms of the body, its flesh, skin, blood, sinews, veins, glands, organs, cells, or senses. . . . I employ the scenery of the island to describe the scenery of my thoughts, the earthquakes of the body to describe the earthquakes of the heart.[10]

It is obvious here that Thomas was interested in the *descriptive* potential of the concept for his poetry, but that he also had an awareness of the deeper *analogical* implications of the doctrine. Thomas's use of the imagery of man as microcosm is clear in several poems. In "Light breaks where no sun shines", for instance, it appears in these lines: "From poles of skull and toe the windy blood / Slides like a sea" (ll. 14-15).[11] The extremities of the body represent the poles of the earth, while the blood circulating is a sea made to roll from pole to pole by the wind. The comparison drawn between blood and sea is typical of the "preconceived symbolism" originating from the idea of man as a little world. Thomas also used it in "The force that through the green fuse" when, as part of his argument towards the earthiness of man, he compared his blood to streams: "The force that drives the water through the rocks / Drives my red blood; that dries the mouthing streams / Turns mine to wax" (ll. 6-8).[12] The old-fashioned theory of the microcosm could provide an infinite source of symbols, on which Thomas drew heavily, particularly in some of his early poems. For instance, "Where once the waters of your face" relies on the reader to establish the link between elements of the cosmos which are provided to him, and the corresponding elements of the body, which are not. In order to grasp the meaning of the poem, the reader needs to imagine the inside of the womb as a sea, with "salt and root and roe", "channels", "tides", "weeds", "stones", "corals".[13]

But Thomas's use of the idea of man as a little world, as in "Light breaks where no sun shines", can also be integrated more subtly within his poetic argument so that it is less glaring. In "When once the twilight locks", the poet is specifically describing the skull as a "globe" and seems to play on the ambiguity that this can create:

> I sent my creature scouting on the globe,
> That globe itself of hair and bone
> That, sewn to me by nerve and brain,
> Had stringed my flask of matter to his rib.   (ll. 9-12)

His "creature" sets out to explore the "globe", but the "globe"—"of hair and bone" and "sewn to [him] by nerve and brain"—is apparently his skull, the material part of his being, the "matter". The "creature" carries this "matter", this bodily envelope, in his exploration, as though it was a "flask" tied to his "rib"; the idea of his "flask of matter" having been tied to his rib could be an image of birth, of incarnation. In other words, the creature is "sent" to explore a skull which it is carrying. This suggests that the creature exploring the skull as though it was a globe is, in fact, the narrator himself, in search of inspiration. This possibility is supported by the close-up, in the first few lines of the poem, on the hand ("finger" and "fist") and by the insistence on the idea of dryness associated with the need to send the "creature" on an expedition (ll. 6, 8, 38). The "galactic sea" (l. 7) and "mother milk" (l. 38), might represent an inspirational manna which has ceased to flow. The sea is not "dammed" (l. 3) anymore, it escapes him.[14]

Thus, Thomas has assimilated the idea of man as a little world in his imagery and made use of it without introducing or expanding it for the twentieth-century reader. In "Foster the light", the poet, playing with the concept of turning the moon into "manshape" and being turned himself into the "world", addresses the Creator:

> O who is glory in the shapeless maps,
> Now make the world of me as I have made
> A merry manshape of your walking circle. (ll. 28-30)

The moon is referred to, here, as God's "walking circle", possibly because it moves circularly around the earth. Thomas plays on the common expression "to think the world of" to integrate within the poem the unusual thought of a man being turned into the world, as he relies on the common story of "the man in the moon" to present the idea of the moon being shaped as a man. This is certainly quite remote from the Paracelsian doctrine of the microcosm and the macrocosm, and hardly recognisable as such, but it is because Thomas integrates foreign concepts so well into a seemingly ordinary modern discourse that we may often fail to notice them, to recognize them as such.

III

In his *De Natura Rerum*, Paracelsus described a balm, a type of aerial vital fluid, the loss of which led to desiccation, decay, death, and return of the earthly man to earth:

> The life of man is an astral effluvium, an expression of balsam in form, a heavenly invisible fire, an enclosed essence or spirit. . . . [T]he death of man . . . is the taking away of the aerial element, the disappearance of the balsam, an extinction of natural light, the great separation of body, soul and spirit. [It is] a return into the matrix of the mother. Natural earthly man is from the earth, and earth will be his mother into whom he must return.[15]

In relation to this, three ideas proposed by Donne are also found in Thomas: that there exists a general vital fluid animating every live object in the world, that there exists a human balm partaking of this general vital fluid, and that the loss of that fluid leads to desiccation and death. These points can be seen in "A nocturnall upon S. Lucies day, Being the shortest day":

> Tis the yeares midnight, and it is the dayes,
> Lucies, who scarce seaven houres herself unmaskes,
> The Sunne is spent, and now his flasks
> Send forth light squibs, no constant rayes;
> The worlds whole sap is sunke:

> The generall balme th'hydroptique earth hath drunk,
> Whither, as to the beds-feet, life is shrunke,
> Dead and enterr'd.[16]

Death is described as the receding of the vital fluid into earth. Man, being part of the natural world, shares with it the same vital sap. In that sense, the dying human being, in a deathbed, is portrayed as being literally sucked dry by earth. Life is said to shrink into the earth, and this shrinking is symbolized by the dying person's shrinking down to the foot of the bed.[17]

Thomas also uses the idea of a vital sap, or balm, a life-giving and life-preserving substance. In "In the beginning", for instance, it is referred to as "secret oils":

> Life rose and spouted from the rolling seas,
> Burst in the roots, pumped from the earth and rock
> The secret oils that drive the grass.   (ll. 16-18)

Moreover, the allusion to a shared vital fluid between root or bud and man is discernible in "I, in my intricate image"[18]:

> She threads off the sap and needles, blood and bubble
> Casts to the pine roots, raising man like a mountain
> Out of the naked entrail.   (I, ll. 10-12)

Man's blood is driven by the same world sap, the same vital force, that drives the grass, shrubs, and trees. And it is not unusual to find in Thomas allusions to time as a sponge, or leech, sucking this vital fluid. Thus, in "The force that through the green fuse" he talks of the "lips of time" that "leech to the fountain head" (l. 16). In "How soon the servant sun", time is referred to as "Sir morrow at his sponge" (l. 8), in "Altarwise by owl-light" it is again to a sponge that time seems to be compared in these three lines: "Time's tune my ladies with the teats of music, / The scaled sea-sawers, fix in a naked sponge / Who sucks the bell-voiced Adam out of magic" (VII, ll. 7-9), and in "When once the twilight locks" the "mouth of time" is said to have "sucked, like a sponge" (l. 4). In this same poem, the narrator mentions an episode where someone comes to "rob" him of his "fluids" (l. 42).

IV

Another aspect of Paracelsian thought may have made its way into Thomas's poetry through the influence of Donne. One principle of Paracelsus's alchemic doctrine was that a combination of mercury, sulphur and salt was the origin of all bodies:

The material world is made of three principles: sulphur, mercury and salt.[19]

Moreover, metals had the power to support or maintain life:

> No man likewise can teach that Metals are dead substances, or do want life;
> seeing their oyls, salt, sulphur, and quintessence are the greatest Preservatives,
> and have the greatest strength and virtue to restore and preserve the life of man.[20]

And Paracelsus also explained that, at a high temperature, two solids could penetrate one another through a chemical process of "cementation":

> [A]s a Man loveth his Wife, and the Woman loveth her Husband, so do the
> Philosophers *Mercury* and the quick *Mercury*, prosecute the greatest love, and
> are moved by Nature with a great affection towards us: So therefore the one and
> the other *Mercuries* are conjoyned each to other, and one with another, even as
> the Man with the Woman, and she with him, according to their bodies, that there
> is no difference between them; and they are congruent in their strength and
> proprieties, save onely, that the Man is firm and fixed, but the Woman is volatile
> in the Fire. . . . They are both to be so close luted and covered, that the Woman
> may not evaporate or breath out, otherwise the whole Work will come to
> nothing.[21]

John Carey believes that this type of chemical reaction is what Donne had in mind when he wrote, in the poem "The Ecstasy", about the hands of two lovers which were cemented by the sweat their heat issued (ll. 5-6).[22] In "Elegy 8, *The Comparison*", sexual intercourse is imaged as an alchemical process to produce gold ("a soul of gold", a new life) with fire (which is male) and an alembic (which is the womb):

> Then like the chemic's masculine equal fire,
> Which in the limbeck's warm womb doth inspire
> Into th'earth's worthless dirt a soul of gold . . . (ll. 35-37)

In Thomas's "I, in my intricate image", man is described all along as an image cast in a mould from metal; he is a ghost laid in metal, a "metal phantom", his "blood and bubble" are "cast" to "the pine roots", in other words, poured as though they were molten metal into the mould of the pine roots, or perhaps simply "thrown onto" the roots of the pine trees.[23]

> She threads off the sap and needles, blood and bubble
> Casts to the pine roots, raising man like a mountain
> Out of the naked entrail.
>
> Beginning with doom in the ghost, and the springing marvels,
> Image of images, my metal phantom

> Forcing forth through the harebell,
> My man of leaves and the bronze root, mortal, unmortal . . .
>   (I, ll. 10-16)

Birth is seen as the forming of a metal image in a mould. The "metal phantom / Forcing forth through the harebell" (I, ll. 14-15), is an image of birth. This happens after his "ghost" has been laid in "metal" (I, l. 3), something which seems to refer to his soul having found flesh.[24] Consistent with this is the idea that the miracle of birth is possible through the fusion of two other metal images, of two persons in metal armour; man is, therefore, an "[i]mage of images". It is the fusion of flesh between woman and man, the "fusion of rose and male motion" that creates the "miracle of life":

> I, in my fusion of rose and male motion,
> Create this twin miracle.   (I, ll. 17-18)

The phrase "rose and male motion" refers to sexual intercourse between female and male, but it also extends the idea of man as being partly vegetal. The miracle is a "twin miracle" because the birth is that of both flesh and spirit. The poet then mentions his "half ghost in armour" and his "man-iron sidle" (I, ll. 5-6).

The idea of describing the body of an unborn person in terms of molten metal, which becomes armour once the person is born is also clear in "Before I knocked", where the narrator explains that, before birth, in the womb, he "Felt thud beneath my flesh's armour, / As yet was in a molten form" (ll. 9-10). A similar line of imagery is also seen in "I dreamed my genesis", where Thomas refers to the place before birth, a place under the grass, as "the man-melting night" (l. 8). The narrator is engaged in the process of escaping the wormy ground as though it was a prison (. . . filed / Through all the irons in the grass", ll. 6-7). For Thomas, the liquefaction of man is, generally, that of lead, iron and brass. And the metallic property of blood is considered in unusual ways. In "All all and all" he refers to "the brassy blood" (III, l. 11), while in "I dreamed my genesis" blood is described as "rust" (l. 18).

V

Individual images, gleaned throughout Thomas's early poetry, can be traced back to Paracelsian cosmogony and alchemy as utilized by Donne. But it is the nature of Thomas's magpie-like borrowings that the concepts are never likely to unravel meaning on a large scale. In providing keys to small areas of interpretation, however, they can be helpful tools for understanding the narrative line of some poems.

NOTES

1. T. S. Eliot, "Shakespeare and the Stoicism of Seneca", *Selected Essays* (London: Faber, 1951) 138-39.
2. Paul Ferris, ed., *The Collected Letters of Dylan Thomas*, rev. ed. (London: Dent, 2000) 122.
3. For a brief history of the theory of correspondences, see Nathalie Wourm, "The Smell of God", *Sense and Scent: An Exploration of Olfactory Meaning*, ed. Bronwen Martin and Felizitas Ringham (Dublin: Philomel, 2003) 81-95.
4. Will-Erich Peuckert, ed., *Paracelsus Werke* III (Basel/Stuttgart: Schwabe 1967) 70: "[A]us diesem limo hat der Schöpfer der Welt die kleine Welt gemacht, den microcosmum, das ist den Menschen. So also ist der Mensch die kleine Welt, das ist, der Mensch hat alle Eigenschaft der Welt in ihm, darum ist er microcosmus. Darum ist er das fünfte Wesen der Elemente und des Gestirns oder Firmaments in der obern sphaera und im untern globul". My translation.
5. The translation comes from Walter Pagel, *Paracelsus: An Introduction to Philosophical Medicine in the Era of the Renaissance* (Basel: S. Karger, 1958) 138. The German text can be found in Karl Sudhoff, ed., *Paracelsus Sämtliche Werke* VI (Munich: Oldenbourg, 1922) 340: "lasset euch die cosmographei ein anatomei sein . . . so ir dieselbigen in grund verstehent, so habt ir den microcosmum genzlich in seim wesen. besehent anatomiam terrae, wie ordenlich in ir hend und füß ligen und betrachten, was finger, was principaliora membra . . . seien . . . die anatomei des wassers, schaue was sein corpus sei, demnach wie die mineralia seine glider sind".
6. See Evelyn M. Simpson, *A Study of the Prose Works of John Donne*, 2nd ed. (Oxford: O.U.P., 1948) 127-28.
7. Mary Paton Ramsay, *Les Doctrines Médiévales Chez Donne, le Poète Métaphysicien de l'Angleterre (1573-1631)*, 2nd ed. (London: O.U.P., 1924) 250.
8. John Donne, *Devotions*, ed. John Sparrow (Cambridge: C.U.P., 1923) IV, 16.
9. *Devotions* XII, 63.
10. *Collected Letters of Dylan Thomas* 57.
11. All quotations are taken from Dylan Thomas, *Collected Poems 1934-1953*, ed. Walford Davies and Ralph Maud (London: Dent, 1993).
12. The mouth of a stream or river is usually the point where it issues into the sea. Here, though, the "mouthing streams" are streams that 'suck' at the same "mountain spring" as the poet (ll. 9-10); the mouth of the stream seems to be the point that issues the stream rather than that where it issues.
13. Tindall suggests that "the waters of your face" reverses "the face of the waters", the sea of Genesis. In that case, "your face" in "the waters of your face", should perhaps be understood as meaning "your facing side", "your surface" (as in "the face of the moon" or, indeed, "the face of the waters"); see William York Tindall, *A Reader's Guide to Dylan Thomas* (New York: Octagon, 1981) 45.
14. The general idea of the poem could be one of search for inspiration; the poetic manna escapes the poet who sends out his alter-ego to explore his mind for ideas. The alter-ego, the "creature", falls asleep and dreams a journey through death and the condition of being dead (which can involve "periscoping" through flowers or becoming a "cypress"). Eventually, the poet decides to leave the "poppied" or drowsy creature to its dream and to get down to work.
15. The translation comes from W. A. Murray, "Donne and Paracelsus: an essay in interpretation" in John R. Roberts, ed., *Essential Articles for the Study of John*

Donne's Poetry (Harvester: Hassocks, 1975) 125. The German text can be found in Will-Erich Peuckert, ed., *Paracelsus Werke* V (Basel/Stuttgart: Schwabe, 1968) 78, 82: "Nun ist das Leben des Menschen nichts anderes denn ein astralischer Balsam, eine balsamische Impression, ein himmlisches und unsichtbares Feuer, eine eingeschlossene Luft und ein tingierender Salzgeist . . . Der Tod aber des Menschen ist gewiß nichts anderes als . . . eine Fortenehmung der Luft, ein Verschwinden des Balsams und ein Ablöschen des natürlichen Lichts und eine große Separation der drei Substanzen Leib, Seel und Geist, und ein Hingehen wiederum in seiner Mutter Leib. Denn alldieweil der irdische und natürliche Mensch von der Erde ist, so ist auch die Erde seine Mutter, in die er wiederum muß".

16. John Donne, "A nocturnall upon S. Lucies day, Being the shortest day", ll. 1-8, *The Poems of John Donne* I, ed. Herbert J. C. Grierson (Oxford, 1912) 44.
17. See John Donne, *The Elegies and the Songs and Sonnets*, ed. Helen Gardner, (Oxford: Clarendon P., 1965) 217. Thomas could conceivably have used the 1912 Grierson edition (reprinted in 1929). Grierson does not comment at all on the first stanza of this poem, but Thomas could have come across the theories of Paracelsus in other parts of the Commentary volume. See, for instance, Grierson, ed., *Poems of John Donne* II, 30, 36.
18. See also "All all and all":

   Out of the sea, the drive of oil,
   Socket and grave, the brassy blood,
   Flower, flower, all all and all.   (III, ll. 10-12)

   The poem is extremely obscure so that any interpretation of the meaning of "oil" is hazardous. Judging from the first stanza, the general idea seems to be that all comes from the earth, from its oil or its lava ("All from the oil, the pound of lava", l. 3), whether it be flowers or men. In the three lines quoted above, oil and blood seem to be equivalent. In his story "The Enemies", Thomas talks of "the living grease in the soil"; see Dylan Thomas, *The Collected Stories*, ed. Walford Davies (London: Dent, 1983) 20.
19. Peuckert, ed., *Paracelsus Werke* III 53: "Der greifliche ist aus drei Stücken, aus sulphure, mercurio und sale". My translation.
20. Paracelsus, *The Archidoxes of Magic* (1656; London: Askin, 1975) 93.
21. Paracelsus, *The Archidoxes of Magic* 23-24.
22. John Carey, *John Donne: Life, Mind and Art* (Oxford: O.U.P., 1990) 145.
23. Of course, "[c]asts" may have a double meaning; it could be related to the mention, a few lines below, of the "fortune of manhood", the fate or destiny of man: "This is the fortune of manhood: the natural peril . . ." In this case, "[c]asts" would be understood in the sense of casting dice. Other possible senses of "[c]asts" here, are those related to weaving and fishing. To "cast on" and to "cast off" are used in knitting and weaving and mean to "start" and "end" a row. This idea would fit the image of the Fates spinning the threads of life, "working on a world of petals" as on a weaving loom. But the fishing image is valid, too, for it is possible to imagine that "She" is casting the line ("to the pine roots") and drawing up a body ("raising man like a mountain / Out of the naked entrail").
24. Thomas can use the word "ghost" to mean "soul" of the living rather than "spirit" of the dead. See "If my head hurt a hair's foot", where the narrator, an embryo, is apparently telling his mother that he does not wish to cause her pain during

delivery, and that he will do anything "Before I rush in a crouch the ghost with a hammer, air, / Strike light, and bloody a loud room" (ll. 9-10). See also "I dreamed my genesis": "Rerobing of the naked ghost" (l. 23).

Welsh Writing in English: a bibliography of criticism 2002 and 2003

compiled by
Diane Green
University of Wales, Swansea

This listing covers books, contributions to books, periodical articles and selected theses. Reviews as a category are excluded although longer, review-articles are listed, as are reviews of listed critical writing. Date of publication is usually 2002 or 2003. Some publications in English on Welsh-language authors have been included, as have occasional publications in Welsh on English-language authors. Readers aware of relevant items, published in 2002 or 2003, which have been omitted are kindly asked to forward details to the Editor, *Welsh Writing in English*, Dept of English, University of Wales, Bangor, Gwynedd, LL57 2DG.

GENERAL CRITICISM

Bianchi, Tony. No Place Like Home? *Planet* 159 (2003) 47-55. On space in contemporary Welsh fiction.

Blandford, Steve. "Old Wales is Dead": Film, Theatre and TV Drama in Contemporary Wales. *New Welsh Review* 61 (2003) 84-94.

Bohata, Kirsti. The Rise and Rise of Welsh Writing in English. *New Welsh Review* 62 (2003) 35-41.

—— Postcolonialism revisited: the challenging case of Welsh writing in English. Ph.D. thesis. University of Wales, Swansea, 2003.

Brennan, Catherine. *Angers, Fantasies and Ghostly Fears: Nineteenth-Century Women from Wales and English Language Poetry*. Cardiff: University of Wales Press, 2003. 208p. ISBN 0-70831-764-2.
Reviews: Moira Dearnley. Reassessments. *Planet* 162 (2003/4) 106-7; Sheenagh Pugh. Everything but Music. *PNR* 155 (2004) 91.

Brown, Tony (editor). *Welsh Writing in English: A Yearbook of Critical Essays* 7 (2001-2002). 190p. ISSN 1356-0301.

Contents: "It is our duty to sing": *Y Gododdin* and David Jones's *In Parenthesis*, by Paul Robichaud, pp. 1-15—The Voices of Glamorgan: Gwyn Thomas's Colonial Fiction, by Stephen Knight, pp. 16-34—From Pig-sty to Benin Head: Modernism and Post-colonialism in Emyr Humphreys's *Jones*, by Diane Green, pp. 35-49—Resident Aliens: R.S. Thomas and the Anti-Modern Movement, by Grahame Davies, pp. 50-77—Poetry for the Air: *The Minister, Sŵn y Gwynt sy'n Chwythu* and *The Dream of Jake Hopkins* as Radio Odes, by Rhian Reynolds, pp. 78-105—A Tower of Babel: Heteroglossia, The Grotesque and the (De)construction of Meaning in Glyn Jones's *The Valley, The City, The Village* and Niall Griffith's *Grits*, by Harri Roberts, pp. 106-129—"Language of Light": The Poetry of John Powell Ward, by Fiona Owen, pp. 130-153—"A dislocation called a blessing": Three Welsh/ Jewish Perspectives, by Jasmine Donahaye, pp. 154-173—Note: "Gandhi" and "Beauty's Slaves": Two English Sonnets by Waldo Williams, by Damian Walford Davies, pp. 174-180—Welsh Writing in English: A Bibliography of Criticism, 1999, by John Harris, pp. 181-188. Reviews: Clare Morgan. Tightrope Walking. *Planet* 158 (2003) 106-107; Nathalie Wourm. *New Welsh Review* 58 (2002) 110-112.

Brown, Tony (editor). *Welsh Writing in English: A Yearbook of Critical Essays* 8 (2003). 202p. ISBN 0-70831-829-0.
Contents: From Fictional Nation to National Fiction? Reconsidering T.J. Llewelyn Prichard's *The Adventures and Vagaries of Twm Shon Catti*, by Andrew Davies, pp. 1-28—"He was a queer lad for his age ...": The Crisis of Masculinity in Lewis Jones's *Cwmardy*, by Emma Davies, pp. 29-45—The Social Vision of Dylan Thomas, by Victor N. Paananen, pp. 46-66—"Writing with dreams and blood": Dylan Thomas, Marxism and 1930s Swansea, by Victor Golightly, pp. 67-91—Apostrophes (and Other Endings) in Dylan Thomas's *Deaths and Entrances*, by James A. Davies, pp. 92-106—Swansea's Other Poet: Vernon Watkins and the Threshold between Worlds, by Rowan Williams, pp. 107-120— Making It New: R.S. Thomas and William Carlos Williams, by David Lloyd, pp. 121-140—Poets, Language and Land: Reflections on English-Language Welsh Poetry since the Second World War, by Jeremy Hooker, pp. 141-156— Forum: Alun Lewis and the Politics of Empire, by John Pikoulis, Tony Brown, M. Wynn Thomas, pp. 157-179— Note: Dylan Thomas in Vancouver, by Geoffrey Madoc-Jones, pp. 180-181—Welsh Writing in English: Á Bibliography of Criticism 2000 and 2001, by Claire Powell, pp. 182-199. Review. Richard Poole. From Wells to Puddles. *Planet* 161 (2003) 110-112.

Byrne, Aidan. Urban literature of South Wales: an exploration of urban themes in works by Gwyn Thomas, Rhys Davies and Christopher Meredith. M.A. dissertation. University of Wales, Bangor, 2000.

Curtis, Tony. Playing it cool. *Planet* 162 (2003/4) 80-88. On poetry and jazz in Britain.

Davies, Damian Walford. *Presences That Disturb: Models of Romantic Identity in the Literature and Culture of the 1790s.* Cardiff: University of Wales Press, 2002. xv, 389p. ISBN 0-70831-738-3. Reviews: Mary-Ann Constantine. *New Welsh Review* 60 (2003) 116-117; Robin Young. Dealings with the Radical Subculture. *Planet* 157 (2003) 106-107.

Davies, Emma. Manufacturing men: literary masculinities in industrial Welsh writing in English. M.A. dissertation. University of Wales, Swansea, 2001.

Davies, Grahame. Success against the odds. *New Welsh Review* 55 (2002) 15-21. On the best Welsh-language poets under 45.

Dixon, M. J. Writing the Rhondda: representations of the Rhondda Valleys in the literature of the 1930s. Ph.D. thesis. University of Wales, Aberystwyth, 2002.

Elfyn, Menna and John Rowlands (editors). *The Bloodaxe Book of Modern Welsh Poetry.* Highgreen, Tarset: Bloodaxe, 2003. 450p. ISBN 1852245492. Introduction by John Rowlands, 16-27. Reviews: Tony Bianchi. *Poetry Wales* 39. 2 (2003) 63-65; Christine Evans. *New Welsh Review* 62 (2003) 113-115.

Gramich, Katie and Catherine Brennan (editors). *Welsh Women's Poetry 1460-2001: An Anthology.* Dinas Powys: Honno, 2003. xlv, 500p. ISBN 1-870206-54-1. Introduction by Jane Aaron. Review: Zoë Skoulding. *Poetry Wales* 39. 2 (2003) 66-67.

Gray, Melinda. Grave Matters: Poetry and the Preservation of the Welsh Language in the United States. In *American Babel: Literatures of the United States from Abnaki to Zuni*, ed. Marc Shell (The Harvard English Studies Series). Cambridge MA: Harvard University Press, 2002. xii, 520p. ISBN 0674006445. pp. 307-321.

Hill, Greg. Sisyphus Goes to School. *Planet* 161 (2003) 82-85. On Welsh Writing in English and the education system.

Jones, John Idris. Wales and the Bard of Avon. *New Welsh Review* 56 (2002) 41-44.

Mazelis, Jo. The Short Story in Wales. *Planet* 161 (2003) 91-92.

Price, Angharad (editor). *Chwileniwm: Technoleg a Llenyddiaeth.* Cardiff: University of Wales Press, 2002. 222p. ISBN 0708317235. Essays on technology in literature: two essays in English, 10 in Welsh. Includes material

on digitizing the Mabinogion, on Early Welsh literature, on R.S. Thomas, and on Welsh literature on the Web.
Review: Fflur Dafydd. *New Welsh Review* 57 (2002) 116-117.

Prys-Williams, Barbara. Variations in the nature of the perceived self in some twentieth century Welsh autobiographical writing. Ph.D. thesis. University of Wales, Swansea, 2002.

Roberts, Dewi (editor). *War: an anthology.* Llanrwst: Gwasg Carreg Gwalch, 2002. 93p. ISBN 0-86381-704-1. Corgi Series 4.

—— *Love: an anthology.* Llanrwst: Gwasg Carreg Gwalch, 2002. 80p. ISBN 0-86381-708-4. Corgi Series 8.

Rowlands, Sioned Puw (editor). *Byd y Nofelydd.* Talybont: Y Lolfa, 2003. 180p. ISBN 086243677X. Interviews with Welsh writers, some of whom are writers in English.

Sullivan III, C.W. Lore of the Rings. *New Welsh Review* 56 (2002) 34-40. The use of Welsh legend in fantasy literature.

Thomas, M. Wynn (editor). *Welsh Writing in English.* A Guide to Welsh Literature, Vol. 7. Cardiff: University of Wales Press, 2003. 348 p. ISBN 0-7083-1679-4.
Contents: Introduction, by M. Wynn Thomas, pp. 1-6—Prelude to the Twentieth Century, by Belinda Humfrey, pp. 7-46—"A New Enormous Music": Industrial Fiction in Wales, by Stephen Knight, pp. 47-90—Borderers and Borderline Cases, by John Powell Ward, pp. 91-119—Dylan Thomas and his Welsh Contemporaries, by James A. Davies, pp, 120-164—The Problems of Belonging, by Tony Brown and M. Wynn Thomas, pp. 165-202—Popular Images, by John Harris, pp. 203-221—*Poetry Wales* and the Second Flowering, by Tony Conran, pp. 222-254 —Both in and out of the Game: Welsh Writers and the British Dimension, by Katie Gramich, pp. 255-277—"Pulling you through Changes": Welsh Writing in English before, between and after two Referenda, by Jane Aaron and M. Wynn Thomas, pp. 278-309—Parallels and Paradigms, by Ned Thomas, pp. 310-326.
Review: Meic Stephens. Bringing up the fear. *Planet* 162 (2003) 100-101.

Von Rothkirch, Alyce. Making Play-Texts Live: Teaching Drama as Experience. In *Global Challenges and Regional Responses in Contemporary Drama in English.* CDE Conference Proceedings, ed. Jochen Achilles, Ina Bergman and Birgit Däwes. Wvt- Wissenschaftlicher Verlag: Trier, 2003. pp. 247-264.

—— Annette Pankratz and Kathleen Starck. Learning How to Teach – Teaching How to Learn. http://fb14.uni-mainz.de/projects/cde. 2002.

—— The Last Stand of the *Gwerin*: Welsh National Ideology and Welsh Drama in English in the Beginning of the Twentieth Century. In *Latitude 63° North: Proceedings of the 8th International Region and Nation Literature Conference. Mid-Sweden University College Östersund, Sweden, 2-6 August 2000*, ed. David Bell. Östersund: Mid-Sweden University College, 2002. pp. 163-174.

—— A Welsh National Theatre? Welsh Drama in English before the Second World War. In *Crossing Borders: Intercultural Drama and Theatre at the Turn of the Millennium*. CDE Conference Proceedings, ed. Bernhard Reitz and Alyce von Rothkirch. Wvt– Wissenschaftlicher Verlag: Trier, 2001. pp. 141-150.

Whitfield, Esther. Mordecai and Haman: The Drama of Welsh America. In *American Babel: Literatures of the United States from Abnaki to Zuni*, ed. Marc Shell (The Harvard English Studies Series). Cambridge MA: Harvard University Press, 2002. xii, 520p. ISBN 0674006445. pp. 93-116.

Williams, Daniel. Cymry Ewythr Sam: creu Cymreictod yn yr Unol Daleithiau 1860-1900. In *Cof Cenedl* 18, ed. Geraint Jenkins. Llandysul: Gomer Press, 2003. pp. 147-59. (In Welsh. *Constructing 'Welshness' in the United States 1860-1900*).

—— The Welsh Atlantic: Mapping the Contexts of Welsh-American Literature. In *American Babel: Literatures of the United States from Abnaki to Zuni*, ed. Marc Shell (The Harvard English Studies Series). Cambridge MA: Harvard University Press, 2002. xii, 520p. ISBN 0674006445. pp. 343-368.

—— Coch a'r Du: Moderniaeth a Chenedligrwydd yn Harlem a Chymru. *Gweld Sêr: Cymru a Chanrif America*, ed. M. Wynn Thomas. Cardiff: University of Wales Press, 2001. 253p. ISBN 0-7083-1703-0. pp. 166-203 (In Welsh. *The Red and the Black: Modernism and Nationalism in Harlem and Wales*).

INDIVIDUAL AUTHORS

Dannie Abse

Abse, Dannie. *Touch Wood: Poems and a story*. Llanrwst: Gwasg Carreg Gwalch, 2002. 90p. ISBN 0-86381-701-7. Corgi Series 1.

—— *The Two Roads Taken: A Prose Miscellany*. London: Enitharmon Press, 2003. xxix, 242p. ISBN 1900564688.

—— *New and Collected Poems*. London: Hutchinson, 2003. 426p. ISBN 0091795184.

Reviews:. Greg Hill. Startling Disclosures. *Planet* 160 (2003) 96-98; Jeremy Hooker. *New Welsh Review* 62 (2003) 95-96; J. Lucas. *Poetry Wales* 39.1 (2003) 30-31.

Davies, James A. Dannie Abse's Autobiographical Fiction. *New Welsh Review* 56 (2002) 14-20.

Kiernan, Anna. Homage to Abse. *New Welsh Review* 62 (2003) 42-47.

Glenda Beagan
Greenall, Mary. Walking in Dark Interiors. *Planet* 156 (2002/3) 39-45. Interview.

Sean Burke
Jenkins, Mark. From Barthes to Butetown. *New Welsh Review* 58 (2002) 20-27.

Duncan Bush
Minhinnick, Robert. Interview with Duncan Bush. *Poetry Wales* 38.2 (2002) 46-50.

Williams, Nerys. Duncan Bush: The 'Parasitic' Art. *Poetry Wales* 38.2 (2002) 51-55.

Gillian Clarke
Brookes, Geoff. *York Notes for GCSE: Gillian Clarke and Seamus Heaney.* Harlow: Longman, 2003. 144p. ISBN 05827722648.

Davies, Diane. Beyond the Referential: Rootedness and Fluidity in the Poetry of Gillian Clarke. In *Contemporary Poems: Some Critical Approaches*, ed. L. Jeffries and P. Sansom. Huddersfield: Smith/Doorstep Books, 2000. pp. 108-125.

Thurston, Michael. Writing at the edge: Gillian Clarke's *Cofiant*. *Contemporary Literature* 44.2 (2003) 275-300.

Tony Conran
Conran, Tony. *Castles* and *All Hallows*: The First Two Symphonies of *The Welsh Commoedia*. *New Welsh Review* 57 (2002) 31-46. 2002 Gwyn Jones Lecture.

—— *Welsh Verse*. Translated by Tony Conran. Bridgend: Seren, 2003. Third reprint of 1986 edition. 356p. ISBN 1854110810. Preface to third edition p. 13.

—— *Branwen: and other dance dramas and plays*. Llanrwst: Gwasg Carreg Gwalch, 2003. 300p. ISBN 0863818560.

B. L. Coombes

Coombes, B. L. *These Poor Hands: The Autobiography of a Miner Working in South Wales*, ed. Bill Jones and Chris Williams. Cardiff: University of Wales Press, 2002. viii 207p. ISBN 0708315631.
Review: David Barnes. *New Welsh Review* 60 (2003) 112-114.

Tony Curtis

Barry, Peter. Contemporary Poetry and Ekphrasis. *Cambridge Quarterly* 31.2 (2002) 155-165.

Curtis, Tony. *Considering Cassandra: Poems and a story*. Llanrwst: Gwasg Carreg Gwalch, 2003. 82p. ISBN 0-86381-707-6. Corgi Series 7.

Stevenson, Anne. Tony Curtis, Seamus Heaney and Confidential Poetry. *Planet* 152 (2002) 21-26.

Aneirin Talfan Davies

Reynolds, Sarah Rhian. Aneirin Talfan Davies: Producing a Nation. Ph.D. thesis. University of Wales, Swansea, 2001.

Idris Davies

Adams, Sam. Letter from Wales. *PNR* 155 (2004) 9-10.

Davies, Idris. *A Carol for the Coalfield and other poems*. Llanrwst: Gwasg Gwalch, 2002. 93p. ISBN 0863817025. Corgi Series 2.

Logan, Stephen. Hiraeth and the Recoil from Theory. *Planet* 155 (2002) 78-85.

Perrin, Jim. Introduction. *The Collected Poems of Idris Davies*. Islwyn Jenkins (editor). Llandysul: Gomer, 2003. ISBN 184323307X.

—— The Achievement of *Gwalia Deserta*. *Poetry Wales* 39.2 (2003) 42-46.

James Kitchener Davies

Thomas, M. Wynn. *James Kitchener Davies*. Writers of Wales Series. Cardiff: University of Wales Press, 2002. 128p. ISBN 0708317243.
Reviews: Gareth Alban Davies. No Room For Nostalgia. *Planet* 156 (2002/3) 99-100; Katie Gramich. *New Welsh Review* 59 (2003) 97-99.

John Davies

Davies, John. *North by South: New and Selected Poems*. Bridgend: Seren, 2002. 156p. ISBN 1854113259.
Review: Wayne Burrows. The Journey Home. *Planet* 159 (2003) 97-98.

Williams, Nerys. John Davies: 'The geography of life around here'. *Poetry Wales* 38.4 (2003) 38-41.

Lewis Davies
Pikoulis, John. The Case of the Vanishing Hero: a profile of Lewis Davies. *New Welsh Review* 61 (2003) 35-40.

Stevie Davies
Davies, Stevie. Hearing Voices. *New Welsh Review* 61 (2003) 23-34.

Jean Earle
Minhinnick, Robert. Jean Earle, 1909-2002 (In Memoriam). *Poetry Wales* 38. 1 (2002) 5.

Rhydderch, Francesca. Intimate Moments: Jean Earle 1909-2002. *Planet* 153 (2002) 13-19.

Dic Edwards
Adams, David. Dic kicks against the pricks. *New Welsh Review* 56 (2002) 186-189.

Betts, Torben. Dic Edwards in conversation with Torben Betts, January-April 2002. www.dic-edwards.com. (The site includes reviews of *Franco's Bastard* and Edwards's essay "Theatre for the Evicted".)

Edwards, Dic. A Welsh Pastoral: The Making of *Franco's Bastard*. *New Welsh Review* 57 (2002) 84-91.

Caradoc Evans
Evans, Caradoc. *Capel Sion*, ed. with intro. John Harris. Bridgend: Seren, 2002. xx, 111p. ISBN 1854113089.
Review: Rhian Reynolds. *New Welsh Review* 58 (2003) 115-116.

Smith, Matthew Michael C. 'Whoring the holy text': the religious grotesque in Caradoc Evans and Dylan Thomas. M.A. dissertation. University of Wales, Swansea, 2001.

Niall Griffiths
Roberts, Harri. Tower of Babel: heteroglossia, the grotesque, and the (de) construction of meaning in *Grits* and other Welsh writing in English. M.A. dissertation. University of Wales, Swansea, 2001.

Steve Griffiths
Minhinnick, Robert. Interview with Steve Griffiths. *Poetry Wales* 39.3 (2003/4) 38-43.

James Hanley
Dentith, S. James Hanley's 'The Furies': the modernist subject goes on strike. *Literature and History* 12.1 (2003) 41-56.

Fordham, John. *James Hanley: Modernism and the Working Class.* Cardiff: University of Wales Press, 2002. xii, 315p. ISBN 0708317553. See particularly Ch. 4, Hanley and Wales, pp. 137-233. Reviews: Stephen Knight. A Modernist in the Fo'c'sle. *Planet* 160 (2003) 107-108; Stephen Wade. *New Welsh Review* 60 (2003) 110-111.

Rice, A. 'A peculiar power about rottenness': Annihilating desire in James Hanley's 'The German Prisoner'. *Modernism-Modernity.* 9.1 (2002) 75-89.

James Hawes
England, Iwan. Coc-yp, cocên a Chymru. *Golwg* 17.7 (17 Oct. 2003) 20-21.

Felicia Hemans
Adams, Theresa Ann. 'That strange personal interest': Personality, publishing, and poetry in the 1820s (John Keats, John Clare, Felicia Hemans, Letitia Elizabeth Landon). Ph.D. thesis. University of Wisconsin, Madison, 2002. ISBN 0493638717.

Anderson, John M. Icons of Women in the Religious Sonnets of Wordsworth and Hemans. In *The Fountain Light: Studies in Romanticism and Religion in Honour of John L. Mahoney,* ed. Robert J. Barth. New York: Fordham University Press, 2002. pp. 90-110.

Blair, K. Proved on the pulses: the heart in nineteenth century poetry, 1830-1860. DPhil thesis. Oxford University, 2003.

Cottingham, M. Felicia Hemans's dead and dying bodies. *Women's Writing* 8.2 (2001) 275-294.

Furr, Derek. Sentimental Confrontations: Hemans, Landon, and Elizabeth Barrett. *English Language Notes* 40.2 (2002) 29-47.

Lokke, Kari. Poetry as Self-Consumption: Women Writers and their Audience in British and German Romanticism. In *Romantic Poetry,* ed. Angela Esterhammer. Amsterdam: Benjamins, 2002. 537p. ISBN 9027234507. pp. 91-111.

Sweet, Nanora. 'The Inseparables': Hemans, the Brownes and the Milan Commission. *Forum for Modern Language Studies* 39.2 (2003) 165-177.

—— Felicia Hemans' 'A Tale of the Secret Tribunal': Gothic Empire in the Age of Jeremy Bentham and Walter Scott. *European Journal of English Studies* 6.2 (2002) 159-171.

Sweet, Nanora and Julie Melnyk (editors). *Felicia Hemans: Reimagining Poetry in the Nineteenth Century.* Basingstoke: Palgrave, 2001. xxix, 242p. ISBN 0333801091.
Contents: Foreword: Now *Our* Hemans, by Marlon B. Ross, pp. x-xxvi— Introduction: Why Hemans *Now?* By Nanora Sweet and Julie Melnyk, pp. 1-15—Impure Affections: Felicia Hemans's Elegiac Poetry and Contaminated Grief, by Michael T. Williamson, pp. 19-35—The Fragile Image: Felicia Hemans and Romantic Ekphrasis, by Grant F. Scott, pp. 36-54—The Triumph of Voice in Felicia Hemans's *The Forest Sanctuary*, by John M. Anderson, pp. 55-73—Hemans's Later Poetry: Religion and the Vatic Poet, by Julie Melnyk, pp. 74-92—'Certainly not a Female Pen': Felicia Hemans's Early Public Reception, by Stephen C. Behrendt, pp. 95-114—The Search for a Space: A Note on Felicia Hemans and the Royal Society of Literature, by Barbara D. Taylor, pp. 124-134—'The Spells of Home': Hemans, 'Heimat' and the Cult of the Dead Poetess in Nineteenth-Century Germany, by Frauke Lenckos, pp. 135-151—Hemans and the Romance of Byron, by Susan J. Wolfson, pp. 155-180—Gender and Modernity in *The Abencerrage*: Hemans, Rushdie, and 'the Moor's Last Sigh', by Nanora Sweet, pp. 181-195—Death and the Matron: Felicia Hemans, Romantic Death, and the Founding of the Modern Liberal State, by Gary Kelly, pp. 196-211—Natural and National Monuments—Felicia Hemans's 'The Image in Lava': A Note, by Isobel Armstrong, pp. 212-230.

Underwood, Ted. Romantic Historicism and the Afterlife. *Publications of the Modern Language Association of America* 117.2 (2002) 237-251.

Wolfson, Susan J. (editor). *Felicia Hemans: Selected Poems, Letters, Reception Materials.* Princeton University Press, 2001. xl, 633p. ISBN 0691050295.
Reviews: S. C. Behrendt. *Criticism: A Quarterly for Literature and the Arts.* 44.2 (Spring. 2002) 217-220; Anon. *Virginia Quarterly Review* 77.4 (2001); K. Karbiener. *Keats-Shelley Journal* 51 (2002) 226-229; C. Pettitt. *Times Literary Supplement* 5129 (July 2001); D. Wit. *Wordsworth Circle* 32.4 (2001) 255-256.

Paul Henry
Davies, Lyndon. Behind Glass: An Essay on Paul Henry. *Poetry Wales* 39.3 (2003/4) 58-62.

Emyr Humphreys

Dawkins, Sarah. Home and family in the novels of Emyr Humphreys. M.A. dissertation. University of Wales, Swansea, 2002.

Green, Diane. The Blodeuwedd myth and the dysfunctional family unit in Emyr Humphreys's novels. *Revista Alicantina de Estudios Ingleses* 16 (Nov. 2003). 129-146. Special Issue devoted to New Literatures in English.

Humphreys, Emyr. Negotiating with the Living. *New Welsh Review* 59 (2003) 28-34. On Margaret Atwood's *Negotiating with the Dead: A Writer on Writing.*

Nicholas, Mary. Emyr Humphreys: creator, crusader, catalytic converter. Ph.D. thesis. University of Wales, Swansea, 2002.

Thomas, M. Wynn. *Emyr Humphreys: Conversations and Reflections.* Cardiff: University of Wales Press, 2003. xi, 256p. ISBN 0708317359. Reviews: Jeremy Hooker. Against an Unholy Alliance of Commercial and Political Power. *New Welsh Review* 56 (2002) 153-154; C. Morgan. *Times Literary Supplement.* 5177 (21 June 2002) 29; Owain Wilkins. Flourishing in the Local. *Planet* 155 (2002) 108-110.

Mark Jenkins

Davies, Hazel Walford. The Theatre of Human Obsessions. *New Welsh Review* 56 (2002) 190-202.

Mike Jenkins

Jenkins, Mike. *Laughter Tangled in Thorn and other poems.* Llanrwst: Gwasg Carreg Gwalch, 2002. 106p. ISBN 0-86381-703-9. Corgi Series 3.

David Jones

Aldritt, Keith. *David Jones: Writer and Artist.* London: Constable and Robinson, 2003. xii, 208p. ISBN 1841193798.

Ashley, Scott. David Jones (1895-1974). In *British Writers: Supplement VII,* ed. Jay Parini. New York: Scribner, 2002. 167-182.

Dilworth, Thomas. *David Jones: A Biography.* London: Pimlico, 2003. 95p. ISBN 0224033605.

Jones, David. *In Parenthesis: Seinnyessit E Gledyt Ym Penn Mameu.* New York Review of Books Pub, 2003. 224p. ISBN 1590170369. Foreword by W. S. Merwin.

—— *Wedding Poems,* ed. Thomas Dilworth, with Foreword and Afterword. London: Enitharmon Press, 2002. 144p. ISBN 1900564874. Review. Greg Hill. Aphrodite in the Blitz. *Planet* 158 (2003) 114-115.

Robichaud, Paul. Gothic Architecture in the Poetry of David Jones and Geoffrey Hill. *Mosaic* 35.4 (2002) 181-197.

Wootten, William. At the thirteenth hour. *London Review of Books* 25.18 (25 September 2003) 27-28.

D. Gwenallt Jones
Thomas, M. Wynn. The Welsh anti-capitalist. *New Welsh Review* 56 (2002) 82-88.

Alun Lewis
Lewis, Alun. *The Sentry: poems and stories*. Llanrwst: Gwasg Carreg Gwalch, 2003. 98p. ISBN 0863817068. Corgi Series 6.

Gwyneth Lewis
Williams, Nerys. Gwyneth Lewis: Taboo and Blasphemy. *Poetry Wales* 38.3 (2003) 23-28.

Hilary Llewellyn-Williams
Hart, David. The Thread of Poetry. *Planet* 162 (2003/4). Interview.

***The Mabinogion* and related materials**
Benozzo, Francesco. *Landscape Perception in Early Celtic Literature*. Andover, MA.: Celtic Studies Publications, 2003. 260p. ISBN 1891271113.

Blake, Steve and Scott Lloyd. *Arthur of Wales* (Collected Literary and Historical Sources). Cardiff: Welsh Academic Press, 2002. 400p. ISBN 1860570747.

Breeze, A. Welsh Tradition and the baker's daughter in *Hamlet*. *Notes and Queries* 49.2 (2002) 199-200.

Cusick, Edmund (editor). *Blodeuwedd: An Anthology of Women's Poetry*. Ruthin: Headland, 2001. 93p. ISBN 1902096711. Introduction, by Edmund Cusick, pp. 7-16.
Review. Margaret Lloyd. The Woman Made of Flowers. *Planet* 152 (2002) 111-112.

Greene, V. Who Believes in the Return of King Arthur? *Cahiers de Civilisation Medievale* 45 (2002) 321-340.

Hall, Alaric. *Gwyr y Gogledd*? Some Icelandic Analogues to *Branwen Ferch Lyr*. *Cambrian Medieval Celtic Studies* 42 (2001) 27-50.

Millersdaughter, Katherine. The Geopolitics of Incest: Sex, Gender and Violence in the Fourth Branch of the Mabinogi. *Exemplaria* 14 (2002) 271-272.

Noble, Peter S. (editor). *The Growth of the Tristan and Iseult Legend in Wales, England, France and Germany* (Studies in Medieval Literature). Phillipa Hardman and Françoise H. M. LeSaux (Introduction), Jan J. Kirby (Preface). Edwin Mellen Publishers, 2003. 214p. ISBN 0773468358.

Padel, Oliver James. *Arthur in Medieval Literature*. Cardiff: University of Wales Press, 2000. 144p. ISBN 0708316824. Reviews: E. R. Henken. *Cambridge Medieval Celtic Studies* 44 (2002) 116-117; N. Jacobs. *Notes & Queries* 49.1 (2002) 131-132; S. Knight. *Speculum* 78. 1 (2003) 241-242; C. Lloyd-Morgan. *Cahiers de Civilisation Medievale* 46 (2003) 93-94.; J. Wood. *Folklore* 113.1 (2002) 109-110.

Roberts, Brynley F. Where were the Four Branches of the Mabinogi Written? *The Individual in Celtic Literature. CSANA Yearbook* 1, ed. Joseph Falaky Nagy. Dublin: Four Courts Press, 2001. pp. 61-73.

Sims-Williams, Patrick. Clas Beuno and the Four Branches of the Mabinogi. In 150 Jahre 'Mabinogion': *Deutch-Walische Kulturbeziehungen*, ed. Bernard Maier, Stefan Zimmer, Christine Bakte. Tübingen, 2001. pp. 111-127.

Updike, J. Medieval Superheroes *New York Times Book Review* 22 (28 Januaery 2001) Adapted from the preface of forthcoming edition of *The Mabinogion.*

Arthur Machen
Clarke, David. Rumors of Angels: A Legend of the First World War. *Folklore* 113.2 (2002) 151-173.

Ferguson, Christine. Decadence as Scientific Fulfilment. *Publications of the Modern Language Association of America* 117.3 (2002) 465-478.

Simpson, Jacqueline. Rumors of Angels: A Response to Clarke. *Folklore* 114.1 (2003) 114-115.

Sparks, Tabitha. Medical Gothic and the Return of the Contagious Diseases Acts in Stoker and Machen. *Nineteenth Century Feminisms* 6 (2002) 87-102.

Voller, Jack G. Arthur Machen (1863-1947). In *Gothic Writers: A Critical and Bibliographical Guide*, ed. Douglass H. Thomson, Jack G. Voller and Frederick S. Frank. Westport: Greenwood, 2001. 516p. ISBN 0313305005. pp. 278-282.

Roland Mathias
Adams, Sam. The Poetry of Roland Mathias. *PNR* 28.4 (2002) 49-56.

—— Roland Mathias: probably Wales's foremost literary critic in English. *Poetry Wales* 39.1 (2003) 59-60.

Mathias, Roland. *The Collected Poems of Roland Mathias*, ed. Sam Adams. Cardiff: University of Wales Press, 2002. xvi, 383p. ISBN 0-70831-760X. Reviews: Michael Collins. *Poetry Wales* 39.2 (2003) 57-60; Tony Curtis. *Poetry Review* 93.1 (2003) 95-100; Jeremy Hooker. Serious Pleasures. *Planet* 158 (2003) 101-103; Robert P. Jones. Worth the Record. *PNR* 151 (2003) 69-71; John Lucas. *Poetry Wales* 38.4 (2003) 69-70; Richard Poole. *New Welsh Review* 59 (2003) 95-97.

Gary Owen
Harris, Simon. "A Cry of Rage". *New Welsh Review* 60 (2003) 44-50. Conversation with Gary Owen.

Meic Povey
Llewelyn, Dafydd. "Speaking Two Spokes". *New Welsh Review* 60 (2003) 51-57. Interview.

Katherine Philips
Hodgson, Elizabeth M. A. Katherine Philips: agent of matchlessness. *Women's Writing* 10.1 (2003) 119-136.

Sheenagh Pugh
Bowen, Jo and Mike Ross. *Approaches to the study of Sheenagh Pugh's Selected Poems*. Cardiff: W.J.E.C., 2001. 32p. ISBN 186085443.

Williams, Nerys. Sheenagh Pugh: Exploring Fanfics, life studies and reanimating history. *Poetry Wales* 38.1 (2002) 57-60.

Allen Raine
Milner-Hughes, Glenys. Flowers of the Riverbank: Women and Wales in the novels of Allen Raine. M.A. dissertation. University of Wales, Bangor, 2001.

Alun Richards
Richards, Alun. Scandalous Thoughts and other stories. Llanrwst: Gwasg Carreg Gwalch, 2003. 108p. ISBN 0-86381-705. Corgi Series 5.

Lynette Roberts
McGuiness, Patrick. Frostwork. *New Welsh Review* 62 (2003) 5-16.

Dylan Thomas
Aaron, Jane. "Heddwas ifanc iawn yn ffrwydro": cerddi cynnar Dylan Thomas. *Taliesin* 120 (2003) 97-110.

Allen, David Rayvern. My dear John — Yours ever, Dylan. *Independent* 31 October 2003. Arts and Books Review 2-4.

Bauer, Mathias. 'Vision and Prayer': Dylan Thomas and the Power of X. *From Sign to Signing: Iconicity in Language and Literature* 3, ed. Wolfgang G. Muller and Olga Fischer. Amsterdam: Benjamins, 2002. 441p. ISBN 1588112888.

BBC Audio Books. *Dylan Thomas at the BBC*. 2003. ISBN 0563477326.

Bennett, Gilbert, Eryl Jenkins and Eurwen Price (editors). *"I Sang in my Chains": Essays and Poems in Tribute to Dylan Thomas.* Swansea: Dylan Thomas Society of Great Britain, 2003. viii, 135p. ISBN 0954583906. Contents: Introduction, by Walford Davies, pp. i-viii—Memoirs, by Aeronwy Thomas, pp. 1-7—The House That Jack Built, by Gilbert Bennet, pp. 8-11—The Influence of Children's Literature, A Case Study: Dylan Thomas and Richmal Crompton, by Betty Greenway, pp. 12-23—Portrait of a Friend, by Gwen Watkins, pp. 24-28—The Macnamaras of Doolin and Ennistymon, by Eddie Stack, pp. 29-37—The Green Poet: The Theme of Nature, by Barbara Hardy, pp. 38-52—'Bright Metal on a Sullen Ground': Reflections on Dylan Thomas's Craft, with thoughts of Hopkins, Yeats and Others, by Walford Davies, pp. 53-67—'A Sweet Union'?: Dylan Thomas and Post-War American Poetry, by M. Wynn Thomas and Daniel Williams, pp. 68-79—Possessions and Obsessions: Encounters with Dylan Thomas, by Stewart Crehan, pp. 80-87—Dylan's Spirit is Alive and Well in the 'Handsome Hellhole' of Vancouver, by Ted Langley, pp. 88-99—The Travelling Players Abroad, by Megan Evans and John Rhys Thomas, pp. 100-102—Not in Rolph: Not in Maud, by Jeff Towns, pp. 103-112—Dylan Thomas, Swansea, The Year of Literature, And Me, by David Woolley, pp. 113-117—The Tumbledown Tongue, by Bill Long, pp. 118-123—Heatherslade Close: For Gilbert (poem), by William Greenway, pp. 124-125—The Wreath Laying (poem), by John Goodby, p. 126—Drowning (poem), by Aeronwy Thomas, p. 127—The Dragon Has Two Tongues, by Hugh Price, pp. 128-129.

Bennett, Gilbert and Donna Jones Paananen. Dylan Thomas: the Celebration. *New Welsh Review* 55 (2002) 25-30.

Burke, Sean. The Biographical Imperative. *Essays in Criticism* 52.3 (2002) 191-208.

Campanini, Silvia. *Strategie e metodi della traduzione poetica: Christopher Marlowe, William Shakespeare, Andrew Marvell, Edgar Allan Poe, Dylan Thomas, Iain Crichton Smith (Indiagini e prospettive).* L'Harmattan Italia, 2002. 175p. ISBN 8887605823.

Davies, James A. Glancing Down the Cliff of Time: Pamela Hansford Johnson and Dylan Thomas. *New Welsh Review* 59 (2003) 35-42.

Davies, Walford. Up and Down the Diamond. Review Article. *Dylan Thomas: An Original Language* by Barbara Hardy. *Planet* 148 (2001) 98-100.

—— *Dylan Thomas: An Original Language* by Barbara Hardy. *ANQ* 15.3 (2002) 50-52. Review article.

—— *Dylan Thomas*. New Delhi: Viva Books, 2003. vi, 134p. ISBN 8176494259. A revised edition of the volume first published by the Open University Press in 1986, with quotations now keyed to Walford Davies (editor), *Dylan Thomas: Selected Poems*. Blaine WA: Phoenix, 2000.

Ferris, Paul. I Was Dylan's Secret Lover. *Observer* 17 August 2003. Review section 1-2.

Golightly, Victor. 'Two on a tower': modernism and the influence of W. B. Yeats on Dylan Thomas and Vernon Watkins. Ph.D. thesis. University of Wales, Swansea, 2003.

Holt, Heather. *Dylan Thomas: the actor*. Swansea: Heather Holt, 2003. 84p. ISBN 0952916517. Foreword by Aeronwy Thomas.

Jones, Daniel (editor). *The Poems of Dylan Thomas*. New Directions Publishing Corporation, 2003. 352p. ISBN 0811215415.

Jones, T. James. Dylan Marlais Thomas (1914-1953). *Taliesin* 120 (2003) 111.

Keery, James. 'The Burning Baby' and the Bathwater I. *PNR* 150 (2003) 58-62. II PNR 151 (2003) 49-54. III *PNR* 152 (2003) 57-62. IV *PNR* 154 (2003) 26-32.

Kingston, V. and Paul Ferris. Face to Face. *English Review* 13.3 (2003) 31-33.

Lycett, Andrew. *Dylan Thomas: A New Life*. London: Weidenfeld and Nicholson, 2003. 352p. ISBN 0297607936
Review. J. Morris. A beast, an angel and a madman. *New Statesman* 16.779 (2003) 48-49; Stephen Knight. The need for a work-life balance. *Independent on Sunday* (26 Oct. 2003) 19.

—— Do not go gentle. *New Statesman*. 16.785 (2003) 36.

Maud, Ralph. *Where Have the Old Words Got Me? Explications of Dylan Thomas's Collected Poems, 1934–1953*. Cardiff: University of Wales Press, 2003. xix, 296p. ISBN 0-70831-7804.
Reviews: James A. Davies. Explicating Dylan Thomas. *Planet* 161 (2003) 104-106; John Goodby. *New Welsh Review* 62 (2003) 103-106.

—— Explicating Dylan. *Planet* 162 (2003/4) 89-90.

Morgan-Guy, John. *What Did the Poets See? A Theological and Philosophical Reflection*. University of Wales Centre for Advanced Welsh and Celtic Studies, 2003. 24p. ISBN 0947531963.

Nagy, Joseph Falaky. *The Poetics of Absence in the Celtic Tradition*. University of Wales Centre for Advanced Welsh and Celtic Studies, 2003. 28p. ISBN 0947531122.

Panaanen, Victor. A landmark event. *New Welsh Review* 55 (2002) 31-33. On the launch of a new collection of essays on Dylan Thomas.

Phillips, Ivan. I sing the bard electric. *Times Literary Supplement* 19 September 2003. 14-15.

Rhydderch, Francesca. Dylan Adieu, 9 November 2003. *New Welsh Review* 62 (2003) 2-4. Editorial

Sharp, C. Dylan Thomas: A Return to Milkwood. *British Heritage* 24.6 (2003) 28-37.

Smith, Matthew Michael C. 'Whoring the holy text'; the religious grotesque in Caradoc Evans and Dylan Thomas. M.A. dissertation. University of Wales, Swansea, 2001.

Thomas, David N. Dylan Thomas's New Quay. *New Welsh Review* 56 (2002) 4-13.

—— *The Dylan Thomas Trail*. Talybont: Y Lolfa, 2002. 128p. ISBN 0862436095.
Review. John Harris. To Walk Abroad. *Planet* 154 (2002) 112-113.

—— *The Dylan Thomas Murders*. Bridgend: Seren, 2002. 200p. ISBN 1854113046.
Reviews: Paul Ferris. *New Welsh Review* 59 (2003) 89-90; Richard Jones. The Murderous South-West. *Planet* 160 (2003) 105-107; Rhian Price. Dylan Thomas, yr ysbïwr? *Golwg* (2003) 17.

—— Dylan's Forgotten Mornings. *New Welsh Review* 61 (2003) 41-48.

—— Severed Heads. *Planet* 159 (2003) 81-86.

—— *Dylan Remembered: 1914–1934*. Bridgend: Seren, 2003. 300p. ISBN 1854113429.

Thomas, Dylan. Blithe Spirits. *New Welsh Review* 60 (2003) 11-12. Reprinting of review of Amos Tutuola's *The Palm-Wine Drinkard* (1952). See Daniel Williams, below.

—— *Selected Poems*. Walford Davies (editor). Blaine, WA: Phoenix, 2000. 176p. ISBN 0753810581. Includes 70 poems with introduction and commentary by Walford Davies.

—— *Selected Poems*, ed. Walford Davies. Penguin Modern Classics. London: Penguin, 2000. xxx 160p. ISBN 0140188894. Includes 69 poems with introduction and commentary by editor.

—— *A Dylan Thomas Treasury*, ed. Walford Davies. Blaine, WA: Phoenix, 2001. 208p. ISBN 0753814099.

—— *Dylan Thomas*, ed. Walford Davies. London: Deat, 2003. Everyman Poetry series, xvi, 112p. ISBN 046087831X. Includes 62 poems with introduction and commentary by editor.

—— *The Laugharne Poems*. Llangadog: The Old Stile Press, 2003. n. pag. ISBN 0907664628.

—— *The Love Letters of Dylan Thomas*. Naperville, IL: Sourcebooks, 2002. 112p. ISBN 1570718733.

—— *The Love Letters of Dylan Thomas*. Blaine, WA: Phoenix, 2003. 96p. ISBN 0753812967.
Review. S. C. Fair. The Love Letters of Dylan Thomas. *Library Journal* 126.20 (2001) 123.

Trusso, Francesco. *Words Weaving Wonder: Principles of Semiosis in Shelley, Hopkins, and Dylan Thomas*. (Semiotics and the Human Sciences, Vol. 16) Oxford: Peter Lang, 2002. ISBN 0820442844.

Various. Comments on Dylan Thomas. *Poetry Wales* 39.2 (2003) 14-22, 46-47, 50-51. Raymond Garlick, Niall Griffiths, Seamus Heaney, Bobi Jones, David Lloyd, Leslie Norris, Sioned Puw Rowlands, Manohar Shetty, Iain Sinclair.

Various. *Edward Ardizzone 1900-1979: Nadolig Plentyn yng Nghymru / A Child's Christmas in Wales*, Aberystwyth: Welsh Books Council, 2003. 30p. ISBN 0953732029. A revised edition of the bilingual booklet first published in 1982 to accompany the UK-wide exhibition of Ardizzone's illustrations to Dylan Thomas's text.
Contents: Edward Ardizzone, by Marcus Crouch, pp. 1-11 – Dylan Thomas, by Walford Davies, pp. 12-22 – A Child's Christmas in Wales, by Paul Ferris, pp. 23-28 – 6 coloured and 4 black-and-white Ardizzone illustrations.

Ward. D. C. Three Literary Lives and the Imperatives of Modernism (Dylan Thomas, Stephen Spender, Osbert Sitwell). *Sewanee Review* 109.4 (Fall 2001) 638-642.

Watkins, H. and D. Herbert. Cultural policy and place promotion in South Wales and Dylan Thomas. *Geoforum* 34.2 (2003) 249-266.

Wiggington, C. J. Modernism from the margins: a study of the 1930s poetry of Dylan Thomas and Louis MacNeice. Ph.D. thesis. University of Wales, Swansea, 2003.

Williams, Daniel. Beyond National Literature? Dylan Thomas and Amos Tutuola in 'Igbo masquerade'. *New Welsh Review* 60 (2003) 5-10.

Williams, John. Dylan and Me. *Independent on Sunday*. 9 November 2003. Life section 1-2.

Williams, John Hartley. Dylan Lives! *Poetry Wales* 39.2 (2003) 8-14.

Yonemoto, Yoshitaka. Joisu 'Shishatachi' to good night. *Rising Generation*. 147.11 (2002) 682-688.

Ed Thomas

Radford, A. Provincial Voices. *Cambridge Quarterly* 31.4 (2002) 357-360. Review article.

Richards, Shaun. Cool enough for Lou Reed?: The Plays of Ed Thomas and the Cultural Politics of South Wales. *Across the Margins: Cultural Identity and Change in the Atlantic Archipelago*, ed. Glenda Norquay and Gerry Smyth. Manchester: Manchester University Press, 2002. ISBN 0719057493. pp. 137-153.

Thomas, Ed. *Selected Work, 1995-1998*. Cardigan: Parthian Books, 2002. 450p. ISBN 1902638247.
Review. Alex Carolan. Slippery Characters. *Planet* 160 (2003) 112-113.

R.S. Thomas

Brewster, R. 'Unhappily in love with God': Conceptions of the divine in the poetry of Geoffrey Hill, Les Murray and R.S. Thomas. Ph.D. thesis. Durham University, 2002.

Davies, Damian Walford (editor). *Echoes to the Amen: Essays After R.S. Thomas*. Cardiff: University of Wales Press, 2003. xvi, 233p. ISBN 0708317898.
Contents. Introduction, by Damian Walford Davies, pp. 1-12—Extraordinary Man of the Bald Welsh Hills: The Iago Prytherch Poems, by Patrick Crotty, pp. 13-43—R.S. Thomas's Welsh Pastoral, by Geoffrey Hill, pp. 44-59—Was R.S. Thomas an Atheist Manqué? by John Barnie, pp. 60-75—'The Curious Stars': R.S. Thomas and the Scientific Revolution, by John Pikoulis, pp. 76-111—

'Blessings, Stevens': R.S. Thomas and Wallace Stevens, by Tony Brown, pp. 112-31—Mirror Games: Self and M(O)ther in the Poetry of R.S. Thomas, by Katie Gramich, pp. 132-48—'Double-entry Poetics': R.S. Thomas–Punster, by Damian Walford Davies, 149-82—'Time's Changeling': Autobiography in *The Echoes Return Slow*, by M. Wynn Thomas, pp. 183-205—Suspending the Ethical: R.S. Thomas and Kierkegaard, by Rowan Williams, pp. 206-219.

—— "The Frequencies I Commanded": Recordio R.S. Thomas. In *Chwileniwm: Technoleg a Llenyddiaeth*, ed. Angharad Price. Cardiff: University of Wales Press, 2002. 222p. ISBN 0708317235. pp. 157-69

Davies, Jason Walford. *Gororau'r Iaith: R.S. Thomas A'r Tradddodiad Cymraeg*. Cardiff: University of Wales Press, 2003. 350p. ISBN 0708317995.

Heys, Alistair. Frost's Cruel Chemistry. *Coleridge Bulletin* 20 (2002) 114-121.

Mackay, E. Seeking the heaven-handling hero. *English Review* 12.1 (2001) 32-35.

McEllhenney, John G. My World Stock Fluctuates a Good Deal! *New Welsh Review* 56 (2002) 21-28.

McGill, William. *Poets' Meeting: George Herbert, R.S. Thomas, and the Argument with God*. Jefferson, NC: McFarland, 2003. 208p. ISBN 0786416939.

McKenzie, Tim. *Vocation in the Poetry of the Priest-Poets George Herbert, Gerard Manley Hopkins, and R.S. Thomas*. Ceredigion: Edwin Mellen, 2003. ISBN 0773465707.

Morgan, Christopher. *R.S. Thomas: Identity, Environment, Deity*. Manchester: Manchester University Press, 2003. 224p. ISBN 0719062489.

Ogden, James. Reflections on R.S. Thomas's 'Taste'. *The Swansea Review* 22 (2003) 45-49.

Sloan, Barry. The Discipline of Watching and Waiting: RS Thomas, Poetry and Prayer. *Religion and Literature* 34.2 (2002) 29-49.

Thomas, R.S. *Poems: R.S. Thomas*. Selected and edited by Anthony Thwaite. London: Phoenix, 2002. 122p. ISBN 0753816539.

—— *Residues*. M. Wynn Thomas (editor). Highgreen, Tarset: Bloodaxe, 2002. 80p. ISBN 1852245964.
Reviews: Patrick Crotty. *New Welsh Review* 58 (2002) 93-95; Damian Walford Davies. Truth's Precipitate. *Planet* 158 (2003) 104-106; James McGrath. Waiting for God. *PNR* 151 (2003) 68-69.

Henry Vaughan
Leimberg, Inge. Three Poems by Henry Vaughan Translated. *The Swansea Review* 22 (2003) 82-89.

Rudrum, Alan. Narrative, Typology and Politics in Henry Vaughan's 'Isaac's Marriage'. *Connotations: A Journal for Critical Debate* 11.1 (2002-3) 78-90.

Thomas, Peter and Anne Cluysenaar (editors). *Scintilla* 6. Usk Valley Vaughan Association (2002). 223p. ISBN 0953067459.
Includes: Henry Vaughan and the Glance of Love: Thoughts on 'The Favour' by Glyn Pursglove, pp.7-20—Vaughan and the Mundus Imaginalis, Alex Cadogan, pp. 110-21—F. E. Hutchinson, Louise Guiney and Henry Vaughan, by Jonathan Nauman, pp. 135-47—A New Language, A New Tradition, by Roland Mathias, pp. 161-82—'How Shall I Get a Wreath … ?: Some Implications of Vaughan's Question for Contemporary Poetry, by Kim Taplin, pp. 194-204.

Thomas, Peter and Anne Cluysenaar (editors). *Scintilla* 7. Usk Valley Vaughan Association (2003). ISBN 0953067459.
Includes: "A Deep but Dazzling Darkness": Writing Poetry in Extremity, by Myra Schneider, pp. 53-61—Gender and Politics in the Writings of Henry Vaughan, by Holly Faith Nelson, pp. 99-115—The Identity of Rebecca Archer Vaughan, by Donald R. Dickson, pp. 129-42.
West, Philip. *Henry Vaughan's 'Silex Scintillans': Scripture Uses*. Oxford: Oxford University Press, 2001. 284p. ISBN 0198187564.
Reviews: Stevie Davies. *New Welsh Review* 62 (2003) 109-111; B. Horne. *Journal of Theological Studies* 53 (Oct. 2002) 775-777. IDDS 610QL.

Vernon Watkins
Golightly, Victor. 'Two on a tower': modernism and the influence of W. B. Yeats on Dylan Thomas and Vernon Watkins. Ph.D. thesis. University of Wales, Swansea, 2003.

Watkins, Vernon. *Poems for Dylan*. Llandysul: Gomer, 2003. ISBN 18433232367. Includes an Afterword by Gwen Watkins.
Reviews: Victor Golightly. *New Welsh Review* 61 (2003) 107-108; Hilary Llewellyn-Williams. *Poetry Wales* 39.2 (2003) 69-71; Ralph Maud. A True Picture Restored. *Planet* 162 (2003/4) 112; Rhian Price. Y cyfaill cymhleth. *Golwg* 15.30 (10 April 2003) 18-19.

Charles Way
Williams, Jeni. The How and Why of Enchantment: Charles Way's Fairy Tales. *New Welsh Review* 61 (2003) 95-102.

NOTES ON CONTRIBUTORS

Sam Adams's many publications in the field of Welsh writing in English include three monographs in the Writers of Wales series, the most recent of which was on *Thomas Jeffery Llewelyn Prichard* (U.W.P., 2000). He is the editor of *Seeing Wales Whole: Essays on the Literature of Wales* (U.W.P., 1998) and of Roland Mathias's *Collected Short Stories* (U.W.P., 2001) and *Collected Poems* (U.W.P., 2002), His "Letter from Wales" appears regularly in *PN Review*.

Sue Asbee is Staff Tutor in Arts and Lecturer in Literature at the Open University. She is currently working on a new edition of Margiad Evans's *The Wooden Doctor* for Honno. Recent publications include chapters on Kate Chopin in *The Nineteenth-Century Novel: Identities*, ed. Dennis Walder (Routledge/Open University, 2001). Her "Popular Culture and American Poetry: Frank O'Hara and Alan Ginsberg" is forthcoming in *Texts and Debates*, ed. David Johnson (Routledge/Open University).

Malcolm Ballin is a Research Associate at University of Wales, Cardiff. After graduating from Cambridge, he entered a career in the British steel industry. After retirement in 1996, he returned to academic life, taking an MA in English at Cardiff in 1997 and a Ph.D. in 2002. He has published numerous articles and reviews on Irish, Scottish and Welsh periodical literature.

Jackie Benjamin was awarded an MA (with Distinction) from the Centre for Research into the English Literature and Language of Wales, University of Wales, Swansea. She is currently undertaking doctoral research at the Centre, on theoretical approaches to the writing of Dylan Thomas.

Joseph P. Clancy is Emeritus Professor of English Literature and Theatre Arts of Marymount Manhattan College, New York City. Since retirement in 1990 he has lived in Aberystwyth; he is an Honorary Fellow of the University of Wales, Aberystwyth. His most recent books are a collection of poems *Ordinary Times*, *Other Words: Essays on Poetry and Translation* (U.W.P., 1999) and a volume of translations, *Medieval Welsh Poems* (Four Courts P., 2003).

Tony Curtis is Professor of Poetry at the University of Glamorgan. He has published nine collections of poetry and has written on contemporary and twentieth-century writing and art in Wales. His annotated edition of *Related Twilights* by Joseph Herman was published in 2002 by Seren, who are also scheduled to bring out a second printing of his *Welsh Painters Talking* (2005).

Geraint Evans teaches in the School of English, Art History, Film and Media at the University of Sydney, where he has also taught on the Celtic Studies programme and been Director of the University's Language Centre. He has published on David Jones as well as on various aspects of publishing history, including Welsh-language publishing in Australia. His "The Death of the Diaspora" appeared recently in *Planet*.

Diane Green was awarded her doctorate (University of Wales) in 2000 for her thesis on the fiction of Emyr Humphreys. She has continued to work and publish on Humphreys, as well as on contemporary fiction. Her post-colonial reading of Humphreys's *Jones* was published in *Yearbook 7*.

Nicholas Jones, a graduate of the University of St. Andrews, is completing doctoral research on the writing of Harri Webb at University of Wales, Swansea. He was awarded the 2003 Melbern G. Glasscock Center for Humanities Studies Research Prize at the South Central M.L.A. Conference.

Sally Roberts Jones was Royal Literary Fund Fellow at University of Wales, Swansea, 1999-2001, and is currently an R.L.F. Project Fellow. She is currently researching the literary tradition of the Neath and Afan Valleys and Tir Iarll. Her publications include *Allen Raine* (U.W.P., 1979), *A History of Port Talbot* (Alun Books, 1991) as well as bibliographies and numerous essays on Anglo-Welsh literature and local history.

D. Densil Morgan is Reader in Theology and Head of Department at the University of Wales, Bangor. He is the author of *The Span of the Cross: Christian Religion and Society in Wales 1914-2000* (U.W.P., 1999) and, with A. M. Allchin, a study of the poetry of D. Gwenallt Jones. His book *The Humble God: An Invitation to Christian Doctrine* (SCM Canterbury P.) is due this year.

Nathalie Wourm teaches French at Birkbeck College. She wrote her Oxford D.Phil. on Dylan Thomas's early poetry and has published several papers on him. She specializes in poetry, in English and French, since the late nineteenth century, especially Symbolist, Modernist and contemporary avant-garde writing. Her current research is in the field of French avant-garde poetry since 1995 and she has several papers in print and forthcoming on this material.